Subcultures

This book presents a cultural history of subcultures, covering a remarkable range of subcultural forms and practices. It begins with London's 'Elizabethan underworld', taking the rogue and vagabond as subcultural prototypes: the basis for Marx's later view of subcultures as the *lumpenproletariat,* and Henry Mayhew's view of subcultures as 'those that will not work'. Subcultures are always in some way non-conforming or dissenting. They are social – with their own shared conventions, values, rituals, and so on – but they can also seem 'immersed' or self-absorbed. This book identifies six key ways in which subcultures have generally been understood:

- through their often negative relation to work (as 'idle', 'parasitical', hedonistic, criminal, etc.)
- their negative or ambivalent relation to class
- their association with territory (the 'street', the 'hood', the club, etc.) rather than property
- their movement away from home into non-domestic forms of belonging
- their ties to excess and exaggeration (as opposed to restraint and moderation)
- their refusal of the banalities of ordinary life and in particular, of massification.

Subcultures looks at the way these features find expression across many different sub-cultural groups: from the Ranters to the riot grrrls, from taxi dancers to drag queens and kings, from bebop to hip hop, from dandies to punk, from hobos to leatherfolk, and from hippies and bohemians to digital pirates and virtual communities. It argues that subcultural identity is primarily a matter of narrative and narration, which means that its focus is literary as well as sociological. It also argues for the idea of a *subcultural geography*: that subcultures inhabit places in particular ways, their investment in them being as much imaginary as real and, in some cases, strikingly utopian.

Ken Gelder is Professor of Literary Studies and Cultural Studies at the University of Melbourne, Australia. His books include *Reading the Vampire* (1994), *Uncanny Australia* (1998) and *Popular Fiction: The Logics and Practices of a Literary Field* (2004). He is editor of *The Horror Reader* (2000) and *The Subcultures Reader Second Edition* (2005).

Subcultures

Cultural histories and social practice

Ken Gelder

 Routledge
Taylor & Francis Group

LONDON AND NEW YORK

First published 2007
by Routledge
2 Park Square, Milton Park, Abingdon, Oxon OX14 4RN

Simultaneously published in the USA and Canada
by Routledge
270 Madison Ave, New York, NY 10016

Routledge is an imprint of the Taylor & Francis Group, an informa business

Typeset in Perpetua by Saxon Graphics Ltd
Printed and bound in Great Britain by MPG Books Ltd, Bodmin

British Library Cataloguing in Publication Data
A catalogue record for this book is available from the British Library

Library of Congress Cataloging-in-Publication Data
Gelder, Ken, 1955–
  Subcultures : cultural histories and social practice / Ken Gelder.
    p. cm.
  Includes bibliographical references and index.
1. Subculture. 2. Subculture—History. 3. Culture—Study and teaching. I. Title.
  HM646.G45 2007
  306'.1—dc22
                              2006025762

ISBN10: 0-415-37951-2 (hbk)
ISBN10: 0-415-37952-0 (pbk)
ISBN10: 0-203-44685-2 (ebk)

ISBN13: 978-0-415-37951-9 (hbk)
ISBN13: 978-0-415-37952-6 (pbk)
ISBN13: 978-0-203-44685-0 (ebk)

Contents

Acknowledgements

This book has been simmering away for a long time: emerging out of an early idea for a Reader in subcultural studies and my collaboration on the first edition of that project with Sarah Thornton back in the mid-1990s, and then developing out of further work I had since done on the revised second edition in 2005. My thanks go to various people at Routledge, past and present – Rebecca Barden and Natalie Foster in particular – for encouraging me to write in much more detail on the subject. Claire Knowles has helped me with some research material for this book, and I'm very grateful indeed to her. I want to thank Clara Tuite for so kindly looking at some of the chapters and offering excellent suggestions; and thanks, too, to Justin Clemens for his encouraging reading of Chapter 4. My department has given me the time and space to do this project, and I'm especially grateful here to John Frow. I must also thank all the students who've studied with me over the years in an Honours course about subcultures, some of whom have subsequently published very fine work in and around the area of subcultural studies. Writing a book is an intense process and, as authors are well aware, it requires a great deal of planning, commitment, hard labour and focus. You affect some people more than others when you do it, in which case I must especially thank Hannah, Christian and Julian for their patience and support as well as their occasional and much-appreciated curiosity.

INTRODUCTION

THIS IS A BOOK ABOUT SUBCULTURES, their cultural histories and their social logics and practices. I wrote it in Melbourne, Australia, where I live, a city which – like so many other cities around the world – no doubt has its fair share of subcultural activity. Skateboarders use the steps and benches in front of Melbourne's austere public library and they criss-cross the surrounding streets, roaming in their small groups back and forth from pavement to road and in between moving cars and pedestrians. Goths congregate in the inner-city suburbs; for a few recent years a representative magazine, *Goth Nation*, was published out of Melbourne and circulated through the various Goth boutiques and specialist nightclubs. Melbourne in fact has an extensive nightclub 'scene', far too elaborate to go into here. It also has a number of drag nightclubs and gay and lesbian bars, along with a wide range of gay and lesbian niche media activity. In the outer suburbs there is the reclusive Seahorse Club, founded in 1975, for older crossdressing participants. There is a widespread 'underground' of strip joints and brothels, as well as street-based male and female prostitution. There is a criminal underworld, which police in Melbourne have had great difficulty in regulating – and there are street gangs of one kind or another right across the city. The Ozanam Community in North Melbourne services homeless and 'marginal' street people and now publishes a magazine, *Subterrain*, which pays tribute to its itinerant population, describing it, too, as an 'underworld' which most of Melbourne almost never sees. The city has its hippies and its ferals, its fregans (who recycle and re-use waste), its neo-punks and its metal (death metal, especially) enthusiasts. Most of the inner city and surrounding suburbs testifies to a remarkably active graffiti subculture; indeed, Melbourne has even been claimed as a 'stencil graffiti capital' (Smallman and Nyman 2005), with the work of graffiti artists in the city documented, and celebrated, in Nicholas

Hansen's 2005 film, *Rash* ('Scratch it and it spreads...'). The Australian and New Zealand hip hop magazine *Out4Fame* is published in Melbourne, which also has a lively local hip hop scene. Various 'Hell-Fire' clubs and leatherbars have opened and closed in Melbourne at various times over the last thirty or so years, catering to S/M and fetish interests. There is the Cave Clan, a loose federation of underground travellers who would sign their name in the fashion of the Coca-Cola logo and explore and territorialise Melbourne's extensive underground drainage systems – literally inhabiting an underworld, rather like the Parisian *cataphiles*. And there is the Melbourne branch of Critical Mass, activist cyclists who protest the way in which the city is dominated by roads and cars but who also arrange cycling events as leisured get-togethers: a small-scale social movement, although arguably still subcultural through its 'disaffiliated' structure and 'attitude'. Automobile dragsters around town, on the other hand, are constantly being moved on by police, encouraged to do what they do elsewhere or not at all. Melbourne has seen its teenage subcultures clash in the streets: like the Mods and Sharpies in August 1966 (Sparrow and Sparrow 2004: 73–77). It has also played host to various literary and artistic Bohemian communities, identified as far back as the 1860s by the novelist and journalist Marcus Clarke and again more recently by the writer and poet Alister Kershaw (1991).

Each of these subcultures – and one can think of many more – creates its own geography, a set of places or sites (some of which last longer than others) through which it gains cohesion and identity. This book will develop the notion of a *subcultural geography* as it charts a range of subcultures and – just as importantly in a study like this – a range of approaches to subcultures. It is true that subcultures have been around in one form or another for a very long time. But they have been chronicled by others for a long time, too: documented, analysed, classified, rationalised, monitored, scrutinised, and so on. In some cases, societies at various times and for various reasons have legislated against them and attempted to regulate and/or reform them, sometimes successfully, often not. Every subculture – every social group, large or small, which can be considered as in some way subcultural – carries a set of narratives about itself, some of which are generated internally while others, usually more visible and pervasive, are developed and deployed in and by the society around it. The notion that subcultures are a matter of *narration* will also be important to this book (which generates a further set of narratives about subcultures in its turn). How accurate or real a narrative about or even by a subculture might be is a question that has rightly preoccupied researchers and commentators. From another perspective, however, accuracy is beside the point. Narratives by or about a subculture come into being and produce a set of effects (or, affects) and reactions: fascination, envy, anxiety, disdain, revulsion, legislation, social reform, etc. They are never neutral. Every narrative by or about a subculture is a matter of position-taking – both within that subculture and outside it – a feature this book will spend much of its time accounting for.

The most common narrative about subcultures is, of course, one that casts them as nonconformist and non-normative: different, dissenting, or (to use a term sometimes applied to subcultures by others) 'deviant'. This book will give this particular narrative a history, tracing it back to accounts of the 'Elizabethan underworld' in order to establish the primary cultural logics through which subcultures have for so long been understood. It is worth noting that the most influential modern study of subcultures – Dick Hebdige's *Subculture: The Meaning of Style* (1979) – looks almost exclusively at post-1950s activities and has very little to say about subcultures before this time. It is, in other words, a synchronic study, reading a set of British youth subcultures in their contemporary moment and, indeed, celebrating the sheer *fact* of their contemporaneity as a way (so it seemed) of revitalising a moribund and demoralised cultural predicament in Britain under the Conservative Prime Minister Margaret Thatcher – who came to power the same year Hebdige's book was published. The present book might very well have a similar sort of purpose: speaking up for subcultures in the context of a neo-conservative cultural and political shift in the contemporary landscape, one which (in my own local context) routinely lends its privileges to 'ordinary' or 'mainstream' Australians at the expense of social minorities. My aim, however, is to be diachronic, giving subcultures and, in particular, *approaches* to subcultures a deeper history. There are at least six prevailing cultural logics about subcultures – that is, six ways of accounting for and identifying subcultures, culturally speaking – that we can list here. First, subcultures have routinely been understood and evaluated negatively in terms of their relation to labour or work. Many subcultures might not work at all (which means they are 'idle' or 'unproductive', or 'at leisure', or pleasure-seeking, hedonistic, self-indulgent); or, their relation to labour might be understood as parasitical, or as a kind of alternative 'mirror-image' to legitimate work practices (so that one might even speak, in a certain sense, of a subcultural 'career'); or, whatever labour a subculture undertakes might simply be understood as in some way unsanctioned or even criminal. In the late eighteenth century, for example, a set of narratives built themselves around the prostitute's 'career' along exactly these lines, as I shall note in Chapter 1. Second (and this point follows on from the first), subcultures are often understood ambivalently at best in relation to class. In some accounts, subcultures are seen as having deviated from their class background altogether, disavowing class affiliations or even 'transcending' class as a result of the particular cultural adjustments they have made. On the other hand, for Karl Marx around the middle of the nineteenth century – as I shall also note later on – subcultures were in fact the *lumpenproletariat*: that is, groups of people *below* class-based identity and without class consciousness, self-interested rather than class affiliated: a view that has persisted. Third, subcultures are usually located at one remove from property ownership. Subcultures territorialise their places rather than own them, and it is in this way that their modes of belonging and their claims on place find expression. Fourth, subcultures generally come together outside of the domestic sphere, away from home and family. A typical subcultural narrative, as we shall see, is precisely that of one's initial deviation from home and the subsequent adjustment into subcultural forms of homeliness and belonging *outside* of the family circle. A fifth cultural logic tends to equate subcultures with excess or exaggeration, registering the 'deviance' of a subculture through a range of excessive attributes – behaviour, styles and dress, noise, argot or language, consumption, and so on – which are then contrasted with the restraints and moderations of 'normal' populations. We shall also see this cultural logic at work throughout this book, although its explanatory force can ebb and flow (allowing some subcultures, in fact, even to be identified with restraint itself, with austerity, self-discipline, etc.). Finally, a sixth, related cultural logic – put to use in Dick Hebdige's book, for example – develops out of the late nineteenth century and casts modern subcultures in opposition to the banalities of mass cultural forms. Here, subcultural identity is pitched against the conformist pressures of mass society and massification. At the same time, however, it is also understood as a structured refusal of one of mass society's prevailing 'symptoms', alienation.

The kinds of narratives through which these various cultural logics are conveyed are not new and, as I have said, this book will in fact give them a history: a cultural history, or perhaps I should say, a subcultural history. But there is one more point to make about subcultures in this Introduction, before the book properly begins. Subcultures are social 'worlds' and their nonconformity or non-normativity must always be understood in social terms. Researchers from the Department of Sociology at the University of Chicago, the so-called 'Chicago School' – so important to subcultural studies during the first half of the twentieth century – rightly insisted that subcultural 'deviance' is not a matter of individual pathology, nor is it an individualised 'refusal' of normative social practices, moralities, and so on (so that strictly speaking, the opening account in Hebdige's *Subculture: The Meaning of Style*, of Jean Genet's alienated act of nonconformity in prison, is not in itself an instance of subcultural practice at all). Subcultural 'deviance' or difference is instead a matter of social affiliation. But the *social* here is understood in a particular way. This book will outline a set of key terms for understanding the social aspects of subcultures – community, scene, network, tribe, club, gang, and so on. Each of these terms has a particular application and relevance, depending on the subculture, the predicament in which it finds itself and the kinds of meaning or significance that commentators invest into it. If there is such a thing as 'subcultural studies' – and I think that there is, although it hasn't quite achieved a legitimate disciplinary identity – then this is its primary focus: the analysis of subcultures in terms of their sociality and social practice. This, too, is as much imagined and narrated as it is experienced and indeed, as this book will suggest, the one constantly works to inform the other.

Chapter 1

SUBCULTURES
A vagabond history

The Elizabethan underworld

THE BEST PLACE TO BEGIN a cultural history of subcultures (although medievalists may disagree) is in mid-sixteenth-century London, with the emergence here of an 'Elizabethan underworld' and the popularisation of a genre of pamphlet-writing loosely referred to as 'rogue literature', devoted to the chronicling of criminal types and criminal activities in and around the city. Criminal underworlds certainly existed before this time and in many other places. However, early modern London saw not only the rise of a myriad of discrete, underground criminal networks but also a proliferation of imaginative narratives *about* them. Gilbert Walker's *A Manifest Detection of the most vile and detestable use of Dice-Play, and other practices like the same* (1552) was an 'exposé' of card and dice cheats, while John Awdeley's *Fraternity of Vagabonds* (probably 1565) was an account of various criminal orders ('Cozeners and Shifters', 'Knaves') and criminal types (the ruffler, the whipjack, the forgerer, the ring-faller, and so on). We might also think of the playwright Robert Greene's various 'Cony-catching' pamphlets from the 1590s, concerned with thieves and blackmailers and confidence-tricksters. Thomas Harman, a Justice of the Peace and author of *A Caveat or Warning for Common Cursitors, vulgarly called Vagabonds* (1567), is credited with coining the word 'rogue', a broadly applicable term describing vagrants and thieves who 'used disguise, rhetorical play, and counterfeit gestures, to insinuate themselves into lawful and political contexts' (Dionne and Mentz 2004: 1–2). The term thus already carries with it imaginative possibilities: implying a kind of performative act, the creation of a fictional self, as well as linguistic display. Perhaps not surprisingly, then, the sixteenth-century London rogue has attracted the attention of literary scholarship in particular, going back as far as Edward Viles and Frederick J. Furnivall's *The Rogues and Vagabonds of Shakespeare's Youth* (1880) and F.W. Chandler's two-volume *Literature of Roguery* (1907). In 1930, on the other hand, an especially influential anthology of rogue literature was compiled by a Professor of the History of Education from King's College, London: A.V. Judges's *The Elizabethan Underworld*. 'The tendency in literary criticism', he complained, 'has been, on the whole, to overlook the historical value of these descriptive writings. Historians themselves have hardly glanced at them...' (Judges 1965: xiii).

Judges's anthology of rogue literature, produced during the Depression in England, worked as a defence of the rogue and the vagabond, regarding them as victims of punitive Elizabethan social laws: 'Tudor despotism', as he called it. The word *vagabond* was given legal definition during Elizabeth's reign, tied to idleness and vagrancy, crimes which elicited harsh penalties. Poor laws, along with enclosure laws and laws requiring proof of residency (a 'principle of settlement'), underwrote an 'elaborate system of central control' (xxxvii), which excluded itinerant or displaced people from citizenship and in many cases treated them as nothing less than 'enemies of the community' (xv). At best, their relationship to the state was cast as parasitical, a feature strikingly expressed in William Harrison's account of vagabonds in *Description of England* (1597) which had characterised them as 'the caterpillars in the commonwealth' who 'lick the sweat from the true labourers [*sic*] brows' and 'stray and wander about, as creatures abhorring all labour and every honest exercise' (cited in Dionne 1997: 36) . Even so, Judges wrote,

> still they came, tramping singly or in groups along the country highways, sneaking into barns and hovels on the fringes of the towns, adapting themselves to city life to swell the ranks of the criminal classes of London...everywhere unsettling the common folk, and disturbing the conventions of an orderly regime.
>
> (Judges 1965: xv)

Here is a powerful expression of the ability of underworld people to survive the legislation against them, form themselves into 'classes' and continue to 'disturb' the dominant social order. Judges's long introduction to this important anthology was mostly devoted to the ways in which Elizabethans upheld and applied the law. In a later anthology of rogue literature, however – this time compiled by a literary critic – the focus was on the *nature* of those criminal classes and whether or not they might indeed be understood as subcultural. Gamini Salgado's *Cony-Catchers and Bawdy Baskets* (1972) renewed interest in Elizabethan writings about cony-catchers ('cony' being a slang term for rabbit) and various other rogue types. But he also wanted to claim that the underworlds these people inhabited were not only organised but *social*:

Seen through the disapproving eyes of respectable citizens they were nothing but a disorderly and disorganized rabble, dropouts from the social ladder. But seen from within, they appear to be like nothing so much as a mirror-image of the Elizabethan world-picture: a little world, tightly organized into its own ranks and with its own rules, as rigid in its own way as the most elaborate protocol at court or ritual in church.

(Salgado 1972: 13)

This remark is no doubt a reply to E.M.W. Tillyard's influential book, *The Elizabethan World Picture* (1942), which conveyed a sense of the orderliness of Elizabethan life, real and/or imaginary, but had nothing to say about early modern underworlds at all. Salgado doesn't reject orderliness, however. He retains Tillyard's 'world picture', but now transfers it to the criminal underclasses themselves: they are just as orderly and hierarchical as the Elizabethan aristocracy. An important way of understanding subcultures is thus offered here, that even as they appear disorderly to outsiders they are from their own perspective 'tightly organised', their social worlds structured by rules and protocols.

Salgado went on to write a book called *The Elizabethan Underworld* (1977), using the same title as Judges's earlier anthology. It evokes a sense of sixteenth-century London as overrun by underworld folk of various kinds, each of them inhabiting their own zones – the brothel districts, for example – but also flowing freely through the city: segregated in some respects, all too proximate in others. This is a picturesque (and picaresque) account, relishing its rogue characters or types which it describes at some length. But other disciplines were also interested in Elizabethan underworlds. John McMullan's *The Canting Crew: London's Criminal Underworld 1550–1700* (1984) came out of criminology, a discipline which as we shall see has been of particular importance to subcultural studies. I have wanted to suggest that the Elizabethan figure of the vagabond is especially important to subcultural studies because it was understood in terms of its parasitical relations to labour and its rootlessness and the fact that it was not tied to property, even though it might be tied for a time to a particular place. Salgado calls the vagabond underworld a 'society of the road' (Salgado 1977: 130), rather like gypsies who were also of concern to early modern legislators. For McMullan, the rootlessness of vagabonds and rogues was in fact directed at London itself, since the population of the city increased dramatically in the late sixteenth century. We shall also come to see (in Chapter 2 especially) that migration and immigration are so often the foundational events for subcultural identity, and this is certainly how McMullan saw it as vagrant groups moved into London to take advantage of its wealth, its size and its social complexities. Soon, London played host to 'a myriad of diverse social universes' (McMullan 1984: 17). Criminal underworlds flourished, concentrating their skills and teaching them to new recruits. London's geography might even be mapped out in terms of the various underworlds that thrived there: 'Criminal areas came to possess an elaborate yet unofficial social world with its own criminal vocabulary, criminal technology, division of labour, apprenticeship system, criminal haunts, and style of collective life' (157).

There is now, according to Craig Dionne and Steve Mentz, a sub-discipline of early modern historical research called 'Rogue Studies' (Dionne and Mentz 2004: 11). Dionne argues that the rogue literature of the late sixteenth century played a major role in subcultural formation, helping to 'reshape the image of the hapless vagabond into the covert member of a vast criminal underground of organised guilds, complete with their own internally coherent barter economy, master–apprentice relations, secret languages, and patrons' (Dionne 2004: 33). Dionne and Mentz are literary critics, however, and naturally enough they return our attention to the *imaginative* features of rogue literature. They criticise McMullan for 'bestowing authenticity on characters and incidents' from Elizabethan texts that are not necessarily realistic – or authentic. They criticise Salgado, too, for accepting these underworld narratives as real. But just how imaginary *were* the subcultures of Elizabethan London? Dionne and Mentz call for a 'middle position', one that combines fact with fiction and blends real documentation with imaginative effects – perhaps rather as the writers of rogue literature, like Robert Greene, did themselves: 'The basic fact-or-fiction split – between reading the rogue as a historical figure who "reveals" something about the real social conditions of early modern England, or analysing this figure as a cultural construction who "represents" an imagined response to cultural stimuli – remains an active divide in studies of early modern roguery' (Dionne and Mentz 2004: 22). Subcultural studies can also be divided along similar lines, as later chapters will suggest.

Vagabondiana

The figure of the rogue and the idea of rogues' communities – 'canting crews' – persisted in British writing into the Restoration and beyond. Richard Head's *The English Rogue and Other Extravagants* (1665) begins to look fondly at the rogue, chronicling an 'excessive' lifestyle of brothel-cruising and deception. Extravagance becomes the thing that links the rogue to his aristocratic Restoration counterpart, the rake: this is the argument Harold Weber makes, for example, noting that both socio-literary types embodied a 'refusal to accept conventional social restraints' as they pursued financial gain and sexual license (Weber 1984: 15). The rogue moves into picaresque literature in the late seventeenth and eighteenth century – a genre influenced by earlier Spanish models – and is usually cast as an individualised figure moving episodically and nomadically through the world, increasingly sentimentalised as the genre goes on. Other narratives about subcultural types were much less sentimental, however. The famous eighteenth-century English painter William Hogarth produced his well-known series of engravings, *The Rake's Progress*, in 1735: eight plates which represented the rake's rise in fortune and subsequent terrible decline. Hogarth had also produced an earlier set of engravings, *The Harlot's Progress*: the narrative cycle of a prostitute, Moll Hackabout, from her migration into the city and the establishment of a social network through which her career could develop, through to her imprisonment and finally her death, presumably from venereal disease. For Sophie Carter, *The Harlot's Progress* was not a unique work; rather, it reflected a cultural narrative about prostitution already available during the early eighteenth century, familiar but also fascinating enough for many people actually to want to buy the prints for themselves. There was, she writes, 'an established and venerable framework for describing the life of the archetypal London prostitute in use in popular print culture since the late seventeenth century at the very least' (Carter 2004: 33). The prostitute is understood here in a particular way, vulnerable at first but also drawn to vice, an aberrant figure whose innate 'deviance' is all too easily revealed – and which works to condemn her at the end. Elsewhere, Tony Henderson has suggested that London's prostitutes in the early eighteenth century were in fact networked and adaptable, retaining a certain amount of agency and choice in their work, preferring 'the relative independence' of streetwalking in pairs or groups (rather than alone, like Hogarth's harlot) – heavily policed and always risking infection but experiencing, as their careers as prostitutes came to an end, 'little difficulty in reintegrating into a part of society which the great majority of them had never really left' (Henderson 1999: 51). As we have seen with rogue literature, however, fact and fiction – narrative and reality – are not so easy to disentangle. And the persuasiveness of a culturally available narrative may indeed be great enough to make whatever realities one might uncover pale into insignificance.

Certainly the image of the prostitute as a figure migrating into the city and then inhabiting particular zones within it retained – and still retains – its cultural force. The prostitute here also parallels the narrative of the vagabond, a rootless character similarly understood as innately drawn to vice. Rogues and vagabonds preoccupied social legislators and moral crusaders in Britain throughout the eighteenth century and into the Regency period: a period which, as Donald A. Low remarks in his book, *Thieves' Kitchen: The Regency Underworld*, might otherwise conventionally be associated with the novels of Jane Austen, that is, 'with social poise…an ideal of elegance and moral alertness' and a classical sense of order (Low 1982: 1). Low's account of the Regency underworld in London recalls Salgado's account of the Elizabethan underworld in that city, as well as Kellow Chesney's earlier popular study, *The Victorian Underworld* (1970). Each of these books provides a counter-narrative to any investment in a 'world picture' of metropolitan order and stability.

Like Salgado, Low emphasises the rapid increase of London's population at this time and the way it played host to large numbers of itinerant people. He chronicles a range of moral and legal concerns amongst respectable citizens and officials; but he also notes the ways in which rogues and vagabonds worked as a kind of spectacle, eliciting fascination just as much as repulsion. In 1817, the Keeper of Prints in the British Museum, John Thomas Smith, published *Vagabondiana, or Anecdotes of Mendicant Wanderers through the Streets of London*. Smith wrote rather sternly about beggars in London as a public nuisance and worried in particular about how difficult it could be to distinguish 'industrious' beggars from 'sturdy impostors' – that is, reality from fiction – although he also characterised begging as a declining phenomenon, with new Vagrancy Laws designed to remove them from the streets. But he sketched them, too, in the already well-established tradition of what were called 'Cries', artistic renderings of urban outcasts and 'anchorless' people (see Shesgreen 2002), and his pictures conveyed a sense of the street-based beggar's often quite elaborate costume aesthetics. Lionel Rose has suggested that beggars in Regency London were so 'varied and raggedly picturesque...that a picaresque literary sub-culture grew up around them, a product of myth and folklore in which the "Jovial Beggar" was somewhat enviously depicted as the carefree antithesis of the work-bound "flats" (mugs) they preyed upon' (Rose 1988: 23). The gypsy, too, figured in this way, especially through the romantic autobiographical novels of the English linguist George Borrow, *Lavengro* (1851) and its sequel, *The Romany Rye* (1857), which see the author leaving London to go out on the open road to mix with gypsies and celebrate their wanderlust. The narrative emerging here is quite different to Hogarth's representation of the eighteenth-century prostitute. It shows that the beggar and vagabond – as well as eliciting moral disapproval from many – could also find themselves inhabiting a certain kind of romance, built around one's attraction to (or nostalgias for) a 'carefree' existence and a wandering life free from the duties of family and work.

Subcultures are sometimes sentimentalised, sometimes not; and the narratives they are given are therefore sometimes romantic, sometimes anti-romantic, depending on the case or, rather, depending on the uses to which a subculture is put and the investments being made in them. If vagabond and rogue communities are cast as largely parasitical and self-interested, in pursuit of financial gain and 'extravagance', then it might be difficult to make a politically progressive investment in them, for example. Around the middle of the nineteenth century, Karl Marx had argued that the *working* classes or proletariat carried with them the possibility of revolution precisely because their labour both organised and defined them: making them conscious of their classed position and therefore enlightened about the level of their exploitation. But the vagabond underclasses – what Marx unflatteringly called the *lumpenproletariat* – only attracted his scorn. Marx's *The Eighteenth Brumaire of*

Louis Bonaparte (1851–52) was a commentary on the French *coup d'état* carried out by Napoleon I's nephew in December 1851. To lend support to his cause, Louis Bonaparte had gathered together not a revolutionary working class but a ragtag of vagrant subcultures, which Marx lists as follows:

> On the pretext of founding a benevolent society, the *lumpenproletariat* of Paris had been organized into secret sections, each section being led by Bonapartist agents, with a Bonapartist general at the head of the whole. Alongside decayed *roués* with doubtful means of subsistence and of doubtful origin, alongside ruined and adventurous offshoots of the bourgeoisie, were vagabonds, discharged soldiers, discharged jail-birds, escaped galley-slaves, swindlers, mountebanks, *lazzaroni* [Italian idlers and beggars], pickpockets, tricksters, gamblers, *maquereaux* [procurers], brothel-keepers, porters, *literati*, organ-grinders, rag-pickers, knife-grinders, tinkers, beggars, in short the whole indefinite, disintegrated mass thrown hither and thither, which the French term *la Boheme*.
>
> (Tucker 1972: 479)

Far from having organised revolutionary potential, the *lumpenproletariat* were instead, for Marx, susceptible to whatever reactionary ideologies and movements came along, self-interested rather than class conscious, 'unenlightened' and therefore easily led – which explained, for Marx, why they so readily gave their support to Louis Bonaparte's 'bourgeois' claim to power.

By the mid-nineteenth century, however, the problem for political and social theorists, among many others, was that itinerants and vagabonds of various kinds were increasingly inhabiting the major cities across Europe and in the United States – and it was proving difficult (just as it still is, today) to know exactly what to do with them. What does a city do with its prostitutes and brothels? Or its beggars and vagrants? Or its street gangs? Or its criminal underworlds? Policing is one way of dealing with these phenomena, typically with little success; but social classification and identification has been another, and by the later part of the nineteenth century these kinds of projects could also be tied to large-scale programmes of social reform. Studies of subcultures as we know them today find their origins in several of the human sciences emerging during this period: criminology and social reportage, as well as anthropology and ethnography, those classificatory human sciences which had gained momentum in the wake of colonialism and the spread of the various European empires into other countries. In England in the late 1840s and 1850s, these disciplinary positions were wonderfully combined in the work of Henry Mayhew, a journalist for the *Morning Chronicle* newspaper who travelled across London interviewing and chronicling its many underclasses. His work – a massive project of social classification – was published in 1861–62 as *London Labour and the London Poor*.

The subtitle, *A Cyclopaedia of the Condition and Earnings of Those That Will Work, Those That Cannot Work, and Those That Will Not Work*, gave expression to exactly those relations to labour and productivity that had worked to distinguish mainstream or respectable society from vagabond subcultures for so long. But Mayhew invoked another powerful distinction drawn from nineteenth-century anthropology, which had conventionally characterised civilised people as settled or sedentary, and 'native' and uncivilised populations around them or elsewhere as nomadic: that is, vagrant. For Mayhew, this binary also seemed to distinguish the myriad street folk he interviewed and chronicled – street vendors, performers, runaways, prostitutes, itinerant workers, various kinds of criminals, and so on – from respectable metropolitan Londoners. Here is part of a section titled 'Of Wandering Tribes in General', which opens Mayhew's great study:

> Of the thousand millions of human beings that are said to constitute the population of the entire globe, there are – socially, morally, and perhaps even physically considered – but two distinct and broadly marked races, viz., the wanderers and the settlers – the vagabond and the citizen – the nomadic and the civilized tribes.... The nomad is...distinguished from the civilised man by his repugnance to regular and continuous labour – by his want of providence in laying up a store for the future – by his inability to perceive consequences ever so slightly removed from immediate apprehension – by his passion for stupefying herbs and roots, and, when possible, for intoxicating fermented liquors – by his extraordinary powers of enduring privation – by his comparable sensibility to pain – by an immoderate love of gaming, frequently risking his own personal liberty upon a single cast – by his love of libidinous dances – by the pleasure he experiences in witnessing the suffering of sentient creatures – by his delight in warfare and all perilous sports – by his desire for vengeance – by the looseness of his notions as to property – by the absence of chastity among his women, and his disregard of female honour – and lastly, by his vague sense of religion – his rude idea of a Creator, and utter absence of all appreciation of the mercy of the Divine Spirit.
>
> (Mayhew 1968: 1–2)

This remarkable tally of (mostly negative) character traits entrenches a number of cultural logics we have already seen in relation to vagabonds – rootlessness, the refusal of organised labour, detachment from property, self-interest – as if they are now embedded in a readily available discourse through which such people are eternally condemned to be represented. And it adds some more, such as the potential for drug addiction and intoxication. But Mayhew wasn't remote from his subjects: he talked to them, close up. Andrew Tolson has looked at Mayhew's role as an interviewer, seeing the interview itself as a new social 'technology' in the later nineteenth century and a 'special journalistic genre', a way of evoking (in this case) a street's 'lived culture' for a reading public (Tolson 1990). Mayhew's chronicles allow his subjects to speak, to express themselves, a fact that radically distances his work from commentaries about subcultural life which remain remote from their subjects – or, as Elizabethan rogue literature sometimes did, which might actually invent or fabricate a subcultural speaking subject.

On the other hand, drawing on the work of Michel Foucault, Tolson suggests that even an interviewer as sympathetic as Mayhew nevertheless worked within a larger framework of governmentality and social regulation: positioning his subjects, othering them, 'subjectifying' them. Mayhew preserved his own distinction from street cultures – consistent with the distinction he had made between the settled and the vagrant – even as he interviewed them and walked amongst them. Later on, however, it was not unusual for outsiders to *masquerade* as vagrants or tramps in order to chronicle metropolitan underworlds at first hand. In the mid-1860s, the newspaper journalist and hack novelist James Greenwood wrote a series of lurid pieces for the *Pall Mall Gazette* based on his overnight experiences in a London workhouse. For Seth Koven, this is an example of *slumming*, where otherwise respectable middle-class 'adventurers' leave their homes and transform themselves (what Koven calls 'self-fashioning') into a member of the vagrant underclass in order to experience first hand, if only for a moment, the 'true' nature of vagrant life. The accounts that slummers such as Greenwood produced were not neutral or dispassionate: quite the opposite, it would seem. Even the fact of visiting these underclasses at night has a narrative or rhetorical effect: 'The darkness of night and his imposture as a casual [i.e. one of the "casual poor"] make possible the "true" revelations Greenwood offers readers, whereas the light of day and the sanctioned apparatus of state inspection can only produce concealment and hypocrisy' (Koven 2004: 46). Darkness reveals here, while light conceals: this is a typically subcultural inversion, but it is also a part of the project of the Enlightenment, that is, the need to shine a light on (or, to enlighten) the many dark corners of the world. Later 'slum explorers' masquerading as vagabonds included the novelists Jack London and George Orwell, an Eton-educated writer who went on the road as a tramp to experience first hand what it meant to be 'down and out'. Slumming again has something anthropological about it and, indeed, it is also associated with the slummer's experience of racial difference. Kevin Mumford (1997) has used the term to describe white participation in the sex districts of Harlem in New York in the 1920s, with their speakeasies and jazz clubs – and Mumford and Koven both note the prurient interest in sexual activity, promiscuity (rather like Mayhew's 'absence of chastity') and homosexuality in particular, that slummers could bring to bear on the people they visited.

Argot, slang and cant

Mayhew was fascinated by the often obscure languages of London's street cultures, their 'argot' – a word originally used to refer to thieves' slang. There has been, for many years, extensive interest from linguists – amateur and professional – in the argot of subcultures, as in the example of George Borrow noted above. A word used to describe the argot of swindlers and cony-catchers by the chroniclers of Elizabethan underworlds was 'cant', from the Latin *canere*, to sing, a word perhaps associated with the singing (for alms) of beggars and wandering friars. In the first volume of her excellent two-volume study, *A History of Cant and Slang Dictionaries*, Julie Coleman draws some important distinctions between what she calls different 'language labels' (Coleman 2004a: 3). *Standard English* is widely understood and shared, generally giving 'no indication through vocabulary, grammar, or syntax of its users' regional origins or social status' (3). *Jargon* is usually used by distinct professional working groups and/or those with an interest in technical matters. *Slang* is used 'by a closed group of people, often united by common interests' (4), not attached to work or profession and therefore, potentially at least, subcultural. It might be associated with youth and fashionable trends, as in Max Décharné's informative but rather nostalgic *Straight From the Fridge, Dad: A Dictionary of Hipster Slang* (2000). Another word for fashionable slang was *flash*. But slang was also associated with vagabond communities and criminal underworlds, as in Eric Partridge's *American Tramp and Underworld Slang* (1931) or Gary Simes's *Australian Underworld Slang* (1993). For Coleman, *cant* 'goes one step further' than *jargon*: 'Its primary purpose is to deceive, to defraud, and to conceal. It is the language used by beggars and criminals to hide their dishonest and illegal activities from potential victims' (2004a: 4). Her first volume begins with the 114-word glossary of Elizabethan vagabond cant attached to Harman's *A Caveat or Warning for Common Cursitors*, and the various instances of cant dialogue Harman supplies (e.g. 'I couched a hogshead in a Skypper this darkemans' [25]). Harman drew on some earlier sources for his glossary which was then used in turn as a source to be modified and extended by others, such as Richard Head, later on. The eighteenth century saw the publication of some stand-alone canting dictionaries, liberally used (as the earlier glossaries of cant words had also been) in much of the rogue and vagabond literature produced during this time.

Samuel Johnson's *Dictionary of the English Language* – his great, authoritative compilation of modern Standard English words – was published in 1755. Thirty years later, with Johnson's dictionary still very much in circulation, Captain Francis Grose, an antiquarian, published his *Classical Dictionary of the Vulgar Tongue* (1785): a compilation of cant terms drawn from many sources as well as what Grose, in his preface to the second edition, called 'burlesque phrases, quaint allusions, and nicknames for persons, things and places' (Grose

1963: 7–8). For Coleman, Grose's dictionary worked in quite the opposite way to Johnson's, especially through its celebration of the ephemerality of subcultural language:

> While Johnson viewed change as regrettable but unavoidable, Grose saw the mutability of language not only as essential, but also as something to be celebrated. Johnson avoided listing short-lived terms and those not dignified by tradition. For Grose, the more novel, the more transient terms are, the more reason there was for recording them…Grose's *Classical Dictionary* is in some ways an antidote to Johnson's: its contents are neither uplifting nor educational; its purpose is to amuse and entertain.
>
> (Coleman 2004b: 4–5)

This is a Dictionary without a higher purpose, in other words, cut loose from pedagogical imperatives. Further elaborations soon followed. In 1819, the confidence trickster James Hardy Vaux – who was twice transported to Australia as a convict – published a lengthy glossary of slang and 'flash language'. A few years later, Pierce Egan, who had written about Regency underworlds in his popular *Life in London* series begun in 1824, produced a new edition of Grose's dictionary. The interest in slang languages began to diversify – and so did the various 'underworlds' which spoke them. Perhaps the most prolific recorder of slang was Eric Partridge, who had published his *Dictionary of Slang and Unconventional English* in 1937. Partridge had studied Classics, French and English in Queensland, Australia, serving in the army in the First World War – his first book was a collection, *Songs and Slang of the British Soldier (1914–1918)*. He then became a full-time writer and researcher, well known for occupying the same desk in the British Library almost every day. Partridge compiled or assisted with a number of specialised slang dictionaries, including the elaborately titled, *A Dictionary of the Underworld, British and American: Being the Vocabulary of Crooks, Criminals, Racketeers, Beggars and Tramps, Convicts, the Commercial Underworld, the Drug Traffic, The White Slave Traffic, Spivs* (1949).

Not least because of their amateur status, dictionaries of underworld slang were not always reliable or accurate. They certainly paid tribute to the ephemerality of language but they could also create a nostalgic, discrete view of underworld language as it once was – or might have been. We can see nostalgia at work in the remarkable glossaries of a contemporary of Partridge's. David W. Maurer was a professional sociolinguist from the United States, well known for his bestselling account of confidence tricksters, *The Big Con* (1940). Like Partridge, Maurer had chronicled the slang of many different social groups, not always underworld subcultures: fishermen, for example. But he also worked with criminal, gambling and drug underworlds. In his essay, 'The Argot of Narcotic Addicts' (1936), Maurer defines underworlds in a now-familiar way as 'parasitic on the dominant culture' and then makes the argument that underworlds develop specialist, secretive languages because they are organised outside or against 'legitimate society', and because their sense of solidarity and the level of their internal organisation is therefore necessarily heightened (Maurer 1981: 274–75). Underworld argot, for Maurer, reflects an underworld's social structure (which means that it is never used individualistically: it is *always* social). Moreover, it is 'spoken almost exclusively in the presence of other members of that group' and 'seldom used at all in the presence of outsiders' (276), even though some aspects of it may become popularised and shared more broadly. His essay is concerned with narcotic addicts who are linked to a criminal underworld through dealers or 'pedlars' and other activities. His primary focus is on opium addicts and – consistent with his own professional identity as a linguist – Maurer identifies them first and foremost as *talkers*:

> Where opium is smoked, a chef (either professional or amateur) is always available to cook the pills for the smokers. In these establishments (usually referred to in literature as 'opium dens' but known to the addicts as *hop joints* or *lay down joints*) conversation is lively and addicts enjoy associating with their friends. Among opium smokers, especially where the smoking is done in groups, conversation is a notable concomitant to smoking; the general sense of well-being and mental relaxation tends to stimulate conversation. This tendency to converse, often on a high intellectual level, has been noted by non-criminal opium smokers – such as the artists and writers of Paris and other bohemian centres – but seems to be notably absent among needle addicts, who like to 'coast' and enjoy the drug subjectively.
> (280–81)

This is in some ways a surprising passage. It rests on an important distinction, subculturally speaking: between opium addicts as social (and therefore conversational), and 'needle addicts' as solitary (and therefore, literally, speechless). It then produces a hierarchy of drug use, valorising opium addiction over those other, needle-based forms. The hierarchy is in effect a distinction between the intelligent and the frivolous, those who care about language and those who don't: 'The conservative, sometimes dignified and intelligent opium smoker has given way to an increasing number of cool needle-pushers and marihuana smokers who are not only playing havoc with the drugs of addiction, but with the argot as well' (281–82). Maurer is especially scathing about the argot of marijuana smokers, which seems 'thin, obscure and affected', 'naive' and 'unseasoned' – as opposed to the opium smoker's argot which is 'cynical, sharp-witted, mature and rich in life experience' (293–94). This is a variation on a conventional distinction drawn between youth and age, shallowness and depth. But in writing off newer narcotic user-based argots, Maurer produces

a resonant elegy for the social world of the opium addict: less like the frivolous and ephemeral language realms charted by Francis Grose so much earlier
on, and more like the dignified, uplifting moral impetus that had underwritten Samuel Johnson's project.

Along with Coleman's categories of *cant* and *slang*, the British linguist
Paul Baker gives us other, more precise designations for subcultural argot: for
example, *Lingua Franca* (a kind of simplified language spoken by sailors which
entered beggar and rogue argot during the eighteenth century), *Romani* (used
by gypsies but also influencing vagabond and underworld argots), and *Parlaree*.
The word *Parlaree*, Baker notes, is derived from the Italian *parlare*, to speak,
but it is more specific in its lexicon than the broader colloquial term, *parley*. It
emerges from earlier vagabond and sailor argots to become a language – or an
'anti-language', that is, a highly coded way of speaking – used by gay men. But
Parlaree is also associated with the theatre and with 'camp' performance. Baker
in fact focuses on its more recent manifestation as *Polari* – shown off during
the late 1960s on the BBC radio show, *Round the Horne*, in sketches featur-
ing two unemployed and very camp actors, Julian and Sandy, the latter played
by the flamboyant English comic actor, Kenneth Williams. Popularised in this
way, *Polari* was nevertheless historically specific. By the early 1970s – when
it became politically important to be openly gay – camp, theatrical expressions of male homosexuality 'became stigmatised' and *Polari* soon 'appeared
to have become moribund, so that by the 1980s it was more forgotten than
remembered' (Baker 2002: 155). It is now a 'lost language', as Baker puts it,
although it is also occasionally revived. Indeed, although it was once important to gay male self-fashioning, allowing its users 'to create the world as they
saw it' (160), it is now cast by Baker much as Maurer had cast the argot of the
opium addict, as a matter of linguistic heritage. His study is a celebration of a
moment which no longer exists during which it seemed right and necessary
to draw on a 'secret language' in conversation with those people sharing the
same socio-cultural affiliations.

Street visibility

In his classic study undertaken during the Depression, *Boy and Girl Tramps of
America* (1934), the US sociologist and slummer Thomas Minehan describes
some of the many children and teenagers (of an estimated several hundred
thousand) who abandoned – or were abandoned by – their families at this
time and took to the road and the railroad. Minehan talks about the argot of
child tramps and sees it as a function of what he calls 'their tribal life':

> The first thing to notice about the tribal life of the boys and girls is
> the numerical size of the unit. The young tramps divide into gangs of a

dozen or less.... This unit, like all tribal units, has at its head a chief....
Some tribes are developing nocturnal habits. They sleep or travel by day
in box cars or brush jungles [meeting places or camps], and prowl by
night. It is a good time to prowl.... Almost all gangs of boys and girls
on the road have, as tribes have everywhere, a restricted geographical
location. Young tramps, as well as older ones, tend to remain fairly close
to the spot of their origin.... Every tribe, anthropologists tell us, has a
distinctive language or dialect. The child tramps are rapidly developing
one. Basically the language is English, with the addition of slang words
and terms. Yet what foreigner using a grammar and the Oxford dictionary could understand!

(Minehan 1934: 210, 211, 214, 217)

These remarks show us once again just how close the sociological study of subcultures was (and still so often is) to anthropology: close enough to register
a local vagrant subculture as a 'tribe'. Minehan's affectionately primitivising
terminology is consistent with earlier studies of tramps and hobos, including
that of Nels Anderson's famous study of homeless, migratory men in Chicago,
The Hobo (1923), to which I shall return in Chapter 2. The tramping children are 'tribal', they meet in 'jungles', and so on: this is how their sociality
is expressed. Away from the home and family, they are also potentially threat-
ening, nocturnal and prowling. Timothy J. Gilfoyle has given a similar, more
recent account of the child and teenager pickpockets in New York City during
the later part of the nineteenth century: those 'street rats and gutter snipes'
who lived 'outside the paradigm of middle-class domesticity, enjoying few, if
any, traditional familial influences' – and so, 'almost by necessity', developing a 'confrontational and oppositional subculture relative to adult authority'
and cultivating 'their own conception of freedom and independence' (Gilfoyle
2004: 870).

We can think about the understanding of subcultural identity as something formulated away from home and family but which compensates for this
lack by organising new, alternative kinds of sociality, however they might be
described. The 'street' is one destination for those who deviate from the
home, and Gilfoyle talks at length about the 'street culture' of New York's
gutter snipes. But the street is also a key aspect of organised urban planning,
and it is heavily policed and patrolled, monitored, regularly cleaned, and
so on. Legitimated notions of what is appropriate to the street, and what
is not, structure the visible and public landscape of modern cities. Indeed,
a city may be 'divided' along exactly these lines. Judith R. Walkowitz, in
her book *City of Dreadful Delight* (1992), looks at various accounts of the
street prostitute in London during the late nineteenth century, capturing the
home/away-from-home binary:

> The symbol of female vice, the prostitute established a stark contrast to domesticated female virtue.... She was also a logo of the divided city itself...prostitution appeared in two guises: in disorderly behaviour on the part of 'soiled doves', sauntering down the city thoroughfares, dangerous in their collectivity; or as the isolated activity of the lone streetwalker, a solitary figure in the urban landscape, outside home and hearth, emblematic of urban alienation...
>
> (Walkowitz 1992: 21–22)

This passage conveys two powerful images of the late nineteenth-century prostitute, one as part of a social group, the other as isolated and alone: rather like Maurer's distinction between opium and needle addicts. Streetwalking can certainly be a solitary pursuit, even though it might also participate in a lived 'street culture'. Another emblematic figure of nineteenth-century metropolitan alienation is the *flaneur*, the 'man on the street', an otherwise aimless city stroller who looks at and observes the people around him while 'maintaining a detached, anonymous and essentially distant relation to the urban landscape he moves through' (Turner 2003: 29): a spectator of other people's 'lived culture' rather than a participant. The *flaneur* emerges as a Parisian figure, credited to the poet Charles Baudelaire who had translated, and been influenced by, Edgar Allan Poe's short story, 'The Man of the Crowd' (1840) – a story about a convalescing urban stroller who finds himself observing the crowds around him and then, as night falls, compulsively follows a man through the city streets. But the *flaneur* is not subcultural. It is understood, instead, as a man who distinguishes himself from the crowd – from the tangible signs of mass society – in order to preserve his individuality. Mark W. Turner has distinguished the *flaneur* in turn from the *cruiser*, a different mode of male streetwalking whereby (usually) homosexual men aim to *connect* with strangers in the street, rather than remain aloof or apart from them. 'The cruiser's intention', he writes, 'is to find in the passing glances in the streets that person whose gaze returns and validates his own' (2003: 59). A connection is made through a set of shared 'signals' (60); even so, as we have already seen with the masquerades of slummers or with beggars who could be 'sturdy impostors', not everyone on the street is as they seem. How do you recognise another cruiser? How do you know if the signals you give out or receive are the right ones? Cruisers might themselves be on the edge of subcultural identity, sometimes connecting with others, sometimes not. Cruising is an individualised practice that at the same time doesn't *want* to stand out in a crowd, which also makes it difficult to observe sociologically or anthropologically. Turner asks, 'how do we know cruising when we see it?' (51), and his inability to answer this question with confidence allows him to draw attention instead to the ambiguities and uncertainties that structure the often fleeting cruising experience. (Dianne Chisholm has interestingly talked about the 'cruising flaneur', combining the two positions outlined here; she also describes the 'lesbian flaneur' in queer urban neighbourhoods: see Chisholm 2005: 49.)

Street-based homosexual or queer subcultures may or may not be easy to recognise, and indeed, the question of the extent of homosexual 'visibility' in public places has preoccupied many researchers as well as, of course, many of those in the subcultures themselves. William Reichard has written about what it was like to go into Kirmser's, a workingman's bar in Minnesota that during the evening became a 'hidden sanctuary for homosexual men and women':

> We never just walked into Kirmser's, nothing as simple as that. We scouted the terrain first to see who might be watching us. If the coast was clear, we stepped forward quickly, yanked the door open and lunged inside.... If there were too many people on the street or too many cars, we might walk past Kirmser's, as if we didn't know it existed...
>
> (Reichard 2003: 3, 5)

The gay men and lesbians using this bar 'dressed like everyone else' (5), blending into the street crowd rather than distinguishing themselves from it. Their social and sexual difference, in other words, was not a matter of visibility at all. It is often noted that homosexual subcultures were mostly *invisible*, avoiding recognition and persecution as much as possible – a view in part expressed through the title of an influential collection of contemporary essays in gay and lesbian studies, *Hidden from History: Reclaiming the Gay and Lesbian Past* (Duberman *et al.* 1989), which also responds to the way homosexuals have been elided from historical research. Indeed, for John D'Emilio there was no realised sense of 'gay history' until around the 1970s, partly because of homosexual invisibility but also because homosexual men and women were almost never regarded in social terms, that is, subculturally: 'Homosexuality had no history. It was a medical condition, a psychopathological state embodied in aberrant individuals. It had been and remained hidden, isolated, and marginal, a set of disconnected and fragmentary life stories' (D'Emilio 1992: 96). Gay and lesbian historians over the last thirty years or so, however, have recovered that history and insisted on the *social* aspects of homosexual life. But the view of homosexual invisibility in public places has also been contested. Michael Sibalis has noted the conventional stress on concealment in accounts of homosexual subcultures. But his analysis of the homosexual subculture in the Palais-Royal in the heart of Paris during the nineteenth century gives a very different picture: 'the most startling feature of Paris's homosexual subculture in this earlier period is not how invisible it was, but, on the contrary, how conspicuous it could be, at least at certain times and in certain places' (Sibalis 2001: 117). The gardens and cafés were well-known meeting places for homosexuals, but they were also places at which they could be seen and chronicled, *flaneur*-like, by others: 'Tens of thousands of Parisians must have

observed for themselves at least some of the conspicuously public homosexual activity that took place there…and thousands more would have read about
it in books and newspapers in the mid-nineteenth century' (127). Public visibility was a matter of being chronicled, performed and publicised by others
– think again of the BBC's *Round the Horne*, with Julian and Sandy – as well
as a matter of self-expression. Leslie Choquette has also looked at gay and
lesbian 'neighbourhoods' and public visibility in Paris in the late nineteenth
century, and she comments on the rise of gay and lesbian autobiographical
writing and memoir, as well as the increasing interest in gay and lesbian social
life among the French novelists, such as Zola and Guy de Maupassant. By this
time, the Palais-Royal 'had given way to the Hotel Drouot, boulevard, and
theatre lines by day, the perennial Champs-Élysées by night' (Choquette 2001:
154). Journalists and novelists continued to chronicle gay, lesbian and cross-
dressing subcultural activity, testifying to its prolonged visibility in public life.
George Chauncey makes the same point about 'Gay New York' around the end
of the nineteenth century and up to the First World War, charting 'a highly visible, remarkably complex, and continually changing gay male world' in the
city, across a number of neighbourhoods and public precincts (Chauncey 1994:
1). So public, and so publicised, was this world that Chauncey wonders how
it subsequently came to be so forgotten: 'How did we lose sight of a world so
visible and extensive in its own time that its major communal events garnered
newspaper headlines and the attendance of thousands?' (8).

Travellers and communities

This chapter has wanted to give subcultures a 'vagabond' history, turning to
the rogues and vagabonds of Elizabethan England as a point of origin and identifying a set of cultural logics through which subcultures have historically been
understood: as organised social worlds which might even have their own languages; as 'parasitical' on labour and the economy, self-interested rather than,
say, class conscious; as deviating from home and family; linked more to the
street or the road than to a 'settled' existence and property ownership; as
impoverished in some respects, extravagant or excessive in others; and as in
some ways secretive while in other ways all too visible. The notion of vagabond subcultures has persisted into the present day with the examples of New
Age Travellers and post-hippie communal living. We might recall that around
the late 1960s it was not unusual to describe the entire lifespan of a North
American hippie as, precisely, a 'trip', as the eminent US sociologist Lewis
Yablonsky had done in 1968: 'A trip in the hippie world can be more than
one or a series of psychedelic experiences – it can refer to a person's total life
voyage' (Yablonsky 1968: 21). Hippies are usually understood as counter-cultural rather than subcultural: as John Robert Howard has put it, they 'posed

a fairly well thought-out alternative to conventional society' and, importantly for the notion of a counter-culture, there was some sense that this alternative mode of living 'would induce change in the rest of society' (Howard 1969: 43; see also Roszak 1970). Very few subcultures have widespread social change on their agenda, nor (with some exceptions) do they imagine that society's values ought somehow to reflect or absorb their own. But counter-cultures do, so that it is commonplace to suggest, for example, that the hippies 'made a lasting impact on the ethos of America' (Miller 1991: 3) or that 'hippie values' are indeed broadly shared or sympathised with (see also Spates and Levin 1972). Howard identifies four hippie 'types' along these lines: the *visionaries* ('utopians who pose an alternative to existing society', repudiating in particular the conventional values of 'work and commerce'), *freaks* and *heads* (drug-oriented hippies who relish the 'trip'), *plastic hippies* (those for whom being a hippie is merely a matter of 'fashion' or appearance, that is, 'inauthentic' hippies), and *midnight hippies* – considerable numbers of usually older people 'integrated into straight society' who are nevertheless in sympathy with the bohemian values that hippies espouse (Howard 1969: 43, 50).

Hippies from the late 1960s might have relished the 'trip' but they also developed alternative modes of *settlement* through communal living: producing what Speck *et al.* had called 'new families', made up of groups of peers and radically distinguished from the conventional nuclear family at home (Speck *et al* 1974: 34). In his study of more contemporary 'cultures of resistance', *Senseless Acts of Beauty* (1996), George McKay mixes post-hippie social movements together with New Age Travellers and various neo-tribes to produce an affectionate tribute to British counter-cultures *and* subcultures during the 1980s and early 1990s that talks about rootlessness and settlement at the same time. What for Henry Mayhew were two opposed modes of living – the vagabond and the sedentary – are here brought together under a new kind of tribal identification. In fact, McKay understands the emergence of New Age Travelling precisely in the context of a 'crisis in housing' in Britain during the early 1980s, producing a marked increase in the numbers of urban squatters and rural travellers, two available solutions to the problem of homelessness (McKay 1996: 46). His descriptions of Rainbow Fields Village at Molesworth, England, as a 'traveller-related community', and the Native American-influenced Tipi Valley settlement in South Wales with its 'traveller-type people', evoke a sense of communal living at its most marginal and precarious (53, 60). These are transient, provisional settlements, its inhabitants constantly facing eviction; even so, McKay writes that he was 'struck by the extent to which they *are* living spaces, vibrant and imaginative' (71). Other accounts of New Age Travellers in Britain stress their nomadic lifestyle and contrast them with life in more conventional village settlements. For Kevin Hetherington, Travellers are nothing less than the descendents of those early modern vagabonds, unkempt strangers who in their large, slow convoy passed through the villages of Wiltshire, Dorset and Hampshire.... They had a dirty, dishevelled look that was taken as a sign that they had transgressed the boundary of respectability and should be given no quarter.

(Hetherington 2000: 13–14)

McKay had also drawn attention to dirt as a 'signifier' of the New Age Travellers' social difference, distinguishing them from the generally clean and tidy realms of respectable English village life (McKay 1996: 66). But Hetherington elaborates the point, linking his discussion to the anthropologist Mary Douglas's definition in *Purity and Danger* (1966) of dirt and pollution as 'matter out of place' and then reading the New Age Traveller iconically as a 'scapegoat' and a 'stranger' in society – or as a 'folk devil', a term he takes from Stanley Cohen's important study, *Folk Devils and Moral Panic: The Creation of Mods and Rockers* (1972), which had looked at media reactions to two rather different, but equally troublesome British subcultures, in the 1960s.

Both Hetherington and McKay examine New Age Travellers in terms of their use of *space* (as they travel) and the way they create *place* (as they camp or settle), understanding these practices as transgressive. To a degree, they also register the utopian aspects of New Age Travelling, as a kind of 'disordering' of conventional, taken-for-granted binaries (between clean and dirty, authorised and unauthorised, property and trespass, etc.). Hetherington also draws on the earlier work of anthropologist Victor Turner and his idea of *liminality* to account for the New Age Travellers' predicament, and it is worth returning to Turner for a moment to explain this idea because his writings have been useful to other analyses of subcultures, too. Born in Glasgow in 1920, Turner studied literature at University College, London. During the Second World War, he lived in a gypsy caravan with his wife and children, becoming increasingly interested in anthropology. Turner studied under Max Gluckman at the University of Manchester and did his fieldwork in central Africa on the Ndembu people, where he explored notions of ritual, symbolic action and social conflict. Later on, he went to the United States, becoming a Professor of Anthropology and Social Thought at the University of Chicago in 1968, after which he worked at the University of Virginia where he developed his interests in performance as a group practice. Turner's literary background heavily informed his anthropological work, in particular, his notion of *communitas*. His most influential book, *The Ritual Process*, was published in 1969 at the high point of the hippie counter-culture in the United States. Here, he wrote about 'liminal *personae* ("threshold people")' and *liminality*, a kind of space or moment in which one is suddenly marginal or decentred, 'betwixt and between the positions assigned and arrayed by law, custom, convention and ceremonial' (Turner 1995: 95). This was where one would find examples of *communitas*, and Turner drew on the example of hippies, among others – alongside his extensive commentaries on the rituals of those central African tribes he had studied – to illustrate the idea. *Communitas* was not quite the same thing as *community*, and it was to be distinguished from *structure*, which Turner associated with the law, custom and convention etc., as well as with rank and hierarchy, and with property ownership. To be liminal is to be, for a moment at least, without property, outside the law, free of social conventions, and so on. At one point, Turner quotes the character Gonzalo from Shakespeare's play *The Tempest* to give literary expression to the ideals of *communitas*:

> I' the commonwealth I would by contraries
> Execute all things; for no kind of traffic
> Would I admit; no name of magistrate;
> Letters should not be known; riches, poverty
> And use of service, none; contract, succession
> Bourn, bound of land, tilth, vineyard, none;
> No use of metal, corn, or wine, or oil;
> No occupation; all men idle, all;
> And women too, but innocent and pure…
> (Act II, scene 1, lines 141–49; cited Turner 1995: 134–35)

Gonzalo's 'structureless' vision of the commonwealth is a matter of spontaneity; permanence, on the other hand (or at least, an ideology of permanence, accumulation, investment etc.), belongs to *structure*. *Communitas* relationships are personal and immediate, rather than a matter of contract or obligation – something Turner saw in the hippie movement with its emphasis on 'togetherness', 'the now' and the 'happening' (113). He also saw it in the works of prophets and visionaries such as the poet William Blake, in the music of vagabond musicians from Bengal, in Zen Buddhism, and in the Franciscan order of the Catholic Church, which rejected the latter's structured system, disowned property and embraced poverty. 'While our focus here is on traditional preindustrial societies', Turner wrote, perhaps a little optimistically, 'it becomes clear that the collective dimensions, communitas and structure, are to be found at all stages and levels of culture and society' (113).

Rather like Henry Mayhew, then, Turner reads his own contemporary culture – western culture – in the framework of anthropological readings of indigenous tribes elsewhere, in this case Africa. Now, however, the 'unstructured' features associated with them (rootlessness, spontaneity, the unconventional, living outside the structured realms of work, production, property ownership, etc.) are invested with positive values rather than negative ones. There is certainly something 'primitive' or at least preindustrial about Turner's *communitas*, which is then often condemned to function either nostalgically or as utopian or otherworldly, or as a fleeting, idealised moment. (Ned Polsky, in his rather phlegmatic account of the Greenwich

Village beatniks published around the same time as Turner's work, had dismissed this approach as '"spontaneity" nonsense' [Polsky 1971: 178].) Although Turner had separated the term from *community*, in fact *communitas* owes a great deal to this term as it was (and still is) commonly understood. Just as *communitas* is opposed to *structure*, so *community* is routinely juxtaposed with *society*: this is the binary we find crystallised in Ferdinand Tonnies's early, influential sociological work, *Gemeinschaft und Gesellschaft*, first published in 1887. We shall come to see the term *community* used extensively as a way of expressing the social worlds of subcultures: the jazz community, the zine community, the virtual community, the tattoo community, and so on. For Tonnies, community (*Gemeinschaft*) is defined emotionally in terms of close-ness of relationships, most obviously through family, marriage and kinship ties or through 'fellowship' and co-operation. It is taken as a local expres-sion of neighbourhood and associated with rural life or folk life: for Tonnies, the German *Volk*. By contrast, relationships in modern society (*Gesellschaft*) are rationally, rather than emotionally, configured and a matter of contracts and agreements rather than fellowship. In society, people are individualised and competitive, rather than collective and co-operative. Authority-figures in the community are close by: the father, the priest. Society, however, is governed remotely by the state, by capitalist bureaucracy, by legislation and convention. Tonnies saw social relationships in the community as 'natural' and 'authentic', an organic expression of social belonging – whereas modern society is 'mechanical' and impersonal, leading to the experience not of a sense of belonging but of *alienation*. Infusing the *Gemeinschaft* with nostal-gia, he registered the transition from the one to the other in this haunting expression of the modern predicament, 'One goes into *Gesellschaft* [society] as one goes into a strange country' (Tonnies 1955: 38).

As Miranda Joseph has suggested, 'One might plausibly argue that the oppositional sequencing of community and society is constitutive of the field of sociology' (Joseph 2002: 6). Such a sequencing might help us to make sense of subcultures, too: as social worlds that can also understand themselves – and be understood by others – as 'oppositional' to, or an 'alternative' to, or even 'outside' of, society (whether early modern, or late modern). As I have noted, the term *community* is indeed sometimes invoked as a synonym for subcultures of one kind or another, helping to convey a Tonniesian sense of belonging, of 'fellowship', and of 'authentic' social relations. But we have also seen in this chapter that subcultures have often been understood as *antithetical* to Tonnies's *Gemeinschaft*. They can formulate themselves well away from the family and home, for example, like the 'gutter snipes and street rats' that Timothy J. Gilfoyle had described in New York City around the mid-nineteenth century, oppositional to rather than regulated by parental authority, their sense of belonging provisional and transient, their sociality (as Gilfoyle describes it) lacking 'any long-lasting system of reciprocal obligation fundamental to group cohesion and solidarity'

(Gilfoyle 2004: 871). This is quite different to Tonnies's sense of the community as a place of kinship, 'fellowship' and co-operation. Subcultural movement is also often charted as a movement *away* from rural communities, a migration into the metropolis, like that of Hogarth's Harlot – a migration which marks the beginning of her own alienation, even though it also provides her with a certain kind of sociality along the way. I have talked in this chapter about *vagabond subcultures*, territorial in many respects but defined primarily by movement – and in this sense again quite different to the Tonniesian notion of community as a stable form of settlement. Even so, the two can be drawn together, as we saw with the hippies' communal living and with McKay's work on New Age Traveller villages in Britain. We shall see Tonnies's influence again in this book, not least on Robert E. Park and Chicago School sociological work on subcultures, the subject of the next chapter. But *community*, although often useful, remains a problem for subcultural definitions. Its origins in the rural village or neighbourhood can be at odds with a subculture's metropolitan 'career'. It can work to produce 'anthropological' narratives about subcultures that are themselves – rather like Turner's *communitas* – nostalgic or idealised, and sometimes even 'primitive', and we shall see accounts of subcultural otherworldliness and utopias along these lines later on in this book. The vagabond aspects of some subcultures, as I have noted, can generate a romantic investment in them: an idealisation of life 'on the road' or of the bohemian disdain for work, for example: what Steven Connor has called the 'romance of the marginal', although he wrongly sees this only as a contemporary characteristic (Connor 1989: 228). In the same way, Tonniesian notions of *community* can also lend subcultural narratives a certain kind of romance, underwriting a subculture's distinction from 'mainstream' or 'conventional' society and reproducing through that subculture a version of Tonnies's binary of 'authentic' (in the subculture) and 'inauthentic' (in society) social relationships. Of course, there are always anti-romantic narratives out there which challenge these descriptions, such as Hogarth's account of the manipulation and fall-into-alienation of Moll Hackabout and Marx's account of the *lumpenproletariat* as self-interested, competitive and easily manipulated by 'bourgeois' interests, just as much a reflection or symptom of an atomised society as anyone else. Miranda Joseph has written *against* the 'romance of the [concept of] community', taking it – rather as Marx himself had done – as an 'oppressive' and 'constraining' category (2002: 16): she has an anti-romantic view of community itself. But *community* retains some force in subcultural studies and we shall see it put to use both as a sometimes richly connotative synonym for subcultures as well as an antithetical category – just like 'society' – from which subcultures are to be clearly distinguished.

Chapter 2

THE CHICAGO SCHOOL AND AFTER
Sociology, deviance and social worlds

Robert E. Park and the 'marginal man'

WHEN THE UNIVERSITY OF CHICAGO was opened in 1892, it included a Department of Sociology that came to dominate sociological perspectives in the United States for the next forty years. The 'Chicago School' was especially important to subcultural studies, with sociologists turning their attention to marginal social groups and 'deviant' social behaviour. They were empirical rather than theoretical in their approach, often going out into the field to do ethnographic research, much in the tradition of anthropology. Chicago was invariably their source and their resource, the second-largest city in the United States at the time and the destination for a wide variety of immigrant populations, not just from Europe and elsewhere but also from the American hinterland. Two famous, turn-of-the-century American novels give a kind of archetypal expression to early immigrant movement into Chicago: the journalist Theodore Dreiser's *Sister Carrie* (1890), about an ambitious young provincial woman who comes to Chicago in 1889 from a small mid-Western town, and Upton Sinclair's *The Jungle* (1906), about a family of Lithuanian immigrants who arrive in Chicago and find themselves put to work in the notorious Union Stock Yards. In these novels, the gulf between rich and poor in Chicago was charted through the carefully rendered lives of outsiders, new arrivals. The literary genre they used was naturalism, a 'sociological' genre which was drawn simultaneously to the ordinary and the aberrant and which, at this time, was also built around the 'muckraking' exposé of slum life on the one hand and corruption at the top on the other.

One of the key early figures from the Chicago School of sociology was another provincial immigrant, Robert E. Park, originally from Red Wing,

Minnesota. But Park came to Chicago in a roundabout way. He worked as a newspaper reporter in New York, studied at Ann Arbor and spent a year reading philosophy at Harvard. Then he travelled to Europe, going to Germany where he completed a Ph.D. dissertation on 'The Mass and the Public' and attended lectures in Berlin by Georg Simmel – 'my only formal instruction in sociology', he later wrote in an autobiographical note (Park 1950: vi). Back in the United States, Park worked with the African-American educationalist, Booker T. Washington, where he developed his interest in racial issues – having earlier written passionately against the Belgian colonial atrocities in the Congo. When he finally joined Chicago's Department of Sociology in 1914 at the age of fifty, his first course was in fact on 'The Negro in America'. But by the 1920s, along with Ernest W. Burgess, Park had developed a distinctive form of sociology that focused on Chicago itself, built around the idea of social 'ecology' – that is, seeing the city as a kind of ecosystem – and responding in particular to the fortunes, and misfortunes, of immigrant populations in that city in terms of their social difference and the 'problem' of cross-cultural contact.

Park thought about culture itself in grand, global terms, no doubt as a result of his own travels outside America but also because of Chicago's predicament as an immigrant destination. He drew on Tonnies's distinction between *Gemeinschaft* and *Gesellschaft* – outlined in Chapter 1 – in order to describe two kinds of places in the world, each of which is defined in social terms. The first is 'typically, a small, isolated community', unaffected by others around it and socially stable, where there is social consensus and very little internal conflict; but the second refers to those places, like Chicago, defined by movement and migration and which can seem to have very little social consensus at all. For Park, this distinction could be very broadly applied, so much so that it seemed to him even to account for the apparent differences between East and West, Orient and Occident: 'The unchanging East', he remarked, 'is the antipodes of the mobile West' (9). Park saw the stability of isolated communities as desirable in one sense, since it meant that a shared culture – built upon a stable society – could flourish. Indeed, *culture* itself, for Park, was tied to stable, ethnocentric social groups and societies: a point consistent with anthropological views at the time. Migration and mobility, on the other hand, tend to 'complicate social relations' (13), undoing social cohesion as people disperse and mix – but in the process they produce what Park thought of as *civilisation*, defined by movement and cross-cultural contact and communication. There may be no social consensus here – and there may in fact be a great deal of social conflict – but Park took this to be a defining feature of modern, western nations and, in particular, large, 'open' cities like Chicago. In a famous essay titled 'Human Migration and the Marginal Man' (first published in 1928), Park drew on Georg Simmel's notion of the 'stranger' to argue that those people who do migrate out of their isolated communities are 'emancipated' and even 'to a

certain degree become cosmopolitan' (1950: 351). Migration is 'the breaking of home ties' (350): this, for Park, is the beginning of the civilisation of
the modern world and Chicago was taken as the city in which, for better or
worse, its consequences most strikingly play themselves out.

Chicago in fact became iconic for Park – so that his 1925 collection of
essays, written with Burgess and Roderick D. McKenzie, could call itself *The
City* as if its findings applied to all metropolises everywhere. Park's opening
essay was first published in 1915 in the *American Journal of Sociology* – inaugu-
rated by Albion Small, the first Head of Chicago's Department of Sociology
– and it talked in a rather practical-minded sort of way about the city not as
an homogeneous place but as a place divided into various 'zones' and defined
by vocational specialisation and social difference. Forms of transportation and
mass communication, like the newspaper, can bring people together, but new
immigrants into the city may well try to preserve their social and cultural
autonomy. Under these conditions the city sees two opposing forces simultaneously at work, proximity (where different kinds of people intermingle)
and segregation (where social and cultural differences set people apart from
one another). Park put it this way, in a remarkable passage that sets the scene
for the Chicago School's interest in subcultures and introduces the notion of
a 'moral milieu':

> The processes of segregation establish moral distances which make the
> city a mosaic of little worlds which touch but do not interpenetrate.
> This makes it possible for individuals to pass quickly and easily from one
> moral milieu to another, and encourages the fascinating but dangerous
> experiment of living at the same time in several different contiguous,
> but otherwise widely separated, worlds. All this tends to give to city
> life a superficial and adventitious character; it tends to complicate social
> relationships and to produce new and divergent individual types. It intro-
> duces, at the same time, an element of chance and adventure which adds
> to the stimulus of city life and gives it, for young and fresh nerves, a
> peculiar attractiveness. The lure of great cities is perhaps a consequence
> of stimulations which act directly upon the reflexes. As a type of human
> behaviour it may be explained, like the attraction of the flame for the
> moth, as a sort of tropism.
>
> (Park 1925: 40–41)

The city may be full of 'little worlds', but it also enables people to move *through*
those worlds and to be transformed as a result. As the last sentence suggests,
Park saw this as a matter of youthful attraction and stimulation, a kind of sur-
render to the romance (or the libido) of the city in all its complexity. His view
rested on a powerful binary that saw the provincial community, with its stable,
unchanging social identity, as a place of convention, a *normalising* place – while

the modern city actively encourages people to become unconventional, divergent, exceptional and 'eccentric' (45). To explain this, however, Park turned from sociology to Freud, offering up a narrative to do with human behaviour that folded into his distinction between the community and the city. The community imposes discipline and restraint upon people: social controls, accepted moral codes, laws, social conventions. In doing so, however, it suppresses divergent impulses which inevitably leak out to produce 'eccentricity'. This may well be tolerated in the isolated realms of the community; but in the city, Park suggests, eccentricity can positively flourish. This is part of his notion that the city 'emancipates' its human subjects. The eccentric and the exceptional, far from being alienated in the city, find likeminded people and moral support there, forming their own 'moral milieu', developing their own 'divergent moral code', and inhabiting their own 'moral region'. They become social; they are marginal, rather than alienated; and they might very well be *difficult* to control or restrain, being defined instead by 'excess' (46). The problem for Park was that they might also, as a result, be just as segregated in the city as the community from which they departed.

In his book *The Pig and the Skyscraper: Chicago: A History of Our Future* (2002), Marco D'Eramo comments on the way in which Chicago has so compulsively studied itself not because of its uniqueness, but because it has understood itself 'as an *exemplary* city...as a representation of The American City' (D'Eramo 2002: 255). For the Chicago School sociologists, the city became a 'laboratory', 'one huge real-time experiment' (256). D'Eramo notes the influence of the University of Chicago philosopher John Dewey's notion of 'pragmatism' on Park, a concept also taken up by Dewey's influential colleague George H. Mead 'for whom an individual's "self" was a social structure, the internalisation of the process by which a group of individuals interacted with other groups' (257). Pragmatism suggests that people adjust to their social predicaments; but they *make* their predicaments too, enabling pragmatism to account for social marginality just as effectively as it could account for self-made success. D'Eramo talks about the fondness at the Chicago School for 'real-life stories' (257), but he criticises the way in which *everything* became exemplary for these sociologists. Individuals were understood as socially representative, as ideal types: *the* Italian, for example. 'The risk here', D'Eramo writes – expressing one of the key problems for subcultural studies – 'is that the individual's situation becomes the group's destiny; a transitory state comes to define a human type' (257). D'Eramo is also critical of Park's notion of urban 'ecology', which viewed the modern city essentially in organic terms and seemed to take its various, different social 'zones' as naturally occurring phenomena. Chicago may indeed still be 'the most segregated city in the United States' (267), but for D'Eramo the Chicago School sociologists understood segregation not just as typical but as an expression of the natural order of things.

The British sociologist Chris Jenks, in his book *Subculture: The Fragmentation of the Social* (2005), is much more critical still of Park and Chicago School sociology. He is right to note that Park developed a 'social-psychological' perspective, a 'micro-sociology' that was 'person-centred' and which saw people and place as organically tied together (Jenks 2005: 52). But it is this micro-sociological approach itself, grounded in a sense of Chicago as an 'exemplary' city, that attracts Jenks's strongest criticism:

> it details, elaborately details, particularity and difference. Now this kind of detail…provides a wealth of background data and examples but it is, in essence, a-social or non-sociological. In one sense the Chicago School had no theory of society greater than a theory of Chicago…[Chicago School sociology] then, is unashamedly micro in its approach, never looks to the bigger picture and is unfortunately ill-equipped to level a critique of the social structure or the going order much beyond its own parish boundaries.
>
> (68)

It seems odd to find that a book about subcultures actually speaks *against* a sociology that describes 'particularity and difference'. But in fact Jenks's book speaks out against subcultures, too, as well as subcultural studies, the kind of work that conceptualises subcultures and describes them – casting this as 'a kind of conceptual parochialism', the outcome of a restricted sociological 'mindset' (71). Since, as we have seen, Park had understood Chicago precisely as an 'open' city, where immigrants could *lose* their parochialism and become 'cosmopolitan', this criticism may be a little unfair. But for Jenks, the Chicago School's micro-vision meant that they concentrated their efforts on 'little worlds' – communities – while utterly ignoring 'the bigger picture', society itself. So Jenks rejects their approach and turns instead to quite a different kind of American sociologist, this time from Harvard University where Park had once studied philosophy: Talcott Parsons. Parsons' most influential book was *The Social System* (1951), a 'functionalist' work of macro-sociology which looked in abstract terms at the 'top-down' forces of society and the way they worked to normalise individuals. For Parsons, society must stabilise itself and must therefore impose a set of 'functional imperatives' on its citizens: requiring them to adapt to its norms, achieve its goals, integrate into its social system, and conform to social expectations. This kind of sociological perspective could not be further away from the Chicago School approach. Whereas Park looked at 'divergent' types who do *not* seem to conform or adapt, Parsons describes the systemic social forces that (as Jenks puts it) 'must, perforce, *consume* difference and divergence' (Jenks 2005: 81, my italics). While Park had focused on the sheer fact of social difference, Parsons turns to social norms and 'the ground rules of social life' (79). Jenks is a neo-Parsonian: for him, Parsons supplies the 'missing narrative' (73) that exposes the 'parochialism' of subcultural studies. It means, amongst other things, that Jenks's book is remarkably conservative, an appeal after the fact of subcultures for an end to social difference and the recovery of the sort of overarching social 'norms' that everyone (nationally? globally?) can somehow share. 'It is only by having a strong sense of the "together"', Jenks writes – in a distant echo of hippie argot – 'that we can begin to understand and account for that which is outside, at the margins, or, indeed, that which defies consensus' (144). In one sense this is true: one must have a sense of prevailing normativities in order to identify divergences. But can a 'sense of the "together"' ever hope to properly account for 'that which defies consensus'? Sociology is Jenks's master discourse, a theorised, abstract way of looking at the world that advocates norms over difference, integration over divergence, 'constraint' (144) over excess, society over subculture. In relation to this, the detailed studies of subcultures by Chicago School sociologists (as we have seen from the quote above) can thus seem to be 'a-social or non-sociological': outside the parameters of his discourse. Or perhaps they are on the *margins* of his discourse. Despite its title Jenks's book in fact barely looks at or mentions any subcultures at all: they are literally on the margins of his own study. At one point, he writes 'that subculture, as an idea, has always signalled or marked out the limits of sociological reason' (131). In this revealing comment, subcultures appear at the point at which a normative or 'functionalist' sociology dissolves away: as if they are something *un*reasonable, something divergent or exceptional in sociology itself.

Hobohemia and ganglands

The kind of sociology Jenks advocates is remote and abstracted, avoiding the 'details' of 'real-life stories' – we might even say, *suppressing* them – in order to underwrite its normative vision of society. But those 'real-life stories' kept on returning, and not just in sociological accounts of subcultures. As I have noted, imaginative literature in the United States had also turned its attention to Chicago, charting the stories of immigrant populations as they moved into the city through the 'sociological' literary genre of naturalism or realism. Both Carla Cappetti and Timothy B. Spears have noted that some Chicago-based literary novelists – such as James T. Farrell and Richard Wright – were in fact well aware of Chicago School sociology, drawing their 'conceptual' ideas from it as well as using it to consolidate the 'urban realism' genre that they wrote in (Spears 2005: 260; Cappetti 1993: 60–64). Literature can indeed be 'micro-sociological', investing in the details of everyday lives. But it is also an imaginative project, infusing those lives with rhetorical force and lending them an iconic register. For Spears, one of the 'most famous representations of Chicago's status as a magnet for hinterland migrants is Carl Sandburg's image of '"painted women under gas lamps luring the farm boys" in his poem "Chicago" (1914)' (Spears 2005: xiv). Here, the city is cast as a prostitute, drawing out the sort of excitement and libido in newcomers that Park later identified with modern American city life broadly speaking. We might think that the dialectic of sociological description and imaginative force is particular to literature; but it also appears in the work of other Chicago School sociologists, and it works to transform Chicago itself as a place through which urban realism is (to a greater or lesser degree) folded into a set of compelling romantic tropes. We can see this especially through the work of Nels Anderson on Chicago's 'hobo' population, and Frederic M. Thrasher on Chicago's 'ganglands'.

Nels Anderson's famous study, *The Hobo* (1923), was the first in the University of Chicago Press's Sociological Series — but Anderson himself remained quite literally on the margins of sociology as a discipline. He was born in Chicago but left home to become an itinerant worker, moving across the country, occasionally begging. Later he enrolled himself into school and then studied at Brigham Young University in Utah — an institution tied to the Church of Jesus Christ of Latter-day Saints and missionary projects in America. Anderson arrived back in Chicago by freight train at the age of twenty-one, and was admitted into the University of Chicago's Department of Sociology. Raffaele Rauty describes him as 'the most atypical of the young students' at the Chicago School, however, not least because of his interest in the plight of the 'hobo', that is, the homeless, itinerant and casual worker (Anderson 1998: 4). Having experienced hobo life himself, Anderson moved fairly easily amongst the many homeless men coming into Chicago — collecting many real-life stories along the way, and helping to pioneer the method of analysis known as 'participant observation'. This method of ethnography is quite different to slumming: there is little or no need for masquerade or impersonation because one is observing one's *own* social group, even if one might no longer be a part of it. I want to make two points about Anderson's remarkable study. First, he produced a clearly delineated subcultural geography for Chicago, built around the movement of the hobo through and around the city. He described the main 'stems' through the city, the various streets and precincts and parks frequented by hobos where a kind of hobo community flourished: 'The veteran of the road finds other veterans; the old man finds the aged; the chronic grouch finds fellowship; the radical, the optimist, the crook, the inebriate, all find others here to tune in with' (Anderson 1923: 4). Anderson called this *Hobohemia*, a bohemia of the homeless. Various 'characteristic institutions' gave Chicago's Hobohemia its materiality: cheap hotels and lodging houses, barber shops, missions, employment and welfare agencies, the occasional radical bookstore. On the outskirts of the city were the hobo camps, the *jungles*. Cut off from respectable social networks and set apart from other workers, the 'stem' and the 'jungle' were the only 'established social centres' available to the hobo.

The second point about Anderson's study is that he turned Hobohemia into a kind of utopia. As we saw with Maurer and the opium addict in Chapter 1, one key feature here is to do with the ease and the skill with which hobos converse:

> This vagabond existence tends to enrich the personality and long prac-
> tice has developed in some of these men an art of personal narrative that
> has greatly declined elsewhere. Many of them develop into fascinating
> raconteurs in the literal as well as the literary sense of the term…anyone
> who thinks may speak.
>
> (19, 26)

Real-life stories were easy to collect because, for Anderson, the hobos seemed to be natural storytellers, laden with experiences but also gifted with literary proficiency – keeping the art of 'personal narrative' alive and, we might even say, embodying narrative. Hobohemia had its radical politics, too, but it wasn't internally anarchic. 'Jungle laws are unwritten', Anderson noted, 'but strictly adhered to' (20): as if the hobos, as a social group, were remarkably self-disciplined and organised. More important, however, was Anderson's sense that Hobohemia was a place in which different racial groups – in particular, white Americans and African-Americans – could freely and comfortably cohabit, without reproducing the racisms and social hierarchies found in mainstream society. 'Absolute democracy reigns in the jungle', Anderson asserted: 'The jungle is the melting pot of trampdom' (19). Hobohemia is cast here as a special kind of place, a utopia, where 'the hobo enters into this life as he does no other. Here he turns his back on the world and faces his fellows, and is at ease' (19). Real or rhetorical, this is a moment of pure sociality – an example of Jenks's 'strong sense of the "together"' – that comes into being precisely because it is not a part of normative society.

Frederic M. Thrasher's *The Gang: A Study of 1,313 Gangs in Chicago* (1927) is still regarded in 'gang studies' (if I can call this criminological subdiscipline by this name) as its foundational text. Thrasher received both his MA and his Ph.D. from Chicago, and then moved to New York University where he taught from 1927 to 1960, becoming a Professor of Educational Sociology. His classic study of Chicago gangs took a long time to complete, understandably enough given its remarkable scale. It involved field observations – and a lot of slumming – as well as interviews with gang members and associates, personal reflections, anecdotes, and the use of a range of official documents from court records to census statistics. Like Anderson with Chicago's hobos, Thrasher produced a map of gang territories across the city, which he referred to as 'Gangland'. Each gang, he wrote, was different – a matter of ethnic difference primarily (although racially, gangs were usually homogeneous), with varying degrees of coherence, differing tendencies towards violence, gang 'traditions', and so on. Although Thrasher asserted that gangs were a prod-uct of a *modern* city – the outcome of immigrant movements into the city along the lines described by Park – nevertheless he gave them a certain 'prim-itive' definition. They are 'tribal and intertribal'; they, too, live in 'jungles' as well as 'wildernesses' and 'badlands'; given to 'wanderlust', they can seem 'like gypsies roaming the city wilderness' (160); and their social organisation is 'medieval and feudal', with gangs presiding over 'kingdoms' and 'empires' (Thrasher 1927: 6). Gangs, for Thrasher, were produced in the city but set apart from it and, indeed, in an actively conflictual relationship with it. (They were also almost entirely made up of boys and men, much like Anderson's hobos: 'Gangs composed entirely of girls', Thrasher wrote, 'are exceedingly rare' [228], although a few gangs were mixed.) Their ganglands were what Thrasher called 'interstitial', places in the 'cracks' and 'fissures' of the city, those places the city seemed to have forgotten or ignored: slums, impover-ished areas, 'no-go' areas. He was certainly alert to the social disadvantages of gang members, speaking among other things of their 'demoralisation'; but like Anderson again he also thought that gangs could be at least in part utopian. Here is his famous definition of the sociality of the gang:

> The gang is an interstitial group originally formed spontaneously, and then integrated through conflict. It is characterised by the following types of behaviour: meeting face to face, milling, movement through space as a unit, conflict, and planning. The result of this collective behav-iour is the development of tradition, unreflective internal structure, *esprit de corps*, solidarity, morale, group awareness, and attachment to a local territory.
>
> (57)

A much later view of the ethnic gang, from Chicago sociologist Gerald D. Suttles' *The Social Order of the Slum* (1968), remains consistent with Thrasher in its emphasis on 'primitive' features and, especially, on sociality: 'The func-tion of the named street corner group is rudimentary and primitive: it defines groups of people so that they can be seen as representatives rather than indi-viduals' (Suttles 1968: 220). More recent criminological studies of gangs naturally argue with Thrasher in various ways (e.g. Jankowski 1991), but his study covered what are still the key areas of gang studies: delinquency, rela-tions to the local (and wider) community, support networks and institutions, ethnicity, poverty, involvement in organised crime.

A rather different key area of Thrasher's study, however, has on the whole been routinely ignored by criminological commentators. He thought that gangs began in childhood, through groups at play who, later on, develop the kind of group solidarity that becomes conflictual. Play is important to Thrasher's study, and it is tied to his sense of gang members as 'primitive', that is, outside of the disciplinary and civilising regimes of society: defined by 'energy that is undirected, undisciplined, and uncontrolled', seeking 'stimulation' and opportunities for 'expression in the freest, the most spontaneous and elemental manner possible' (1927: 101). A chapter on entertainment in his book suggests that gang members enjoy reading adventure fiction and, even more, watching movies. Movies are a social event and gang members bond together through them. But a gang's 'elemental' character also means, for Thrasher, that members are easily influenced by what they see, imitating their screen heroes, reproducing adventurous scenarios, and so on. The boys and young men in gangs are role-players in this account, naturally 'romantic' and imaginative. 'Not only does the gang boy transform his sordid environment through his imagination', Thrasher wrote,

> but he lives among soldiers and knights, pirates and banditti. His enemies are assigned special roles: the crabby old lady across the alley is a witch; the neighbourhood cop becomes a man-killing giant or a robber baron; and the rival gang in the next block is a hostile army.
>
> (117–18).

We have seen that, for Anderson, the hobo was also involved in storytelling. The problem with gangs, however, is that the sources for their stories come not from experience and 'personal narratives' but from the movies and cheap popular fiction. The hobo remains grounded in reality which is then a source for his narratives and conversation; the gang member, on the other hand, is 'fanciful' and, for Thrasher, actually finds it difficult to 'distinguish between what is real and what is not' (130). The dominant genre used by Chicago-based sociologists and novelists during the early twentieth century was, as I have noted, an investigative form of urban realism or naturalism: a genre linked to 'muckraking' journalism and reportage (Park often advised ethnographers at the Chicago School to be, first and foremost, good reporters), similarly designed to reflect or capture the social and personal details of the real world. But gang members seemed instead to be influenced by romance and adventure, genres conveyed through the Hollywood films they enjoyed watching. Their 'romantic' tendencies led Thrasher to conclude that they must therefore be 'unreflective', that is, unable to properly understand the conditions of their own social predicament. This is close to Marx's view of the *lumpenproletariat* as noted in Chapter 1, a sub-class of people who – because they have no broader class allegiances – are easily led by the bourgeoisie (just as gangs might throw their numbers behind certain politicians on election day). So how does a sociology which invests in realism deal with such 'romantic' subjects? How much role-play and imagination can the kind of sociology which details a subculture's real predicaments hope to account for? If to be 'fanciful' is therefore also to be 'unreflective', then in a certain sense – to recall Jenks's commentary again, quoted above – it is not the sociology that is 'non-sociological', it is sociology's subjects, the gang members themselves.

Taxi-dancers, social worlds and subcultural careers

While he was at New York University in the early 1930s, Thrasher in fact took part in a series of projects examining the effects of movies on boys. These Motion Picture Research Council/Payne Fund Studies were some of the earliest systematic analyses of the social effects of mass media forms, unfolding in a moral and educational climate anxious about the influence of movie sex and violence (e.g. gangster movies) on 'impressionable' young viewers (see Jowett *et al.* 1996). Thrasher had worked on one of these, 'Boys, Movies, and City Streets', with a new recruit at NYU, Paul G. Cressey, although it was never published. Cressey came to NYU with a reputation, the author of a remarkable book, *The Taxi-Dance Hall: A Sociological Study in Commercialised Recreation and City Life* (1932), which was the result of his MA research in the late 1920s while at the University of Chicago. This research was atypical at the time because it focused almost entirely on women: the so-called taxi-dancers who worked in dance clubs in Chicago and who were hired by men to dance with them and keep them company. The venues were also sometimes called 'dime-a-dance halls', and they were found in many cities across the United States, although usually away from the main entertainment precincts. Cressey's study was a dense, ethnographic project, full of women's 'real-life stories', their many anecdotes and recollections. But as Jowett *et al.* note, it also attracted scandal and perhaps accounted for Cressey's later decision to move out of that city:

> Accusations had been made that the unmarried Cressey had acted with impropriety in order to collect autobiographical data from the taxi dancers: he had instructed his student assistants to pay to dance with the girls, walk them home, buy them sandwiches and coffee to loosen their defences and extract more of their stories. Jessie Binford of the Juvenile Protection Association charged sexual misconduct, and Cressey had left Chicago under a cloud.
>
> (1996: 85)

The Taxi-Dance Hall is certainly a striking study, the outcome of an ethnographic project that might today seem at the very least ethically compromised. Cressey and his assistants practised slumming, or what we might think of as *covert* participant-observation, in order to meet and converse with the taxi-dancers:

> Observers were sent into the taxi-dance halls. They were instructed to mingle with the others and to become as much a part of this social

world as ethically possible.... The investigators functioned as anonymous strangers and casual acquaintances. They were thus able to obtain
this material without encountering the inhibitions and resistance usually
met in formal interviews.

(Cressey 1932: xxxiv)

Cressey's view of the taxi-dance hall as a 'social world' is the key to its value
as a subcultural study. The girls would migrate there, leaving their homes and
families for whatever reasons to find themselves (as Cressey puts it) 'set adrift
in a careless money-mad city life with little effective moral instruction to
guide them and with no money-making skill or training' (47). The taxi-dance
hall was one destination for these girls, a more legitimate one than, say, prostitution. Even so, various 'moral agents' had for some time been attempting
to control and regulate (or even close down) what was a flourishing dance hall
scene in the city. Randy D. McBee reports that Chicago's Juvenile Protective
Association had investigated 278 of them in 1915 alone (McBee 2000: 55).
Taxi-dance halls themselves may have originated in San Francisco's red-light
district; the first one opened in Chicago in 1921, and they were soon found
in most other major cities across the United States. By 1925, McBee notes, 'a
survey in New York reported that eight thousand women worked as taxi dancers and earned about thirty dollars a week, a wage significantly higher than the
average office worker' (57).

For Cressey, the taxi-dance hall was a 'distinct social world', existing in
'moral isolation', with 'its own ways of acting, talking, and thinking...its own
vocabulary, its own activities and interests, its own conception of what is significant in life, and – to a certain extent – its own scheme of life' (Cressey
1932: 31–32). It gave the girls 'stimulation', but also a set of opportunities
that – as the girls took advantage of them – led to a 'career'. Cressey may well
have been the first sociologist to map out a subcultural career amongst his subjects. He did this in two ways. First, the taxi-dance hall offered what he called
'commercial recreation' for both girls and patrons. The girls could exploit this
feature rather than be exploited *by* it, by becoming 'opportunistic', sometimes
engaging in a 'battle of wits' with patrons, and (as one girl notes) 'making the
most of what you've got' (48). The combination of stimulation and opportun-
ism leads to a certain amount of shared 'satisfaction' amongst the girls, but
also divides them in terms of their successes and advancements in the dance
hall. In this respect, the taxi-dance hall reflects the broader life of the city, and
society, itself: so that this isolated social world is also a kind of microcosm of
capitalistic exchange elsewhere. Second, girls may at various times become
romantically involved with their patrons – and so run counter to the dance
hall's commercial practice (by favouring one patron over another, offering free
dances, spending too much unpaid time with a man, etc.). Careers may also
be mapped through the various romances, even marriages, that arise out of

the taxi-dance hall. So this is a subculture in which commercial imperatives and 'the romantic impulse' – the impersonal and the intimate, exploitation and affection – sit uneasily alongside each other.

Cressey's view of the taxi-dance hall as a place of 'stimulation' recalls Robert Park's earlier account of the city's libidinal influence on new immigrants ('like the attraction of the flame for the moth') as well as Sandburg's image of Chicago's 'painted women under gas lamps' luring young men into the city. The taxi-dance hall encapsulated the modern urban problem of alienation – men and women alienated from each other, in this case – which it then attempted to resolve commercially. The male patrons themselves were also invariably new immigrants into the city, a wide mixture of races and ethnicities: what one of Cressey's assistants colourfully called 'the most speckled crew I'd ever seen: Filipinos, Chinese, Mexicans, Polish immigrants...' (31). Cressey noted that many of the girls considered 'Oriental' men to be the most easily exploited. But he also notes that, in order even to *begin* to exploit these men, the girls – most of whom were white and provincial – first had to put aside their racial prejudices. The extent to which the girls would dance and co-mingle with (for example) Chinese men also determined the trajectory of their career at the dance hall. Sometimes, girls would become romantically involved with these men; at other times, their relationship would be a strictly 'sensual' transaction, a matter of the 'cold, impersonal' exchange of money. Whatever it was, Cressey took the same view that Park had taken about what it means to break the home ties and migrate into the city, namely, that it is in effect a kind of 'emancipation' which sees people become as a consequence something close to 'cosmopolitan'. The taxi-dancer may continue to migrate from city to city, finding that the dance halls there are 'all essentially alike': another instance of Chicago's exemplary or representative status. At one point Cressey comments on 'this new type of feminine migration' – this 'mobile group of a new variety' – and quotes one of the taxi-dancers:

> I've been all over the country because of these halls. My home's Chicago, but I've been in New York, New Orleans, Kansas City, Seattle, and Los Angeles...
>
> Everywhere I went, though, I'd meet somebody I'd known somewhere else. In New York I saw some Flips [Filipinos] I used to know here in Chicago. When I was in Los Angeles I met a girl that used to be out on the West Side. The other night I met a Flip here I used to know out in Seattle. It's a small world, after all.
>
> (105–6)

These remarks work to draw the subcultural interests and cosmopolitan ideals of the Chicago School together. Migratory subcultures have as one point of origin the movement away from home and family, obviously enough. But it can also seem as if these subcultures simply exchange one localised, parochial identity for another. The Chicago School's emphasis on migration and mobility solves this problem by understanding the subculture as a microcosm of society at large, even as it insists on that subculture's distinction from it. Proximity and segregation co-exist here; the 'small world' of the United States and the isolated social world of the taxi-dance hall thus appear in these remarks to have somehow converged – as if the former has shrunk precisely because the latter now seems to be all over the place.

Assimilation, adjustment, deviance

Subcultural studies is necessarily involved in a debate over the prioritising of norms and differences. The Chicago School is no exception here, and it is worth remembering that although Park was fascinated by the 'eccentric' and the 'marginal', he also spoke up for social integration. In *Old World Traits Transplanted* (1921), Park and his co-author, Herbert A. Miller, suggested that assimilation in the United States 'is as inevitable as it is desirable; it is impossible for the immigrants we receive to remain permanently in separate groups' (Park and Miller 1969: 308). One of the first sociologists to use the term *subculture* in its social sense, Milton M. Gordon, was also the author of one of the most important books on social integration, *Assimilation in American Life: The Role of Race, Religion and National Origins* (1964). In 'The Concept of Sub-Culture and Its Application', published in *Social Forces* in 1947, Gordon had talked about the need to look beyond the conventional sociological categories of ethnicity, class, and so on, to more nuanced collective arrangements – although he didn't tie this to any sense of non-normativity or nonconformity. He recast Park's phrase 'marginal man' as 'marginal sub-cultures', emphasising the social aspects of difference in an increasingly pluralised, modern United States (Gordon 1947). Even so, his later book outlined the various ways in which assimilation occurs and presented a sense – more typical of the early 1960s than later on in the decade – that most ethnic groups would eventually and inevitably find themselves 'structurally incorporated' into the mainstream of American cultural, economic and political life.

Chicago School sociology was influenced by, and bled into, work in other disciplines: anthropology, for example, where the notion of 'acculturation' helped Park to think about a sense of some future moment of assimilation. It also developed hand-in-glove with criminology. But criminology took the Chicago School back to the problem of *difference*. The primary interests at the time were in criminal acts, delinquency, and deviance: all of which resisted social integration. Two key figures are worth noting here. Clifford Shaw didn't finish his doctorate at Chicago, but by 1927 he was director of the university's newly created Department of Research Sociology where he consolidated his ongoing work with local juvenile delinquents. His autobiographical study of a delinquent named Stanley with whom Shaw remained closely associated, *The Jack Roller* (1930), is a classic criminological text, a remarkable 'real-life story'. Edwin Sutherland, who *did* complete his sociology Ph.D. at Chicago, was hired to write what became the discipline's most influential textbook, *Criminology* (1924). Sutherland also turned to the problem of the delinquent, which had conventionally been cast as a matter of individual pathology ('feeble-mindedness' etc.). Like Shaw, Sutherland met a criminal, Broadway Jones, a Chicago grifter or confidence man whose life-stories Sutherland similarly documented in *The Professional Thief* (1937), where Jones (harking back to those eighteenth-century nicknames for subcultural types, like Moll Hackabout) was aptly renamed 'Chic Conwell'. Sutherland realised that criminal behaviour was not an individualised, pathological form of behaviour but, rather, a matter of what he called 'differential association': arising out of one's social connections with *other* criminal types, with those who commit crimes rather than with those who do not.

This view of criminal activity as a social practice was influential for criminology and is especially important to subcultural studies. It is taken up later on in Albert K. Cohen's *Delinquent Boys: The Culture of the Gang* (1955), which is indebted to Sutherland as well as to Talcott Parsons – since Cohen had gained his Ph.D. from Harvard University, not Chicago. Parsons notwithstanding, however, Cohen uses the term *subculture* with confidence. 'Every society is internally differentiated into numerous sub-groups', he writes, 'each with ways of thinking and doing that are in some respects peculiarly its own' (Cohen 1955: 12). Like Sutherland, Cohen argues against psychiatric approaches to delinquency which individualise and pathologise it. Delinquency, he insists, is a social phenomenon, with 'gangs of boys *doing things together*...deriving their meaning and flavour from the fact of togetherness and governed by a set of common understandings, common sentiments, and common loyalties' (178). Delinquents – either by choice or (more likely) by predicament – cannot adjust to prevailing social norms or accept social goals. But they are not therefore socially alienated. Rather, they find what Cohen had called a 'subcultural solution': that is, they associate and interact with other people '*with similar problems of adjustment*' (59). This view of delinquency as a social outcome of nonconformity was very different to the prevailing view of nonconformity as a matter of alienation. Another of Parson's students, Robert Merton, had taken up Emile Durkheim's notion of *anomie* in an earlier, influential article, 'Social Structure and Anomie' (Merton 1938). The emphasis here is on social goals, norms and aspirations which, when people cannot meet them, produce 'strains', dysfunctionality and alienation (*anomie*). For Merton, individuals therefore had to be able to derive satisfaction not just from the social goal or norm itself, but from the actual means of achieving it. That is, the journey towards social conformity and normativity, which had to be worked at, itself had to be an inherently satisfying one. Nonconformity, then, was an expression of social dissatisfaction, where one might resign oneself to *not* attaining social goals etc. Cohen's view, however, was quite different, and very much in the pragmatist tradition of the Chicago School. He saw that nonconformity was not so much a form of maladjustment as *re-adjustment*. One may very well reject society's dominant norms and goals, but that doesn't mean to say that one is therefore norm-less (or even goal-less). Instead, one adjusts to the logic of *different* norms and, more important, one finds social groups where these norms prevail and persist. They may be non-normative from society's point of view, but they are norms just the same. Cohen's view of the 'subcultural solution', then, is a bit like Park's notion of the 'moral milieu'. The nonconformist interacts with others who, perhaps paradoxically, share or sympathise with the norms of his or her nonconformity – because they, too, have experienced similar problems of adjustment and similar processes of re-adjustment. Even though society's norms and goals are dominant, the 'numerous sub-groups' that make up society demonstrate that subcultural solutions are more common than one might at first imagine.

A keyword for criminology, underscoring its emphasis on social difference and nonconformity, was *deviance*, and its best and most eloquent exponent was another Chicago School graduate, Howard S. Becker. Most of the material in his classic book, *Outsiders: Studies in the Sociology of Deviance* (1963), had been written in the early 1950s, around the time of Cohen's *Delinquent Boys*. *Outsiders* looked in particular at marijuana use, especially among Chicago's jazz musicians. But, like Cohen again, Becker also wanted to make a set of more general points about nonconformity. He once more rejected the 'functional' sociology of Parsons and Robert Merton, distancing himself from their remote perspective: 'it is harder in practice than it appears to be in theory to specify what is functional and what is dysfunctional for a society or social group' (Becker 1963: 7). Just as Cohen had suggested that society consists of 'numerous sub-groups', so Becker notes that the social is always a matter of difference and stratification, with people often belonging 'to many groups simultaneously' (8), as much ruled by factionalism and conflict as they are by consensus. Indeed, the emphasis on difference and conflict carries with it a heightened sense of political awareness – whereas the Parsonian notion of norms, stability and consensus (Jenks's 'togetherness') can by contrast seem politically naive. Deviance itself, for Becker, is the *result* of social norms and the rules they create. It isn't a thing-in-itself; rather, '*social groups create deviance by making rules whose infraction constitutes deviance*' (9). Deviance is therefore 'an interactive process involving both deviants and non-deviants' (2), not an action but a 'transaction' – in which case, studying deviancy means looking at those who make the rules as well as those who fall foul of them. Like Cohen again, Becker saw that social groups outside the frame of normative rules, like 'the homosexual community', nevertheless have their own normative logics which they may then 'rationalise': adopting principles built around them, giving them historical depth (producing genealogies of homosexuality, for example, invoking earlier experiences, anecdotes, etc.), 'normalising' their own non-normativity even as they continue to distinguish themselves from prevailing social conventions. Under their own normalised nonconformity, outsiders might very well come to view those who *judge* them as outsiders. The deviant perspective is therefore a relative one, but also always a social one. Becker developed a notion of 'labelling theory', speaking not just about deviant social groups but also about the 'moral entrepreneurs' who judge them — who *label* them as deviant and so turn deviance into a kind of role that gets played out according to the label. But in a paper written in 1971 ('Labelling Theory Reconsidered', published 1973), Becker moved away from labelling theory to prefer, instead, a model of social 'interaction', built around the need to study 'all participants in these moral dramas' (1973: 207). Interaction, moral dramas, role-playing: these things combine together in a sociological approach known as 'symbolic interactionism'.

John Irwin, social actors and the 'scene'

The eminent Chicago School sociologist Herbert Blumer coined the term 'symbolic interaction' in 1937, in order to account for social interaction as a matter of interpretive communication, the decoding of transmitted meanings — and also to emphasise that meaning itself is derived *out* of social interaction (see Blumer 1969). Social interactions are a matter of conveying meaningful symbols, in which case one must interpret those meanings and adjust or respond accordingly. A certain kind of 'moral drama' is acted out as a result, where people perform their social roles in terms of the meanings they derive from social situations and the meanings they convey back in return. Symbolic interactionism is a positioned sociology which looks at particular predicaments, emphasising subjective interpretation rather than subscribing to some kind of remote, 'objective' position. Performativity is important here, so much so that social interaction can indeed be seen as a form of role-playing, or even a form of theatre: as in the 'dramaturgical' sociology of Erving Goffman, another eminent Chicago School graduate, which drew attention to the particular nuances of role-playing action in various social and institutional environments. Different social predicaments elicit different performances from people as well as different logics of interpretation; and the same is true for social groups. Not every social group performs its relation to the world in the same way, a point which may be especially true of non-normative or non-conforming subcultures.

A symbolic interactionist perspective might very well be useful in studying deviance as a performed social response to those who make the rules and invoke the symbols of their authority, Becker's 'moral entrepreneurs' – who likewise in turn perform a social response to *deviance*, offering an equally (but very differently) positioned interpretation of it. On the other hand, symbolic interaction also helped sociology to move *away* from the deviance model, seeing social performance as a much more contingent thing, a question of increasingly fluid, open social relations. Subcultures might be segregated and local, specific to one place and not another, 'distinct social worlds' as we saw with the taxi-dance halls. But – again like the taxi-dance halls – they might also be 'everywhere', and one might move through them with relative ease. The first book to represent and historicise work in what is now called sub-cultural studies was David O. Arnold's edited collection, *Subcultures* (1970). It began with some early criminological work from Sutherland and went on to include extracts from Cohen and Milton M. Gordon, focusing on the deviant and the delinquent in line with prevailing criminological interests. But it also noted that by the end of the 1960s the concept of a subculture had been con-siderably stretched. It seems, Arnold notes in his introduction to the book, 'as if the accelerated use of the concept has caught us unawares' (Arnold 1970: 3). Subcultural studies no longer confines itself to 'deviant behaviour'; rather, it seems to belong 'to most, perhaps all, of the subfields of sociology' (3). One of the more contemporary contributors to Arnold's collection was John Irwin, a sociologist from Berkeley, California, who had written a classic criminolog-ical study, *The Felon* (1970). But Irwin also responded to this growing sense that subcultures might also *not* be deviant as such, and that one's involvement in them might be less the result of conflict and delinquency and more a matter of choice and 'lifestyle'. He worked his views through in a remarkable book called *Scenes* (1977).

Scenes begins by placing itself ambivalently in relation to Chicago School sociology (even though the Foreword to the book was written by Gerald D. Suttles), departing especially from its criminological perspectives:

> [the Chicago School's concepts of] gangs, subcultures, and behaviour systems did not approach the casualness of the worlds I was involved in. All such gangs and subcultures suggested too much commitment, deter-minism, instrumentality, and stability in membership.... Concepts such as milieu, ambience, fad, and craze, on the other hand, did not suggest enough permanence, cohesion, or complexity of form.
>
> (Irwin 1977: 18)

Irwin's project was to examine the contemporary city in the wake of the Chicago School and in the context of an embryonic sense of postmodernity. The city alienates people from each other, producing a space full of 'strangers' who 'do not interact' (25). Far from being normative, it is sometimes over-whelmingly heterogeneous, encouraging impersonalised relationships, even mutual suspicion. The view here is very much in the tradition of Tonnies's *Gesellschaft*, in other words. Even so, people do form 'emotionally sustaining' relationships with others: the question is, how does the sociologist give this formulation? Irwin turned to the word *scene*, relating it to the symbolic inter-actionist perspective. People 'make scenes' in the city, doing certain things together in certain places. They are performative and expressive, 'self-conscious actors' in whatever scene they inhabit – quite different in kind to the 'unreflective' role-play of Thrasher's *lumpenproletariat* gang members. The city for Irwin was much less of a '*social machine*' than it used to be, no longer able to depend on the grand narratives of consensus and conformity and without a 'central, overriding societal purpose' (24). On the other hand, it is much more of an '*entertainment machine*' (21–22), driven by excitement, libido and self-expression – a view not so very different in some respects from Robert Park's, it must be said. The social worlds it offers people are therefore primarily built around leisure, and pleasure – and even a sense of 'risk'. Irwin spoke of the city's 'bar scene', for example, although this could be porous in the sense that one could find oneself sitting alongside strangers in the midst of sociality. The 'disco scene' also drew strangers together, this time in a staged, physical expression of intimacy. Irwin also commented on the trend towards therapy scenes, where people 'get it together' through yoga, group discussions, confessions, and so on. Forms of mass entertainment may or may not be relevant here. Irwin said that television produced a 'pseudo scene' where one interacts passively with, and lives 'vicariously' through, the socialities it conveys – even though television (in a comment which anticipates Benedict Anderson's later notion of mass media and the 'imagined community') may be 'the only urban scene which gives Americans a sense of national collective involvement' (46). But media for Irwin could sometimes be just as important in scene-making as face-to-face contact. Sociality needs to be imagined and created: this is the symbolic interactionist perspective which influenced Irwin's study. It need not therefore be local and immediate at all. Television, cinema, literature: they all contribute to the distribution of 'information about different subcultures' and thereby help to objectify them 'into recognised styles' (59). As we saw above, Thrasher had worried about the influence of cinema on impressionable gang members who then acted out 'romantic' roles of conflict based on what they had seen. Irwin, however, saw that media contributes to the 'expressive' and 'imaginative' nature of subcultural involvement. For 'self-conscious actors', media influence and objectification is one facet among others in the creation of social identity.

Irwin talked about two 'grand scenes' in the United States, hippies and surfers. These were also 'lifestyle' scenes, but they began with particular kinds of investments: in an ideology and world-view (hippies), and in a combination of way-of-life practices and actual skills (surfers). Irwin's account gave these two subcultures a rise-and-fall narrative that would anticipate Dick Hebdige's view of the inevitable incorporation of British punks just a couple of years later (Hebdige 1979). The first phase for a subculture is its formation; this is followed by its expansion, its corruption, and finally its stagnation. The hippie and surfer subcultures expanded too rapidly, each drawing 'more people than it could absorb' (Irwin 1977: 121): 'hangers-on' who were less ideologically committed, less skilful, and so on. But perhaps their diffusion is more typical than unique. Scenes, for Irwin, are 'tightly scripted' in one sense, but they always leave room for 'improvisation' (194). The commitment one makes to them can indeed be 'casual' – a feature that also speaks to the inherent *instability* of a scene. Scenes might have more permanence than fads and crazes, but they do change and they do become undone. This is at least in part because the participant in a scene is also a participant in the diversity of modern life: 'They are "relativists" – that is, they are aware of the cultural diversity of their worlds, and they do not believe that their own culture is the *only* culture' (57). Irwin's study moves away from the Chicago School's notion of segregated subcultures, but it continues with its ideal of cosmopolitanism, its sense that a subcultural experience is also at the same time a cross-cultural experience. For Thrasher, Chicago's gangs were 'inturned' and therefore 'unreflective': this was their problem. For Irwin, the modern city dweller is 'self-conscious' and improvisational, a cultural (or subcultural) relativist, a pluralist. So he speaks against the prevailing view that 'people are generally disillusioned with city life' (225), preferring the segregated security of smaller communities, the stability of religion ('a stable and mystical belief system'), etc. But he also speaks against city life as a matter of privatisation, *anomie* and alienation, just as the Chicago School had done. To become subcultural is to return to a mode of public living *in the city*: it is a way of 'learning to cope with heterogeneity and impersonality' (228).

Chapter 3

BAR SCENES AND CLUB CULTURES
Sociality, excess, utopia

Mohocks, Hell-Fire Clubs and Molly Houses

IT WOULD BE DIFFICULT TO FIND an agreed-upon point of origin for clubs, and there are many reasons for forming them: not all subcultural by any means. Clubs are, primarily, a means of socialising and of giving socialisation some sort of definition, an underwriting cultural logic and a structure and method of organisation. In his history of British clubs, Peter Clark writes that by 1800, 'clubs and other forms of association had become a vital component of the social life of the educated English-speaking classes' (Clark 2002: 3). But he also notes that clubs were common and popular enough well before that time even for writers to satirise them: like the Tory polemicist and humorist Ned Ward, whose *A History of the London Clubs* (1709) began by describing just six of these but soon expanded to account for over thirty. Political and religious associations had their clubs, and so did various trades and occupations; and many of these clubs (like the Whiggish Kit Kat Club, or the Tory Scriblerian Club – see Chapter 4) were essential to the well-being, and successful management, of the nation itself. Kathleen Wilson writes that during the eighteenth century clubs 'were central to structuring and sustaining extra-parliamentary politics, embodying forms of sociability and engagement capable of shaping their members' social and political relations with each other, with civic culture and with the nation-state itself' (Wilson 1995: 71). For Wilson, these clubs also embodied principles of rationality and masculinity, instrumental in the delineation of a 'public political sphere' outside of the feminised home (73). We might think of the Freemasons here, too, although the history of Freemasonry goes back even further, to the fourteenth century and the Guilds or 'Mysteries' of Masons (stone craftsmen) which had gained at this time some political power in London. By the seventeenth century, societies of Masons or Free Masons were admitting members outside of their trades and forming 'fellowships', 'brotherhoods', and so on. In 1717, four Lodges got together and founded the first Grand Lodge of England, which met in taverns in Drury Lane and Westminster. Their knowledges were increasingly mystified and their Lodge meetings were increasingly ritualised, with Freemasonry becoming a matter of secrecy and coded recognition, a means of establishing social and professional hierarchies – even as it tied itself, especially in its North American incarnations, to nation-building and political power. The Grand Lodge of British Columbia and Yukon in Canada has an elaborate and informative website with detailed scholarly histories and genealogies of Freemasonry, as well as a set of documents about its own formation in 1860, its various Grand Masters, its achievements, and so on. This influential Canadian society also posts a number of 'anti-masonic' commentaries which accuse Freemasonry of anti-Christian behaviour or offer 'conspiracy theories' about its political influence, its links to the Ku-Klux-Klan, etc. – all of which are refuted. Freemasonry, it notes, 'has been described as a system of morality, veiled in allegory and illustrated by symbols' <http://freemasonry.bcy.ca/info.html>. By way of contrast, it also links to another informative page about the Hell-Fire Clubs of the eighteenth century. Even though the founder of the first Hell-Fire Club in London, Philip, Duke of Wharton, was also a Grand Master in 1722–23, this page draws a careful distinction between Hell-Fire Clubs and Freemasonry: 'The practices and phi-losophies of the several Hell-Fire Clubs would certainly appear to be antithetical to those of Freemasonry. Where Freemasonry taught moderation, the Hell-Fire Clubs promoted excess; while Freemasonry bound its members to obey the moral law and to be lawful citizens, the Hell-Fire Clubs encouraged drunken-ness, debauchery and a disregard for social convention' <http://freemasonry. bcy.ca/history/hellfire/hellfire.html#george>. We have, in these remarks, a version of a binary we have already seen in relation to subcultures: in par-ticular, as sites of excess to be distinguished from the restraints of mainstream society or 'dominant culture'.

The Hell-Fire Clubs were part of what Wilson calls a flourishing 'radical club life' in Britain during the eighteenth century, populated in this case by aristocratic rakes and libertines. In his study of the Hell-Fire Clubs – subtitled *A History of Anti-Morality* – Geoffrey Ashe describes England after 1688 (the 'Glorious Revolution') as prosperous, classical and enlightened, the embodi-ment of Liberty, tolerance and diversity. London, he writes, 'could put almost any mode of living on an organized basis' (Ashe 1974: 46), and there were indeed already many different kinds of clubs in the city. The numerous coffee and chocolate houses in London at this time, as well as the taverns, encour-aged sociality and would often be claimed (or, we might say, territorialised) by various constituencies, groups of people with specialist interests: poets, for example, or journalists, philosophers, businessmen, political groups and the clergy. On the other hand, there was much political and social 'restless-ness' in the city, a feature given violent expression in 1712 by a group of men called the Mohocks who took their name from a tribe of North American Indians. For Ashe, the Mohocks symbolised the darker side of Liberty, young rakes who bore out the inscription over the door of the abbey owned by Sir Francis Dashwood, the founder of the notorious Permissive Society in 1755: *Fay ce que voudras*, or, Do What You Will. The social historian Daniel Statt sees the libertine as a social type – partly progressive, partly backward-looking – of which the rake is a kind of subset. The rake, he writes, 'may be taken to represent the dark side of the libertine archetype, typically bereft of the wit, refinement, style and sense to which the libertine could at least putatively lay claim' (Statt 1995: 181). The rakish Mohocks were an aristocratic gang, roam-ing the streets and bashing and assaulting both men and women. They had an 'emperor' (i.e. a leader), as well as rituals and charters, and there may well have been a Mohock Club – since the Mohocks certainly met at the coffee-houses and taverns around Holborn and Covent Garden. Statt reserves his judgement about the possibility of an organised Mohock Club, however, not least because so much of the source material about Mohocks is literary rather than, say, eye-witness journalism. The Tory Jonathan Swift was fascinated by them; so was John Gay, and so were the Whig moralists Joseph Addison and Richard Steele, who wrote for the *Tatler* (1709–11) and the *Spectator* (1711–12) – the former of which would print stories under coffee-house headings, appealing to coffee-house patrons as a source of gossip and conversation. But their accounts were probably politically motivated and almost certainly hyperbolic, an early version of what Stanley Cohen – in his book about media reactions to clashes between the mods and rockers in 1960s England – has famously called 'moral panic' (Cohen 1972). For Neil Guthrie in the journal *Eighteenth-Century Life*, the 'hard evidence for *many* rakish clubs is curiously lacking, no doubt because members did not generally record their activities and because the accounts that do survive are often those of unsympathetic or ill-informed outsiders' (Guthrie 1996: 33; my italics). Too many crimes were attributed to the Mohocks, who may in fact have been few in number; and too many fantasies circulated about them, inflamed by writers like Swift who con-sidered them to be 'part of a large and sinister plot' (36). For Guthrie, the Mohocks, like the Hell-Fire Clubs, represented a moment of excess during the early eighteenth century that was then prone to exaggeration by some influential but all-too-imaginative commentators. His article wants to correct this exaggerated view; we might say that, by trying to return to 'what actually took place' (50), he, too – rather like the Canadian freemasons above – speaks up for moderation and restraint.

Ned Ward's *The History of the London Clubs*, the first pamphlet of which was published in 1709, was a satirical account of club life in London which in fact blended real description and imaginative exaggeration together, so much so that it could be difficult to tell them apart. Ward was an early example of a tabloid journalist, sensationalising his topics and entertaining his readers. But he also wanted to account for the range of social practices and character 'types' in London at the time. Howard William Troyer notes that Ward's interest in club life was not:

> in the narrow sense of an organized society holding stated and recurrent meetings in a chapter house, but in the larger and equally current sense of a gathering or grouping of citizens in terms of their activities and habitual places of resort.
>
> (Troyer 1946: 152)

Ward's descriptions of clubs were usually excuses to satirise the behaviour of particular social groups who may or may not actually be gathering together: as in 'The Split-Farthing Club', 'an attack on the avaricious and miserly citizens of Bishopsgate Street', or 'The Surly Club', his 'satirization of the language and behaviour of Billingsgate porters, oarsmen, and lightermen, notorious throughout the city for their obscenity of speech' (158). His lurid account of the rakish 'Man-Hunters Club' may have anticipated, or even pre-empted, the Mohock panic a few years later. Ward satirised establishment clubs, too, like the Kit Kat Club. And he also wrote scathingly about 'The Mollies Club', producing a 'diatribe against a current group of effeminate fops' (153) who met at a tavern that Ward refused to identify (see also Hallam 1993: 111–14). The word *molly* was a common term for homosexual, used by homosexuals themselves, although it had earlier been applied to female prostitutes. 'Molly Houses' – places where homosexual men gather – may have been around as early at 1700: this is where the historian Rictor Norton in fact locates the origins of a gay subculture in England (Norton 1992). Norton's account also turns to a libertine post-1688 England, with subcultural sexual practices pursued not by an underclass but by aristocrats. Charles Spencer, 3rd Earl of Sutherland, was a connoisseur of the arts and a patron of young scholars; he established a 'sodomitical' club frequented by 'Ganymedes', handsome and often cross-dressing young men. Imaginative play here was tied to classical scholarship and aesthetic knowledge. Randolph Trumbach also notes that 'some sodomites in the molly-houses played men to match the role of female prostitutes that others took', staging what he calls 'third gender' performances that also hark back to the earlier connotations of *molly* (Trumbach 1998: 7). The social world of the early eighteenth-century 'sodomites' thus unsurprisingly elicits an outraged and generally exaggerated response from outsiders which may itself take an imaginative form: as in the various verse satires directed against this subculture of sexual 'inverts', like John Dunton's *The He-Strumpets: A Satyr on the Sodomite Club* (1707):

A New Society prevails,
Call'd S[o]d[om]ites; Men worse than Goats,
Who dress themselves in Petticoats.

(cited Trumbach 1998: 51)

By this time, a number of Societies for Reformation of Manners – Reforming Societies – were already active in London, organisations with the moral purpose of suppressing debauchery and homosexuality in the city. Norton describes the raids in 1725 and 1726 on a Molly House kept by 'Mother Clap' in Holborn, as well as the trial that followed; and he charts the ways in which these 'scandalous haunts' were revealed and exposed, usually through a system of spies and informants. At the same time, he argues, these Reforming Societies may well have helped to stimulate the *growth* of the gay subculture. Gay men often cruised around the Royal Exchange and other places. By driving them off the streets, Reforming Societies inadvertently helped them to find other, less public places in which to congregate – and so to become more organised, more self-aware, more *social*. Some meeting-places were exposed and raided, some not; occasionally, the raiders were even repelled. 'The attempt to suppress vice', Norton writes, 'may actually have facilitated the expression of homosexuality', which 'coalesced under the pressures of this reforming environment' (1992: 52). This is where the origins of an identifiable gay subculture in London can be traced.

Lesbian bar histories

The idea that – by labelling and/or suppressing 'deviant' activities – society can at the same time bring social types into being and make them self-aware and self-conscious is also one that we find in the work of Michel Foucault. For Foucault, 'homosexuality' gained its definition not in the early 1700s but in 1870 (or 1869, depending on the account) through the influential work of the German psychiatrist Carl Westphal, whose notion of 'contrary sexual sensations' helped to constitute the male homosexual not just as someone who commits illegal acts but as a sexualised 'type of life', a 'case history' able to be accounted for by medical and psychiatric discourse. 'The sodomite', Foucault famously wrote, 'had been a temporary aberration; the homosexual was now a species' (Foucault 1984: 42). But at least the homosexual is now able to speak on his own behalf, aware of his own predicament and aware of others who share that predicament. Other points of origin for homosexual subcultures are more recent still, however. On 27 June 1969, police raided the Stonewall Inn, a gay bar in Greenwich Village, New York, frequented by gay men as well as lesbians and transgender people and drag queens: white, Hispanic and African-American. Gay bars were legal in New York by this time, but the Stonewall

Inn did not have a liquor license and was also supposed to have links to organised crime in the city – and New York's Republican mayor may have simply wanted to clean it up. The police raid triggered off several days of rioting, soon involving thousands of gays and lesbians. Gay communities were galvanised by 'Stonewall' and by the end of the following month the first Gay Liberation Movement ('Out of the closets, into the streets!') was formed – an organisation that spread rapidly across the United States and elsewhere. Here again, then, we have the formation of homosexual social consciousness, arising out of club life and its persecutions – not entirely unlike the Molly Houses two hundred and sixty-odd years earlier.

If this is where a homosexual self-consciousness – a sense of 'being gay' – emerges, then how can we think about homosexual sociality *before* Stonewall? George Chauncey has charted a 'topography of gay meeting places' in New York between 1890 and 1940 – clubs and bars, as well as streets, baths and restaurants – in order to trace what he calls 'the making of the gay male world' (Chauncey 1994: 23) well before late 1960s 'gay liberation'. From a different perspective, Christopher Nealon has looked at pre-Stonewall gay and lesbian literature in the United States, including lesbian pulp novels from the 1950s, arguing that these writings enabled homosexual readers at the time to imagine homosexuality as both 'an exile from sanctioned experience, most often rendered as the experience of participation in family life and the life of communities, and...a reunion with some "people"...who redeem this exile and surpass the painful limitations of the original "home"' (Nealon 2001: 1–2). Here is a now-familiar expression of subcultural movement: out of the home and into a new kind of sociality. Lesbian pulp novels from the 1950s can be seen nowadays as 'tokens of a pre-Stonewall queer "heritage"' (141), conveying the experience of 'being lesbian' and – as one commentator puts it – reaching 'isolated, small-town lesbians who could read them and see that they were not the only lesbians in the world' (cited 148). Lesbian pulp fiction might have usefully supplied a sense of imagined sociality to lesbians in small-town 1950s North America; but in the larger cities around this time, there were at least a few examples of bars and taverns where lesbians could actually meet face to face. Nan Alamilla Boyd describes the bars in San Francisco's North Beach, which lesbians would share with prostitutes and sex workers. A raid in 1954 on a butch-fem bar, Tommy's Place, demonstrated that lesbians 'remained vulnerable to the whims of politics and police' – but it also helped to create a 'siege mentality' in the bars that galvanised lesbian and gay communities more than a decade before Stonewall (Boyd 2003: 15–17). 'In San Francisco', Boyd writes, 'the roots of queer activism are more fundamentally found in the less organised (but numerically stronger) pockets of queer association and camaraderie that existed in bars and taverns' (10). There are now studies of the histories of lesbian bar culture in Detroit (Thorpe 1997), Montreal (Chamberland 1993) and Colorado (Gilmartin 1996). The History Project's

Improper Bostonians: Lesbian and Gay History from the Puritans to Playland (1998) even provides a map of lesbian and gay bars and gathering places in that city in the years between Prohibition and Stonewall, as a testimony 'to a dynamic and diverse subculture that existed before the Stonewall riots' (History Project 1998: 162). But the most exhaustive and detailed account of this topic – one which took fourteen years to complete – is Elizabeth Lapovsky Kennedy and Madeline D. Davis's oral social history of lesbian bars in Buffalo, New York, *Boots of Leather, Slippers of Gold: The History of a Lesbian Community* (1993).

This is an ethnographic study with around thirty 'narrators', women who recount their first-hand experiences – their 'real-life stories' – in Buffalo's lesbian bars, going back to the 1940s. The focus is on *working-class* lesbians, because this is where the authors locate lesbian bar culture. Aristocratic or upper-class lesbians, they suggest, were 'not dependent on society's approval'; middle-class lesbians in professions such as teaching 'had to be secretive about their identity'; but working-class lesbians 'pioneered ways of socialis-ing together…without losing the ability to earn a living' (Kennedy and Davis 1993: 3). Lesbian and gay bars were already around before the 1940s in some of the major cities in the United States, but were rare elsewhere. The con-ditions at home during the Second World War may have helped lesbians to socialise, but whatever the reasons by the 1940s there were two bars of inter-est in Buffalo: Ralph Martin's, a mixed or 'unsegregated' gay and lesbian bar, and a smaller, lesbian-only bar, Winters, 'the closest thing to a woman-defined space that could be imagined for a public bar of the 1940s' (47). In Chapter 2, I described John Irwin's notion of the 'bar scene' in American cities, as socially porous places where one might find oneself sitting alongside strangers. For Kennedy and Davis, however, the lesbian bar scene offered a 'protected' environment for homosexual women (65), exclusive rather than open, and designed to merge the act of 'public socialising' with the possibility of 'per-sonal intimacy' (5) – although they describe some of the fights and brawls that took place there, too. Working-class lesbians developed social identities through the bar scene structured around the butch-fem (or femme) partner-ship. As Kennedy and Davis note, feminist commentators have often negatively evaluated butch-fem identities as merely imitating or reproducing the conven-tional heterosexist binary of masculine/feminine. Their view is quite different, however: that butch lesbians 'defied convention by usurping male privilege in appearance and sexuality, and with their fems, outraged society by creating a romantic and sexual unit within which women were not under male control' (6). The image of the butch is crucial to their argument about working-class lesbians' involvement in the lesbian bar scene. Far from imitating convention, the butch's carefully cultivated 'masculine' appearance signalled her differ-ence, her distinction: 'the image of the butch, or the butch-fem couple, was the only distinct marker around which a community could be built' (374). The problem here is that, having so positively invested in the butch's distinction, the authors are then not entirely clear about what to do with the fem partner. For fems, they controversially suggest, 'the category lesbian was situational' (385), less of a subcultural commitment and less a matter of a cultivated, different lesbian image. 'Most had lived comfortably at least some of their lives', they write, 'as heterosexuals' (385). Kennedy and Davis thus end their study by creating another kind of distinction which they make internal to the subculture itself: between 'persistent' (butch) and 'fluid' (fem) members of the lesbian community. 'We need concepts', they conclude, making a point that is both important to and problematic for subcultural studies, 'that will take into account the persistent *and* the fluid…' (387, my italics).

The question of how exclusively 'lesbian' lesbian bars actually were (and still are) seems to be an open one, and perhaps some aspect of John Irwin's notion of a 'porous' – or *fluid* – urban bar scene remains true here. As we saw in Chapter 2, segregation and proximity can often trouble each other in the city. Kelly Hankin sees the lesbian bar in exactly this way, 'as a locus of lesbian and heterosexual activity, as well as a site fraught with racial and class divisions' (Hankin 2002: xiv). Hankin's *The Girls in the Back Room* is an excellent study of the way the lesbian bar is represented in mainstream cinema and documentary film, concerned not so much with actual lesbian bars and their histories (like Kennedy and Davis) but, rather, with the 'stories we tell ourselves' about them, the ways in which they are *imagined*. She argues that the emergence of 'lesbian bar representation' in the 1920s and 1930s coincided with a popular and social scientific sense that the lesbian was 'invisible and thus uncontrollable' (2002: xviii). The lesbian bar was therefore a 'site of fascination' which had to be rendered 'authentically' in cinema – but which was also imprinted with 'heterosexual ownership' (xv), contained and segregated by mainstream film-makers in order to keep conventional sexual distinctions between heterosexual and homosexual intact. Hankin analyses Robert Aldrich's film, *The Killing of Sister George* (1968) along these lines – 'the first film to depict an exclusively lesbian bar scene' (xix), shot on location at the otherwise reclusive London bar, Gateways. She also looks at some documentaries about lesbian bars, describing 'the continuously vexed relationship of lesbians to public space' (xxiv). There are nostalgias in these documentaries for the way lesbian bars used to be. But Hankin ends her own study by drawing out another kind of longing, not for the way things were but with how they might become: sliding from nostalgia to utopia as she imagines a place that is *persistent* and *fluid*, segregated and proximate, simultaneously:

I'm inclined to think of bar documentaries less as nostalgic longings for a place we've never been [to] than as utopian desires for a place we hope to have, a place that 'can and perhaps will be': a space free from violence; a space where, treasured rather than maligned for their differences, women of varying races, ethnicities, economic statuses, identities, and age can interact passionately, intellectually, and culturally; and, finally, a place where sex and politics commingle and unite, where 'respectability' does not cancel out desire.

(155–56)

Drag queens and drag kings

The comments above on butch as an embodied expression of female masculinity (rather than masculinity per se), along with Kennedy and Davis's notion of 'persistent' and 'fluid' affiliations to a subculture, can help us to think about another kind of club scene – drag. 'Drag queen scenes' unfold in clubs where (usually) homosexual men dress and perform as women. Two things can be said about these scenes in terms of their social difference. First, they should be distinguished from 'female impersonation', which is commonplace across a range of male social sectors and which is usually not associated with homosexuality. Female impersonation can certainly be performative and is a reasonably familiar feature of popular entertainment, including cinema and television (e.g. the 'variety show'). It can also be tied to clubs: in his study of the history of drag and the theatre, Laurence Senelick describes the 1895 Paint and Powder Club in Baltimore, 'whose members were prominent businessmen, [who] staged lavishly funded, crossed-dressed musicals for the delectation of traveling salesmen' (Senelick 2000: 353). Strictly speaking, however, this is not an example of a drag queen scene: it is, we might say, more 'fluid' than 'persistent'. The Australian transgender activist Roberta Perkins makes exactly this point in her fine, early study, *The 'Drag Queen' Scene: Transsexuals in Kings Cross, Sydney* (1983). Perkins had talked to twelve girls (this is the term used by the transsexuals themselves) who worked in the bars and clubs in the 'Cross', one of Sydney's more notorious entertainment precincts and a 'meeting place of society's nonconformists' (Perkins 1983: 29). Drag queens are not always transsexuals, but they are something more than just female impersonators—performers (like, say, Barry Humphries) who are neither homosexual nor live as women. Perkins's twelve informants *are* transsexual, however. Not all of them had actually undergone surgery, but 'they all lived as women, identified themselves as women and were identified by others as women' (3). The clubs in Kings Cross become places of refuge for these girls, whose families had often rejected them. 'Most of us clung together for support', one girl says, 'needing one another as points of reference' (17). On the other hand, they disperse into particular kinds of 'careers' (to recall Cressey on the taxi-dance girls in Chicago) such as the 'showgirl', the 'stripper' or the 'prostitute', and so create a smaller subset of social worlds, each with its own values: for the showgirl, for example, it is 'prestige'. These drag queens, for Perkins, occupy a 'sexual ghetto', segregated from the prevailing conventions of society and certainly far removed from the 'ordinary' lives of most suburban Australians – even though their clients and audiences are generally men *from* the suburbs. The 'Cross' is a kind of dystopia here; and the girls' experiences lead Perkins to suggest that the drag queen 'is one of the most exploited and oppressed figures in our society' (1).

Second, the male homosexual drag queen should also be distinguished from the broader culture of homosexuality itself. This is not least because drag queens perform a particular kind of relationship to *women*. The novelist Edmund White had noted that:

> a large segment of the lesbian and gay male population frowns on drag queens, who are seen as mocking women, all the more so because they get themselves up in the most *retardataire* female guises (show girls, prostitutes, sex kittens, Hollywood starlets).
>
> (cited in Bergman 1993: 6)

Perkins has also noted that the Kings Cross drag queens played out (albeit in an exaggerated fashion) the 'stereotyped norms' of femininity, becoming 'a curious mixture of conformity and nonconformity' (1983: 159). But drag queens – precisely by performing *as* women – also undo the normative maleness of homosexuality, crossing gender boundaries. Drag queens and their culture were the subject of Esther Newton's classic ethnographic study, *Mother Camp* (1972), the result of ground-breaking fieldwork she did for her graduate degrees in anthropology at the University of Chicago in the mid-to-late-1960s, before Stonewall. The first drag queen show Newton saw was in a small bar on Chicago's Near North Side. The best-known chapter from *Mother Camp* is titled 'Role Models', and here she identifies this sense that the drag queen is in some ways at odds with other homosexuals. For Newton – and it is worth remembering again that this is before Stonewall – homosexuality is something of a public 'stigma' for homosexuals, who prefer their sexuality to remain socially invisible. For the drag queen, however, homosexuality is only *too* visible. 'The drag queen role is emotionally charged', Newton writes, 'and connotes low status for most homosexuals because it bears the visible stigma of homosexuality' (Newton 2000: 23). The drag queen is thus 'a marked man in the subculture' (22) and their theatrical culture is one from which many homosexuals distance themselves.

For Newton, drag queens deal with their alienation through *camp*. Drawing on the sociology of Ernest Goffman, she sees camp not just in terms of role-play but as a 'strategy for a situation': 'the camp ideology', she writes, 'ministers to the needs for dealing with an identity that is well defined but loaded with contempt' (23). Camp has three aspects to it: *incongruity* (i.e. the juxtaposition of features or things – or sexualities – not 'normally' meant to go together), *theatricality* (the performance of that juxtaposition, its exaggeration, its 'stagey' quality) and *humour*. Camp and drag merge into each other here, with camp understood as an ideology – a set of tastes, an aesthetic, a way of living, even a kind of politics – that is specific to homosexuality. The notion of camp as an aesthetic had gained currency in the mid-1960s through Susan Sontag's famous essay, 'Notes on "Camp"' (1964). Here, camp was understood as a modernist, anti-realist expression of 'style-without-content', as surface-without-depth, a celebration of bad taste, disposability, and so on. But in a later essay, Newton notes that Sontag had made 'a serious mistake' in ascribing camp to modernism; it is, she argues, found 'in groups of people in social networks, not abstractions...' (Newton 2000: 39). The view that camp is embodied rather than disembodied is a subcultural one, tying camp not to a 'sensibility' that anyone can participate in, but to a particular kind of social world – the world of the drag queen, in this case – and the way in which this social world manages its 'situation'. For David Bergman, the drag queen's subordinate place in homosexual culture qualifies the kind of camp s/he accesses, as *low* camp: 'Low camp as exemplified by the drag queen has always played a strange and ambiguous role in both the homosexual perception of homosexuality and in the heterosexual perception of homosexuality' (Bergman 1993: 6). Bergman is especially irritated with Sontag's abstraction of camp, her association of it with 'failed seriousness'. She was, he writes, 'never genuinely interested in camp itself' (8) – meaning in this context, she was never genuinely interested in drag.

In their study of working-class lesbian bars in Buffalo, Kennedy and Davis note that although the butch identity is 'also based on gender artifice' (Kennedy and Davis 1993: 383) – like a drag queen's – nevertheless butches seem to have no connection to camp at all. The drag queen's counterpart, however, is not so much the butch lesbian as the drag *king*. Although there is a long and significant history of women performing as men – including the legendary Storme DeLarverie, a pioneering lesbian male impersonator who was also famous for hitting back at a policeman at Stonewall and so igniting the riots – nevertheless drag king shows are a relatively recent phenomenon in lesbian clubs. In *The Drag King Book* (1999), Del LaGrace Volcano notes that drag king acts seemed like 'an entirely new concept in lesbian nightlife' during the mid-1980s, with the drag king as a 'very special species' (Volcano and Halberstam 1999: 10). Judith Halberstam has also commented on the 'relative scarcity' of drag kings and male impersonators in lesbian culture, remarking on 'the lack of a lesbian drag tradition' (Halberstam 1998: 234). Drag kings are distinguished from butch lesbians in these accounts, because the latter is not performative as such even though she has cultivated a 'masculine lesbian' or 'female masculine' identity. Drag kings, on the other hand, make masculinity a central part of their act. Halberstam identifies two 'very distinct sub-types' which exactly reproduce the distinction Kennedy and Davis had drawn above

57

between the butch (*persistent*) and the fem (*fluid*): the 'butch' drag king, who elaborates on stage the 'female masculinity' she cultivates off-stage (which is different in turn to 'male masculinity'), and the 'femme' drag king who takes her masculinity as a matter of performance only and may well leave it behind her when she steps off the stage and 'takes off the fake hair and the boxers and the chest binding' (Volcano and Halberstam 1999: 36).

In her book *Female Masculinity* (1998), Halberstam offers a more nuanced taxonomy of the drag king when she writes about two club-based events in New York during the mid-1990s: the Hershe Bar Drag King Contests, and the weekly drag king show at Club Casanova. Different 'genres of masculinity' are performed by women at these events: it may be a convincing kind of masculinity ('butch realness', 'male mimicry'), or an ironic kind that ends by removing the masculine attire ('femme pretenders'), or a performance of gay masculinity ('fag drag'), or a parody of masculinity ('denaturalised masculinity'). The problem for Halberstam is that, like the butch lesbian, the drag king also doesn't seem particularly attached to camp, even though drag king performances might well express the three aspects of camp that Newton outlines above (incongruity, theatricality and humour). Halberstam wonders whether camp is 'an essentially gay male aesthetic' explicitly conveyed through the drag queen's outrageous performance of femininity – helped along by the fact that femininity itself is 'artificial' and performative (Halberstam 1998: 234, 237). Masculinity, on the other hand, is naturalised as a gendered practice and so is 'non-performative': it 'just is' (234). The drag king's performance of masculinity, then, is almost oxymoronic: the performance of something non-performative. Drag queens exaggerate their femininity, but drag kings therefore *downplay* their masculinity. In Halberstam's account, drag queens are embodiments of excess, but drag king performances are instead about 'restraint and containment' (238) – a feature that goes against the grain of subcultural identity as I have been characterising it (and one we shall see again, also in relation to masculinity, in Chapter 7). Halberstam is herself a 'trans-butch or a drag butch' and in *The Drag King Book* she writes, 'I take my masculinity very seriously, and find it nourished and cultivated by immersions in those queer arenas of Drag King theater' (Volcano and Halberstam 1999: 1). She draws a distinction between drag kings/drag butches and the occasional mainstream media images of 'supermodels with moustaches' or 'playgirls with dicks' in glossy fashion magazines (such as the actress Demi Moore in an issue of *Arena*). This is effectively another version of Kennedy and Davis's *persistent* and *fluid* binary – or, we might say, the binary of the authentic and the inauthentic – and it parallels the distinction drawn above between butch and femme lesbians. Halberstam is 'nourished' by drag king performance and hopes for 'a butch brotherhood behind the Drag King world' (1). That is, she hopes for something *persistent* and authentic in drag king culture. But it doesn't seem to be there. Like her co-author, Del LaGrace Volcano, Halberstam does male drag 'every day' (41). But drag king performance seems to be more *fluid* than she had thought:

> We constantly seek to blur the line between on and off stage, but that porous boundary shifts and warps. If the mainstream media has often been thwarted in its hopeful anticipation that Drag Kings are properly feminine women dressing up for a lark; similarly, our search for what we considered provocative butchness and essential queerness beneath the costumes was also continually thwarted.
>
> (41)

This self-effacing and slightly melancholy confession might remind us of Kennedy and Davis's concluding call for subcultural studies to draw on 'concepts that will take into account the persistent *and* the fluid', the authentic and the inauthentic, the butch and the femme, simultaneously. There is a trace of John Irwin's notion of the 'porous' bar scene in Halberstam's remarks, as if (in this case) the persistent/authentic butch is always destined to find herself sitting beside the fluid/inauthentic femme. But there is also the sense that a search for something real or 'essential' below the surface – 'beneath the costumes', off the stage – is condemned not to succeed, especially in such a cultivated, performative club environment. If camp is surface-*without*-depth, an expression of the 'failure of seriousness' in Sontag's phrase, then this account may very well be casting drag king performance as camp in spite of itself.

Disco and queer life-worlds

Camp has often been associated with disco music, originally an African-American music popularised by DJs at underground clubs for gay men in the late 1960s, crossing over into the mainstream charts in the mid-1970s. Kai Fikentsche notes that 'the first urban venue that made disco rhyme with homo was the Sanctuary on West Forty-third Street' in New York, 'the capital of disco' (Fikentsche 2000: 26, 27). Italian-American Francis Grasso was the pioneering DJ at Sanctuary – the only straight man in the club, it was often said – and the first DJ to 'stitch' records together in sequence, one blending into the next, to produce a non-stop dance experience. Important performers in disco history would include the drag queen combo Labelle and the diva and drag queen Sylvester, whose hit song from the mid-1970s, 'You Make Me Feel (Mighty Real)', became a disco anthem. For Walter Hughes, the song expresses 'not the drag "realness" of the voguing houses, achieved through ironic mimicry of the icons of white fashion culture…[but] a gay "realness" that flickers into being with a "touch" and a "kiss" – at the moment of homosexual physical contact' (Hughes 1994: 154). Disco here is cast as a homoerotic experience, as well as a romantic one – two aspects of disco described by Richard Dyer in his 1979 assessment of this often-maligned musical form. For Dyer, disco is erotic not in a 'phallic' sense (like, it is implied, progressive rock music) but because its effects flow through the whole body: 'the importance of disco in [gay] scene culture indicates an openness to a sexuality that is not defined in terms of cock' (Dyer 1990: 415). Disco also offers an intensity and yearning, a passion, that makes it romantic. It offers a powerful sense of having escaped from the banalities of ordinary life, work especially. For Dyer, it in fact provides an *alternative* to the banalities of work, defined by energy and pleasure and captured through its erotics and its romantic sensibility. In this sense, disco is also therefore utopian, an expression of the 'gap' between 'what is and what should be' (417).

Dyer also notes that disco, for gay men at least, is camp. Not every disco performer is gay or in drag, but if they aren't gays can and do still 'appropriate' their music. 'In this respect', Dyer writes,

> disco is very much like another profoundly ambiguous aspect of gay male culture, camp. It is a 'contrary' use of what the dominant culture provides, it is important in forming a gay identity, and it has subversive potential as well as reactionary implications.
>
> (413)

The notion that disco was important to the creation of a modern gay male identity is compelling and is usually tied to a post-Stonewall moment, as Walter Hughes has noted: 'Historically, disco music was one element in the post-Stonewall project of reconstructing those persons medically designated "homosexuals" as members of a "gay" minority group, and of rendering them individually and collectively visible' (Hughes 1994: 148). The film *Saturday Night Fever* (1977), which so popularised disco as a mainstream musical form, is seen negatively in this context as 'an overdetermined attempt to heterosexualize disco' (147). Fikentsche notes that the film:

> is by no means intended as a documentary of the local dance scene, giving instead a skewed picture of disco dancing in musical, social and sexual terms that, for better or worse, had a long-lasting impression on American audiences. Protagonist John Travolta's character is neither gay nor black, nor musically hip.
>
> (Fikentsche 2000: 27)

New York's famous Studio 54 opened the same year as *Saturday Night Fever* – in April 1977 – again lifting disco out of its gay history and aligning it instead with a hedonistic celebrity culture which became notorious for its mostly heterosexual activity and drug use. This is when disco is supposed to have 'peaked' and then gone into steep decline. Looking at two revisionist 'disco nostalgia' films produced much later on in 1998, *54* and *Last Days of Disco*, Peter Braunstein writes in New York's *Village Voice* that disco's gay history has now been all but wiped away. One might conclude from these films, he suggests,

> that gays were a colorful accessory to an otherwise straight scene.... The cosmetic surgery performed on disco – then and now – can only be undone by exposing its real foundation, laid during the halcyon days just after Stonewall in 1969. To understand the real meaning of disco and the reasons it died involves taking a trip back to the gay coming-out party that launched this scene in the first place.
>
> (Braunstein 1998: n.p.)

We can see in these nostalgic comments another version of the authenticity/inauthenticity or persistent/fluid binary noted above, cast – interestingly enough – in camp, performative terms. The 'real foundation' of disco is found in its gay origins, beneath the surface; in which case, a certain amount of 'cosmetic surgery' is needed to produce disco as a *straight* musical scene. In the comments that follow, the straightening of disco – its mainstreaming – seems in fact to unfold as something resembling a kind of drag queen performance:

> Within a decade of Stonewall, then, straights were compelled to navigate in an inverted cultural order whose terms were set by gays. One writer in a 1977 *Harper's* piece expressed confusion at the presence of heterosexuals in primarily gay discos: 'While they might say they were there only as watchers, only as voyeurs, they were also becoming participants..., outlaws in what had always been an outlaw world.'
>
> The rise of disco had brought with it the mainstreaming of *gay*, possibly the opening salvo in the queering of America. Yet it wasn't homosexuality per se that disco ushered in but a sustained exploration of the sexual self, including the femme side of the male persona. With its fluid structure of crests and flows, disco music allowed men to imagine the wavelike and recurrent quality of the female orgasm, and to enter a world of psychic plenitude where the spartan injunctions of machismo had been overthrown. Needless to say, this world turned upside down made another, discophobic America very nervous.
>
> (ibid.)

Disco, in this endearingly hyperbolic account, is an inverted world where heterosexuals can be gay 'outlaws' too, where machismo is replaced by 'femme', and where men find themselves in imaginative proximity to the female orgasm. John Irwin's notion of the 'porous' bar scene has returned here with a vengeance, applied to nothing less than the nation itself. But it is the gay disco scene that is porous now, a subculture that is made over to heterosexuals on the one hand (straightened, mainstreamed) but which makes heterosexuals over in its turn: inverting them, as it were, or 'queering' them.

The notion of a queer identity can often work to complicate the conventional categories of *gay* and *lesbian*, and can even complicate the binary of homosexuality and heterosexuality. But it also positions itself against normativity and especially hetero-normativity, that is, the *conventionalising logics* of heterosexuality. This is the view of queer that Fiona Buckland draws on in her book, *Impossible Dance: Club Culture and Queer World-Making* (2002), which works to understand 'queer clubs' in New York as non-normative places: places 'in which the heterosexual couple was no longer the referent or the privileged example of sexual culture' (Buckland 2002: 6). For Buckland, these clubs are porous in one sense, and quite distinct in another. She views them as places of theatre and performance, drawing on the symbolic interactionist notion of social identity as a matter of socialised role-playing and meaning-making, discussed in Chapter 2. Queer clubbers, as they dance together, are expressive, creative and playful – play is especially important to Buckland's study. They 'fashion' themselves as queer in the process, so that the club in fact becomes a space in which queer participants are able actually to *become* queer. For example, clubbers will 'dress "queer" to create themselves and to be read by a target audience of other queers, which, in a gay, lesbian, or queer club, can be exploited to the utmost' (39). 'I wasn't attractive', says one of her 'chubby' informants, 'so I made up for it by being outrageous' (cited 40). Dancing and movement are also expressive and creative, connecting clubbers to each other and again enabling them to think of themselves as *social*. For Buckland, queer clubbers are often 'worldless, cut off in many instances from family, church and other instances of community-building' (38). Alienated from other kinds of sociality in this way, they fashion their own 'life-worlds' inside the clubs, places which then form a part of their 'cognitive map' of the city. Buckland prefers the term *life-world* to the word *community*, since the latter doesn't allow for porousness or for the kind of fluidity she ascribes to club life – which confuses the authentic and the inauthentic through its constant 'self-fashioning' and performativity, and sees many different kinds of people interacting with each other. At the same time, community remains as a kind of ideal here: as if one still yearns, as Judith Halberstam had, for something more *persistent*. Queer clubs may not be communities themselves, but they may very well yearn for community. In this sense, the queer club – rather like the lesbian bar for Hankin, above – is utopian, a 'carrier of utopic imagination' where 'the promises of freedom and egalitarianism…may be impossible to realize' (1) even as they are played out ritualistically in the club environment.

Clubbing, distinction, utopia

The view of the dance club as an imaginative, self-fashioning place is not one that is specific only to gay, lesbian and queer clubs, of course. In *Dance Hall Days*, Randy McBee looks at the way women danced and performed in clubs in the 1920s and 1930s, noting that for them 'the dance hall was a world of make-believe, that thrived on spontaneity, embraced flirtation, and had the potential to upset certain gender norms' (McBee 2000: 114). The case for the last point isn't a particularly strong one, however, and we can probably easily agree that heterosexual dance clubs will be a good deal more heteronormative than queer ones. In Sarah Thornton's ethnographic study of British clubbers in the 1990s, *Club Cultures: Music, Media and Subcultural Capital* (1995), 'the axis along which crowds [at dance clubs] are most strictly segregated is sexuality', with gay and lesbian clubs usually posted in listing magazines separately to heterosexual clubs (Thornton 1995: 112). Thornton's study investigates 'predominantly straight and white' dance clubs, those with a 'heterosexual manifestation' (6). Drawing on the work of Pierre Bourdieu, especially his notions of social distinction, taste and 'cultural capital' – the knowledges and competence one has in a particular cultural field, or of a particular cultural practice – Thornton suggests that dance club crowds are in fact stratified and hierarchised, internally divided rather than collective or communal. Club cultures do tend to imagine themselves as discrete 'social worlds' through the distinction they invariably draw between themselves and the 'mainstream' – a distinction which is crucial to their valorisation as a subculture, although it may also be more imagined than real in its effects. But this distinction works in turn to divide club cultures themselves. For Thornton, club cultures are primarily about knowledge and taste – in music, for example. Some people, however, are more 'in the know' than others. And some people's tastes are more hardcore or 'hip' than others. Thornton returns to Howard Becker's study *Outsiders* (1963) for the distinction between being 'hip' and being 'square' – which Becker had noted amongst a group of Chicago jazz musicians. And she modifies Bourdieu's notion of cultural capital to account for this expression of knowledge and taste amongst clubbers, of being 'in the know' and being 'hip', which she calls *subcultural* capital. Subcultural capital is usually a factor of age in the dance clubs: younger participants know more about their scene and are more committed to it. But Thornton suggests that it is gendered, too. Boys seem (or seemed) to go out more, listen more, and read more dance music-related material than girls. Girls might defend their tastes, but in doing so, Thornton writes, 'they acknowledge the subcultural hierarchy and accept their lowly position within it' (1995: 13).

Female clubbers may or may not recognise themselves in this account, which casts them negatively as less 'hip' or hardcore, less 'in the know', and lower in the clubbing hierarchy than boys. Later on, Thornton describes a

popular image of mainstream clubbing, a symbol of an 'unhip and unsophis-
ticated' crowd with 'indiscriminate music tastes': a place where, as she puts
it, 'Sharon and Tracy dance around their handbags' (99). As she notes, this is
a *feminised* image of the mainstream, one of several 'burlesque exaggerations
of an imagined *other*' (101) offered up by clubbers who are more invested in
hardcore tastes. But in her own account, the female clubber is *already* down
the bottom of the subcultural hierarchy, already less 'in the know' and therefore less 'authentic' – so much so that the 'us' (subculture, authenticity) and
'them' (mainstream, inauthenticity) distinction is able also to be expressed as
'masculine culture' and 'feminine culture' (115). For Peter Braunstein, above,
disco enabled an exploration of 'the femme side of the male persona'. Here,
however, women and men are distinguished from one another, the latter val-
orised subculturally at the former's expense. Thornton's account might also
recall the butch/femme distinction discussed earlier, which was similarly tied
to a binary of authenticity (*persistent*) and inauthenticity (*fluid*), as well as to
the distinction between (female) masculinity and femme. But however it is
understood, Thornton's study of club cultures is certainly quite different in
kind to, say, Fiona Buckland's – and not simply because the former's focus is
heterosexual while the latter's is queer. It is much more about the 'dynamics
of distinction' (163) which subdivide club cultures than about their shared,
community-oriented ideals; much more about their hierarchies and elitisms
than about 'the promises of freedom and egalitarianism' that dance clubs
might bring to their participants; and more about clubbing as a managed area
of leisure activity than a site for imaginative play and performance. Recalling
my comments at the end of Chapter 1, we might say that, whereas Buckland's
account of queer clubs in New York is romantic, Thornton's account of British
clubs is anti-romantic.

There *are* romantic accounts of the straight dance club scene, however.
Simon Reynolds has celebrated the myriad of rave, techno and house dance
clubs, configuring their many 'subsubgenres and microscenes' according to
sonic differences and presenting them as hi-energy sites that are indeed *persistent*: 'there's so much yet to come', he writes enthusiastically (Reynolds
1998a: 380, 390) and, in the conclusion to another book, 'there's so much still
ahead' (Reynolds 1998b: 432). Community, sociality and belonging can also
be emphasised here; so can self-fashioning and imaginative play. For Antonio
Melechi, dance clubs 'represent a fantasy of liberation, an escape from identity. A place where nobody is, but everybody belongs' (Melechi 1993: 37):
no social distinctions or hierarchies at all in this heady remark. Ben Malbon's
book, *Clubbing: Dancing, Ecstasy and Vitality* (2001), is also an ethnographic
study of British dance clubs, especially the rave subculture, and again it is
strikingly different to Thornton's. Like Reynolds in *Generation Ecstasy*, Malbon
looks at club activity built around a form of music that, although (or perhaps because) it is without lyrical content, can nevertheless produce an

intensely registered dance experience. Rave culture participants, especially those under the influence of the drug ecstasy (MDMA), seem to feel a sense of heightened euphoria and happiness that is specific to the rave club scene. Drawing on the work of British novelist and journalist Marghanita Laski who had written several books on ecstatic experiences, creativity and everyday life, Malbon describes the way 'altered states' on the dance floor produce a sense of intimacy with other ravers, a 'sensation of oneness' that wipes away one's individuality. Ecstasy literally takes clubbers out of their bodies (*ex-stasis*). Clubbing for Malbon is rendered lyrically or poetically as an 'oceanic experience', transitory and hedonistic, where clubbers experience a sense of flow and movement together. It isn't that the clubbers are out of control, however: a sense of discipline prevails on the dance floor and clubbers also seem to preserve their subcultural values of 'coolness' (like Thornton and Becker's 'hipness'). Even so, Malbon emphasises the role of play and vitality, the release of energy. Distinctions and hierarchies dissolve away: '*it does not matter*', he underscores,

> whether the clubbing crowd is actually diverse in terms of identities or not. Rather…what matters is that many clubbers *understand* the clubbing crowd, of which they are a part, to be diversely constituted, and they crucially find this understanding a rewarding and enriching experience.
>
> (Malbon 2001: 186)

Here, it seems, the *fluid* and the *persistent* fold into each other. Malbon's account is compelling but romantic all the same. He draws on Victor Turner and his notion of *communitas*, although Malbon prefers the term 'commonality' for the kind of social experience that rave clubbing produces. It isn't about the formation of a 'life-world', as it was for Buckland. Instead, it is about the loss of self. Either way, it still seems to offer its participants an idealised experience of club life, a momentary glimpse of an 'earthly utopia or dream world' (128).

Chapter 4

LITERARY SUBCULTURAL GEOGRAPHIES
Grub Street and bohemia

From Ranters to Grub Street scribblers

IN **PREVIOUS CHAPTERS** I have noted that subcultures are, among other things, a matter of imaginative representation. In even those disciplines where one might most expect description to be driven by realistic imperatives – sociology, for example – we find instead a host of tropes and metaphors, as if it is impossible to account for subcultures without them. Subcultures are brought into being through narration and narrative: told by the participants themselves, as well as by those who document them, monitor them, 'label' them, outlaw them, and so on. It therefore makes sense to look at subcultures in terms of their relation to print culture, and in particular, literary culture. As I had suggested at the beginning of Chapter 1, the notion of an 'Elizabethan underworld' in sixteenth-century England was itself caught up with literary representation: the result of a set of sometimes hyperbolic literary effects involving the imaginative (and no doubt often imaginary) representation of marginal and troublesome social types. We have seen a few other examples of literary hyperbole in descriptions of subcultures, too, like John Dunton's poem about *mollies* and club life presented in Chapter 3: 'excessive' representations of 'excessive' subcultural practices. If the subculture is *itself* involved in literary production as a way of expressing its own predicament – and accounting for the world around it – then hyperbole and excess can sometimes come to seem utterly definitive. A striking example can be found during the mid-seventeenth century in a subculture whose very name connotes hyperbole and excess, the Ranters.

By the seventeenth century a number of religious sects or movements had already split from the established Protestant Church. The Puritans, for

example, were 'godly' dissenting Protestants who agitated for social and religious reform, finally gaining ascendancy during and after the English Civil
War (1642–48) – after which, they were known by the broader term,
Nonconformists, accounting for their continued position outside of the established Church. Other nonconforming religious groups also formed around this
time: the Religious Society of Friends or Quakers, for example, or the more
radical social and political agitators, the Levellers, or the Diggers, founded
in 1649 – communistic Christians who occupied commons and attempted to
create small, egalitarian communities there. The Ranters, however, were of a
different order altogether. Regarded as heretical by the established Church,
they were egalitarian, blasphemous and pantheistic (believing that God is in
every living creature), advocates of free love and sexual promiscuity, heavy
drinkers of ale, smokers and swearers: self-indulgent and self-interested. Or
at least, this is how Ranters were commonly represented. Nicholas McDowell
has commented on the 'appearance of pamphlets describing in salacious detail
the blasphemous and licentious behaviour of the Ranters' (McDowell 2004:
25). And Kathryn Gucer has discussed the way anti-Ranter pamphleteers
presented 'exaggerated images of the Ranters by casting them as sensational
characters' (Gucer 2000: 78). One well-known Ranter was Abiezer Coppe, an
Oxford-educated chaplain who never completed his degree and the author of
A Fiery Flying Roll (1649), a wild tirade against social inequality and hypocrisy.
This remarkable *rant* imagines a new 'Jerusalem' in England, literally vomited
out of Coppe's body as he deliriously transcribes the word of God:

> *Go up to London, to London, the great City, write, write, write.* And behold I
> writ, and lo a hand was sent to me, and a roll of a book was within…&
> the Roll thrust into my mouth, and I eat it up, and filled my bowels with
> it, where it was bitter as wormwood; and it lay broiling, and burning in
> my stomach, till I brought it forth in this form.

This is a utopian text, a forerunner to the visionary poems of William Blake:
not so much self-interested as prophetic and transformative – and also, obviously, hyperbolic and excessive. Not long after its publication, the English
Rump Parliament ordered all copies of Coppe's text to be publicly burnt.
Coppe himself was imprisoned and in 1651 he wrote a couple of recantations
(which may or may not have been genuinely felt).

McDowell notes that Coppe's literary style perplexed his critics who
described his work as 'phantastick' or dismissed it as merely 'play, parody and
prankishness' (cited McDowell 2004: 90). But he also notes that the Ranters
took up the negative images of them circulated by their critics and used them
to their advantage: 'these writers actively engage with the hostile images of
themselves circulated in print and appropriate those images in the process of
using the printed text to fashion their own heterodox identities' (27). Self-

fashioning, here, occurs through writing. McDowell emphasises the 'linguistic turn' in social analysis that looks at how people shape their worlds and identities through language: *narrating* their predicament, playing it out textually. He therefore criticises a purely historical approach to the field – the kind we see in J.C. Davis's *Fear, Myth and History: The Ranters and the Historians* (2002), which wonders about the real nature of the Ranters, who exactly they might have been, whether they were a 'mass movement, sect, or loosely co-ordinated group of a handful of individuals' (Davis 2002: 15), and so on. McDowell also criticises the tendency amongst Marxist historians of seventeenth-century England, such as Christopher Hill, to understand the Ranters as spokespeople for ordinary folk, as 'plebeian' or proletariat – not least because of the Ranter's perplexing literary style. (And their supposed self-indulgence: they may be more *lumpenproletariat*.) Far from being representative, the Ranters might well have been idiosyncratic, peculiar, tied to a very particular kind of literary writing. Clement Hawes has looked at what he calls 'enthusiastic rhetoric' in the seventeenth century, the 'manic' writing of Ranters and radical Puritans which saw writers like Coppe endow themselves with an authority (e.g. the voice of God) that was 'otherwise unavailable to those assigned a lowly social authority' (Hawes 1996: 28). Manic writing was linked to religious nonconformity and often pathologised as madness. For Hawes, however, it was instead a special kind of literary expression, with six generic or characteristic features:

> (1) a preoccupation with themes of socio-economic resentment; (2) a 'levelling' use of lists and catalogues; (3) an excessive, often blasphemous wordplay; (4) a tendency to blend and thus level incongruous genres; (5) a justification of symbolic transgression, especially in the context of lay preaching, as prophetic behaviour; and (7 [sic]) imagery of self-fortification against persecution and martyrdom. (9)

These generic features work together to produce (whether it exists in reality or not) a shared, radical subject position, 'determined by the turmoil of the 1640s and 1650s': constructing what Hawes calls 'a subcultural ethos of manic subjectivity' (28).

With the Ranters, then, we see the deployment of a literary *genre* of writing defined by its indulgence and excess, otherworldly and prophetic, oppositional and embattled, always hyperbolic. But by the 1660s – the Restoration – the literary climate in England had changed considerably. There was a veritable print revolution, with the collapse of press controls and the expansion of readerships as people became increasingly literate. As Paula McDowell has noted, even with the Licensing or Printing Act of 1662, 'the English press would never again be as effectively censored as it had been' during and before the Civil War (McDowell 1998: 4). A few years after the Glorious Revolution of 1688, the Licensing Act was in fact 'allowed to lapse for good, ending offi-cial pre-publication censorship and government restrictions on the number of master printers throughout Britain' (4). Printing and publishing became accessible to almost anyone; rapidly-produced broadsheets and pamphlets sold and circulated; and an energetic public sphere emerged, driven by debate (or, often, downright abuse) and involving writers, booksellers, printers and pub-lishers: literally, a print *culture*. It was also a marketplace, where writing – far from being otherworldly and prophetic – found itself grounded in the every-day commonplaces of commercial transaction. This is where we find the 'hacks' and 'scribblers' carving out their literary careers – and they do it in a part of London that, although real enough in one sense, is again best known for its imaginative renderings, its force as an evocative, and excessive, trope or metaphor. This is where we find, as McDowell puts it, the 'emerging profes-sional literary subculture that by the late seventeenth century in England was already popularly referred to as "Grub Street"' (5).

Grub Street is now Milton Street, in the parish of St Giles, Cripplegate – close to the Barbican Centre in today's London. Its original name probably derived from *grube*, a ditch or drain, referring to Fleet Ditch and the marshland environs of its location but also signifying its lowlife identity 'in the seedier and seamier part of London' (Heaney 1995: 1). For Pat Rogers, Cripplegate 'had for some time been known as a haunt of counterfeiters, receivers, beg-gars, foreigners and houses of ill repute' (Rogers 1972: 23). By the early 1700s it was also characterised by its pimps, prostitutes and brothels. But another group of people had made their home there, too: writers, poets, satirists, and booksellers and publishers like Edmund Curll. Curll published a wide variety of cheap books and pamphlets: medical cures, scandals, hack biographies of recently deceased authors, Whig political tracts, a range of pirated, unauthor-ised material, and pornography. In 1724 he published *Venus in the Cloister; or, The Nun in Her Smock*, the translation of a French pornographic work that led to his arrest and conviction for obscenity (possibly the first such conviction in England). For an early biographer, he is 'the unspeakable Curll', an unscrupu-lous but likeable, publicity-seeking rogue who threw himself into the business of publishing and bookselling, a 'not very respectable person, but genuinely keen on books' (Straus 1927: 48). Curll had angered two eminent Tory writ-ers, Jonathan Swift and Alexander Pope, by publishing some of their writings without their permission, and he became involved in a long-running feud with Pope that saw each become a character in each other's work – most famously, with Curll appearing in Pope's brutally satiric poem about Grub Street and the decline of English literary and cultural tastes and standards, the *Dunciad*, the first edition of which appeared in 1728. The dispute between Pope and Curll is generally seen as more structural than personal, however. For Paula McDowell, it signified the difference between 'courtly, manuscript literary cul-ture' and 'the print-based, market-centred [literary] system we know today'

(McDowell 1998: 4). Catherine Ingrassia develops this point by distinguishing between the kind of high Augustan, Tory position Pope embodied – which tied itself to the ownership of property as the key to social worth, and promoted the 'paternal, stable, and rational figure of the landed [i.e. propertied] citizen' – and the emergent but *unstable* world of the literary marketplace, where publication is a matter of risk and speculation, credit and commodities (Ingrassia 1998: 3). It is certainly easy to see the dispute between Pope and Curll in terms of an older literary order defined through its commitment to a polite and leisured mode of literary exchange, and a new literary order investing in a notion of literature as a commercial transaction. Both writers consequently become representative politico-cultural types. Pope had in fact already affiliated himself to a group of like-minded Tory authors through the Scriblerian Club, whose collective project was to satirise hack writing and expose cultural pretensions and fake erudition: establishing a tradition of Tory satire which continues even today to sneer at non-classical cultural forms and practices. Curll, on the other hand, 'was the embodiment of Grub Street' and '*par excellence* the newly-emerged, no-holds barred capitalist publisher of the first half of the eighteenth century' (Heaney 1995: 11).

Pat Rogers's early book, *Grub Street: Studies in a Subculture* (1972), is still a foundational critical account of the world of these hacks and scribblers. He rightly notes that Grub Street – a real place in London – nevertheless flows into literary writing to become symbolic, to serve a set of cultural/political ideologies but also to be imagined, exaggerated, worked into poetry as a cumulative effect. Grub Street, he writes, 'has one foot in the real world, the other in an imaginative realm' (Rogers 1972: 3); it gives us an example of an actual geographical site, an 'urban ecology', that is transformed through literary work. The fact that writers and prostitutes inhabited the same location was useful to the view that hack writing was itself a kind of prostitution, parasitical on the work of others. It was easy to fold the two careers together:

> the satirists did everything in their artistic power to align their victims with low life. The fundamental technique of Augustan polemic is forcibly to enrol one's opponent in the lowest segment of society. One branded his literary effusions as criminal, as prostituted, as pestiferous; and if possible one showed that his actual living quarters (as they might be) were set in a district whose social character partook of the same qualities. One placed him, that is, within the precincts of Grub Street.
>
> (279)

Pope's *Dunciad* gives us an extreme example of this kind of rendering, but it also unhooks Grub Street from its moorings and makes it so hyperbolic that – as Peter Heaney writes – the place 'becomes an infernal, publishing Pandemonium, driven by demonic vendors of literary trash', its hacks and booksellers 'invested with a lunatic energy' and transformed into 'bloated and monstrous gargoyles' (Heaney 1995: 24–25). Rogers also spends a lot of time with Pope, as well as Swift; which leads him to wonder if these Tory authors were responsible for the creation of Grub Street as a coherent literary identity: rather like an early version of Howard Becker's 'labelling theory', discussed in Chapter 2. He then asks how conscious the hacks and scribblers might have been of their *own* coherence as a subculture:

> how closely knit were the brotherhood of Scribblers? Were they conscious of their duncely status before Pope unkindly reminded them of it? Did they have, in other words, a recognisable identity or community of interest other than the fact that they were leagued against the party of Swift [i.e. the Tories]?
>
> (Rogers 1972: 277)

Rogers draws on the work of Milton M. Gordon and Albert K. Cohen to answer in the affirmative, returning to the Grub Street hacks' close proximity to criminal societies and their own regular run-ins with the law: making Grub Street a very particular kind of place, where literary writing and criminal activity exist side by side. Paula McDowell makes a similar point in her study of women in Grub Street, since women also worked there and in the surrounding environs as authors, publishers and printworkers, and also as street hawkers and ballad-singers. Print culture generated 'a new mode of association for women', although McDowell argues that they probably formed a 'series of heterogeneous collectivities, rather than a homogeneous "subculture"'. But they were also routinely vilified, cast as 'scandalous', 'seditious', 'fanatick' and 'crackbrained', and often arrested. Their labelling as lowlife and as pathological lends them a subcultural coherence, in spite of their varied social backgrounds; and like the male hacks and scribblers, they were also 'united by a fear of the law' (McDowell 1998: 11, 31).

Pornography and the literary underground

The concept of Grub Street has also had some currency *outside* of London, able to designate other geographically-identifiable locations for groups or subcultures of hack writers elsewhere. Robert Darnton has used it in Paris, for example, in his book *The Literary Underground of the Old Regime* (1982), a study of struggling writers trying to make a living in the years prior to the French Revolution: the 1770s and 1780s. 'Perhaps the literary world was always divided into a hierarchy', he writes, 'whose extremes might be labelled a *monde* of mandarins on the one hand and Grub Street on the other' (Darnton 1982: 16). Darnton's Parisian Grub Street writers – many of them recently migrating into the city – are unable to access the world of 'polite' French literary culture and the privileges bestowed upon it through the court. Locked out of this closed, elite world, the Parisian hacks are forced to produce sensational, exaggerated literary works – pornography, for example – simply in order to sell copies and survive. But they also vent their anger against 'the *monde* that humiliated and corrupted them' (20) by excluding them from their privileged, court-sanctioned institutions. The *libelle* becomes their favourite genre, expressing the kind of discontent and resentment that helped to underwrite the Revolution not long afterwards:

> The grand monde was the real target of the *libelles*. They slandered the court, the church, the aristocracy, the academies, the salons, everything elevated and respectable, including the monarchy itself, with a scurrility that is difficult to imagine today, although it has had a long career in underground literature.
>
> (29)

Another study by Darnton, *The Forbidden Best-Sellers of Pre-Revolutionary France* (1996), looks more closely at the booksellers, printers and peddlers involved in libellous and often illegal literary production in the Old Regime. He also examines some of the *libelles* themselves: works of 'philosophical pornography', for example. The idea of *pornography* is a modern one, invented in the second half of the nineteenth century according to Walter Kendrick (1987). The hack writer Nicolas Restif de la Bretonne, on the other hand, published his little book, *Le Pornographe* ('The Pornographer'), back in 1769 and took this title as a self-description. His book concerned itself with the question of legalising prostitution, reminding us of the Greek origins of the word *pornography*: *pornographos*, 'writing about prostitutes'. Melissa M. Mowry has gone back further still to the Restoration in England to note that – after the English Civil War – books of antirepublican pornography began to circulate which often took up the figure of the prostitute in order to make the political point 'that women fell into whoring because their fathers had lost everything by siding with Parliament during the civil wars' (Mowry 2004: 9). The prostitute emerges in late Stuart England as a literary-political trope, put to work (or pleasure) in debased popular narratives. As I noted in Chapter 1, the prostitute's life is condemned to be imagined by others, her own voice pretty much wiped away; indeed, as Mowry notes, 'there is now no authentic voice of the prostitute from the late Stuart period, if such a thing ever existed' (15). The greatest English work of pornography built around the imagining of a prostitute's life (narrated in the first person, as if it *is* authentic) is John Cleland's libertine classic, *Fanny Hill* (1748), the publication of which coincided with the outpouring of a 'new cycle' of Parisian pornography during the 1740s as described by Darnton (Darnton 1996: 87). The publishing of pornography soon becomes an underground cottage industry with its own traditions and its specialised audiences, still able to retain at least some of its political edge and libellous force (although, later on, this would drop away as pornography dedicated itself primarily to sexual content and sexual arousal). Iain McCalman has described a 'street tradition' of pornographic publishing in early nineteenth-century England, with satires directed at George IV and various aristocratic figures, as well as the clergy, underpinned by a return to Libertine philosophies that also saw the reprinting of earlier Restoration erotica (McCalman 1988: 210). For McCalman, pornography was tied to the radical press in England, although it was also a symptom of the radical press's decline. The most prolific pornographer of the early- and mid-nineteenth century was William Dugdale, who operated 'under a maze of aliases from premises in Drury Lane and Holywell Street' in London (205). Pornographers were often arrested – Dugdale himself died in prison – and their premises raided and cleared. But they also participated in something like a subculture, operating amongst a network of information-sharing and activity and finding themselves increasingly scrutinised by the law and increasingly segregated in terms of their location in the city. They were, McCalman writes,

> gradually forced…to cluster in professional ghettoes centred around Holywell Street and Wych Street, St Martins Lane and Russell Court, and Leicester Square and its surrounds. These were the kind of milieux that William Dugdale charted in his first obscene publication, *Yokel's Preceptor*, an underworld directory of smut shops, brothels, thieves' dens and gambling hells.
>
> (218)

Segregation in one sense is proximity in another here, as pornography literally maps out its lowlife cultural equivalents to produce a subcultural geography of the city, a set of sites with which it identifies and about which it also knows a great deal. We might even see this as an exercise in what Sarah Thornton had called *subcultural capital*, described in Chapter 3. *Yokel's Preceptor* subtitles itself in slang – 'Being a…show-up of all the rigs and doings in this great metropolis' – and it attaches a glossary of useful slang words to guide the less familiar reader/tourist (those with less subcultural capital) through this urban underworld.

Pornographic publishers have certainly been persecuted and marginalised, especially in relation to the more 'polite' standards of established literary culture. It would be difficult, however, to say that they have been *repressed*. The flowering of pornography during the Restoration, for example, in fact coincided with the liberalisation, rather than the tightening, of censorship laws. Nevertheless, the 'repressive hypothesis' (to borrow Michel Foucault's phrase) lies behind Steven Marcus's influential study of late nineteenth-century pornography, *The Other Victorians* (1964), which drew a sharp distinction between 'the dominant moralistic culture of restraint and the thriving subculture of pornography'. In Marcus's work, these two realms 'are mirror opposites – one repressed, troubled, limited, focused and moral and the other characterised by inexhaustible excess, repetition, plenitude, insatiability, in Marcus's terms a "pornutopia"' (Garton 2004: 4). Foucault's critique of this binary in *The History of Sexuality* has since made Marcus's essentially Freudian view seem naive, or partial. Certainly, the notion of cultural repression as the cause of an underground counter-reaction is in itself too crude to work in broad explanatory terms. But it does have its applications. The brief account I have given above sees pornographic hack publishing as the result of cultural exclusions and economic imperatives, as well as political affiliations – not so much repressed, as segregated. On the other hand, as Jay A. Gertzman remarks in his fine study, *Bookleggers and Smuthounds: The Trade in Erotica, 1920–1940* (1999), the distribution of erotic and pornographic works 'could not have operated without the tacit sanction of established society' (Gertzman 1999: 23): as if repression (or *suppression*) and licensing are two sides of the same coin. He also notes that 'erotica merchants' or 'smutmongers' in the United States often mixed their publishing lists, putting erotic material alongside quality literature: *desegregating* pornography, we might say, but in a way that was consistent with mid-Victorian interests that saw pornography returned to a literary culture of high aesthetics and cultivated tastes. This is one of the arguments made in Lisa Sigel's book, *Governing Pleasures: Pornography and Social Change in England, 1815–1914* (2002): that pornography increasingly re-attached itself to taste and privilege, collected by bibliophiles, enjoyed in exclusive clubs (like the Cannibal Club, patronised by eminent Victorian writers), and sold at high prices, thus sealing itself off from mass consumption until the early twentieth century. The Grove Press was an American publishing house started by Barney Rosset some time later, in 1951. It also mixed quality literature and erotica together, publishing (for example) the unexpurgated version of D.H. Lawrence's *Lady Chatterley's Lover* as well as William Burrough's controversial *The Naked Lunch* in 1959, and reprinting Henry Miller's 'obscene' earlier novel, *Tropic of Cancer* (1934): all of which landed Grove Press in court. It published Samuel Beckett and Brecht and Albert Camus, all respectable highbrow writers. But it also published the Marquis de Sade and much of the Victorian pornography discussed in Steven Marcus's book, as well as Cleland's *Fanny Hill*, which was banned in the United States until 1966 when it finally gained a favourable and famous judgement from the US Supreme Court. Many Beat novelists and poets were published by Grove Press, too, such as Jack Kerouac and Allen Ginsberg. In 1964, FBI agents raided the Cleveland warehouse of one of America's most successful pornographic publishers, Reuben Sturman – who became increasingly involved with criminal organisations as his business expanded, finally dying, much like William Dugdale, in prison. The agents confiscated 590 copies of a pornographic paperback novel called *Sex Life of a*

Cop (Schlosser 2004: 118); but they also took away copies of one of Grove Press's literary publications, a novel by the Beat writer Jack Kerouac called *The Subterraneans* (1958).

Beats and bohemias

A few years earlier in 1957, 520 copies of another, foundational Beat literary work had been seized by US Customs officials on the grounds of its obscenity. Allen Ginsberg's poem *Howl* had originally been printed in England but was published in the US by Lawrence Ferlinghetti, the owner of San Francisco's City Lights Bookstore, in 1956. Customs later released the books but the local police pursued the matter, arresting Ferlinghetti as well as the bookstore's manager, Shigeyoshi Murao, for publishing and selling obscene material. A long trial followed, during which Ferlinghetti gained the support of many other writers as well as the American Civil Liberties Union, finally winning the case when the poem was declared as having 'some redeeming social importance'. *Howl* is, however, a devastating assault on American society, a delirious, hallucinatory and hyperbolic stream of complaint and invective that absolutely distinguishes it from the otherwise polite and restrained realm of American letters, 'the mannered tradition of Henry James, the perspective that carefully applied fineness of sensibility and discrimination of feeling as a source of illumination about character and culture' (Mellon 1999: 9). *Howl* is in three parts, the first of which begins with a vision of Ginsberg's own literary community as social outcasts, expelled from America's dominant cultural institutions, deranged and homeless:

> I saw the best minds of my generation destroyed by
>   madness, starving hysterical naked,
> dragging themselves through the negro streets at dawn
>   looking for an angry fix,
> angelheaded hipsters burning for the ancient heavenly
>   connection to the starry dynamo in the machinery
>   of night,
> who poverty and tatters and hollow-eyed and high sat
>   up smoking in the supernatural darkness of
>   cold-water flats floating across the tops of cities
>   contemplating jazz,
> who bared their brains to Heaven under the El and
>   saw Mohammedan angels staggering on
>   tenement roofs illuminated,
> who passed through universities with radiant cool eyes
>   hallucinating Arkansas and Blake-light tragedy

> among the scholars of war,
> who were expelled from the academies for crazy &
> publishing obscene odes on the windows of the
> skull...

The social position articulated in this poem might well recall that of the hack writers in Darnton's eighteenth-century Parisian Grub Street, also locked out of privileged cultural institutions upon which they then vent their anger: so that Ginsberg's poem is, generically, a modern American version of a *libelle*. But *Howl* is also a visionary poem delivered as a breathless invective, very much like the work of the seventeenth-century Ranter, Abiezer Coppe, discussed above. *Howl* is certainly a piece of 'manic' writing, but it is also a prophetic and mystical one that acknowledges the Ranting tradition through its reference to William Blake in the passage above and in the way it forges a direct connection between its literary community and 'Heaven' (with Ginsberg's 'footnote' to the poem repeating the word 'Holy' over and over). It is a work of divine madness, pathologising *itself*, as it were, in the third section which is directly addressed to a friend Ginsberg had met while he was institutionalised in a psychiatric hospital in New York. Coppe's poem was an attack on England, which he hoped could somehow transform itself. Ginsberg's poem is an attack on modern America – which he calls *Moloch* – and is much less hopeful about the possibility of transformation:

> Moloch whose mind is pure machinery! Moloch whose
> blood is running money! Moloch whose fingers
> are ten armies! Moloch whose breast is a cannibal
> dynamo! Moloch whose ear is a smoking tomb!...
> Visions! omens! hallucinations! miracles! ecstasies!
> gone down the American river!

Much of the Beat sensibility can be found in Ginsberg's poem: its spiritualism, its disenchantment with Eisenhower's America (regarded as materialist, conformist and war-mongering), the sense of its exclusion from establishment cultural institutions, its affinity with the 'street' and the hobo (as well as drug addicts, drop outs, thieves), its view of itself as part of a like-minded community (extended widely enough for people to talk of a 'Beat Generation'), and its affirmation of a radical literary tradition going back to the homosexual American poet Walt Whitman, Dostoevsky, Jean Genet and the French poet Rimbaud. In his study of Ginsberg's *Howl*, *American Scream* (2005), Jonah Raskin notes that in the mid 1950s, 'American poets rarely howled, screamed, ranted, or raved' (Raskin 2005: 44). Although Raskin never actually mentions the Ranters, he chronicles Ginsberg's debt to William Blake and goes on to establish Ginsberg's central position in a 'secret society of poets' (86) and a tradition of civil dissent that found its common expression in Beat Generation writings.

The key Beat writers were Ginsberg, Jack Kerouac, Gregory Corso and William Burroughs, the latter usually taken as the Beat's intellectual mentor – although the literary and cultural affiliations here are much broader. James J. Farrell notes that Kerouac and other Beat writers 'influenced the creation of coffeehouse culture in which poetry, jazz, and folk music came together in a captivating critique of the "Social Lie" of Fifties America' (Farrell 1997: 53). The 'Social Lie' was a phrase coined by Kenneth Rexroth, an influential American poet who came to be based in San Francisco and who served as a witness for the defence at Ginsberg's obscenity trial – and who later wrote a book entitled *Communalism: From Its Origins to the Twentieth Century* (1974), which included a chapter on the Ranters, Levellers and Diggers in seventeenth-century England. Rexroth's phrase gave expression to 'the materialism, mechanisation, militarism, and conformity' (Farrell 1997: 66) of American society, and the capacity of the governing classes to deceive those they govern. The Beats were not revolutionary, however. John Clellon Holmes, who introduced the term *Beat Generation* into print for the first time in an article in the *New York Times* in 1952 after hearing Kerouac use the term, wrote, 'In the wildest hipster…there is no desire to shatter the "square" society in which he lives, only to elude it' (cited 66). The term 'hipster' came to be applied to Beat writers and Beats generally speaking, coming out of the African-American jazz scene. It was defined by the American writer Norman Mailer in a controversial essay titled, 'The White Negro: Superficial Reflections on the Hipster', published the same year – 1957 – as Jack Kerouac's famous Beat novel, *On the Road*:

> the only life-giving answer [to the contemporary American condition] is…to divorce oneself from society, to exist without roots, to set out on that uncharted journey with the rebellious imperatives of the self. In short, whether the life is criminal or not, the decision is to encourage the psychopath in oneself, to explore that domain of experience where security is boredom and therefore sickness, and one exists in the present, in that enormous present which is without past or future, memory or planned intention, the life where a man must go until he is beat, where he must gamble with his energies through all those small or large crises of courage and unforeseen situations which beset his day, where he must be with it or doomed not to swing. The unstated essence of Hip, its psychopathic brilliance, quivers with the knowledge that new kinds of victories increase one's power for new kinds of perception; and defeats, the wrong kind of defeats, attack the body and imprison one's energy until one is jailed in the prison air of other people's habits, other people's defeats, boredom, quiet desperation, and muted icy self-destroying

rage. One is Hip or one is Square (the alternative which each new generation coming into American life is beginning to feel), one is a rebel or one conforms, one is a frontiersman in the Wild West of American night life, or else a Square cell, trapped in the totalitarian tissues of American society, doomed willy-nilly to conform if one is to succeed.

(Mailer 1959: 339)

Mailer's essay was romantic in one sense and crudely racialising in another since it took as the source of its image of the 'psychopathic' hipster an African-American underclass – 'the Negro' – which he cast as utterly sensual, the wild corollary of a 'civilised', but conformist, America. Jazz is the link here, similarly flattened down by Mailer to a matter of pure sensuality ('it is the music of orgasm'). The Beats were primarily associated with bebop, a rhythmically and harmonically complex form of jazz emerging in the early 1940s – which I shall discuss in more detail in Chapter 6. All the bebop musicians were African-American: Charlie Parker, Dizzy Gillespie, Thelonious Monk, Miles Davis and many others. Bebop allowed for improvisation, too, and this connected with the Beats' valorisation of the spontaneous, of flow and digression, and rapid composition (with Kerouac's *The Subterraneans* completed in three days, for example).

The Beats are generally remembered romantically, as nonconformist writers on a spiritual quest (Kerouac's 'beatitude') which was itself romantically conceived. But the broader beat subculture (with a lower case 'b') has been more prosaically dealt with. The sociologist Ned Polsky wrote a famous essay about the beat subculture in New York's Greenwich Village during the summer of 1960, first published in 1961 and reprinted in his book, *Hustlers, Beats and Others* (1967) – which also contains a fascinating essay on pornography. For Polsky, *beat* was a preferable term to *hipster*, even though it seemed to him that beats 'resent any label whatever, and regard a concern with labelling as basically square' (Polsky 1971: 149). Polsky's ethnographic account presented the Greenwich Village beats at the beginning of the decade as reclusive and publicity-shy, an unspectacular subculture who dress 'in an ordinary lower-class manner' and wear 'badges' (e.g. beards on the young men) only as a way of 'identifying themselves to one another', promoting 'a "we" feeling' of self-identification (150–51). The beats seem to share several recognisably subcultural features: they are often 'teenage runaways', leaving their homes to migrate into the Village (152); they consolidate their subcultural identity with other subcultural practices, especially drug-taking; they are 'excessive', sexually speaking, that is, promiscuous; and they 'avoid work', with a conviction that is 'so strong that many beats are willing to starve for it' (157). On the other hand, Polsky rejected the prevailing view of beats as 'apolitical *lumpen*' (159); if anything, he suggested, they are *anti*-political, rejecting both mainstream and extreme political parties even though they are themselves 'keen critics of the society in which they have grown up' (158). Polsky distinguished Greenwich Village beats from the 'small and atypical' Beat writers, since the former seemed to read very little and write even less – what they *did* write, he said, 'is poor when it is not godawful' (177). To recall the quote from Chapter 1, Polsky had no time for the '"spontaneity" nonsense' of Beat composition: his favourite Beat writer was Gregory Corso, not Ginsberg or Kerouac. But the key point of Polsky's long essay is to do with his account of the beats' relationship to African-Americans in the Village. Polsky noted the mutual interest of beats and black Americans in jazz. But he disagreed with Norman Mailer over the notion of the beat as a 'White Negro' and his conflation of the hipster (who refused to be a part of conformist American society) with the African-American (who was refused *by* conformist American society). Polsky made the point that beats, far from wanting to resemble African-Americans (as in the famous passage from *On the Road* where the narrator speaks of 'wishing I were a Negro'), were in fact conventionally American in continuing deep down to despise them. But – anticipating the argument of another Grove Press publication, Franz Fanon's 1967 study *Black Skin, White Masks* – he also argued that, rather than seeing the beat as wanting in some sense to be black, African-Americans in the Village themselves wanted most of all to be '*white*'. It was an argument that Polsky admitted would be 'touchy if not downright offensive' (180n34):

> The several white beats I met who knew my earlier critique of them – unfortunately I met no Negro beats who knew it – all disputed my claim that they accept the Negro only for his 'Negro-ness' (as bringer of marihuana and jazz, etc.)...According to them, they really do accept the Negro in his totality. Maybe so; but I doubt it. White beats should be given credit for the best of conscious intentions, but it is disheartening how often their actions confirm that old Negro proverb, 'Whenever you see a white man with a coloured man, the white man wants something from the coloured man'.

> (180)

Here we have a sociologist who doubts his subjects (even those who have taken the trouble to read his work) in order to register a 'truth' about them that they cannot know themselves: a not entirely uncommon feature of ethnographic sociology. Even so, Polsky's remarks convey an important perception, that people affiliate with racially different groups primarily through *cultural* interests and practices. The question of racial affiliations – relations between whites and African-Americans especially – was of particular interest to those who wrote about, and invested in, the 'bohemia' of Greenwich Village.

The neighbourhood street layout of Greenwich Village is quite different to the grid plan of most of Manhattan, so that it is literally an eccentric geographical site in a major metropolis. By the 1890s, immigrant Italian and Irish communities had consolidated there. But the Village also has a long association with bohemians which flowered in the first two decades of the twentieth century and lent the site its distinctive, nonconformist identity – given a frivolous kind of symbolic expression when, in 1913, the French/American Dada artist Marcel Duchamp and a fellow agitator climbed to the top of the Triumphal Arch to declare the Free Republic of Greenwich Village. The writer Malcolm Cowley – who later, at Viking Press, published Kerouac's *On the Road* – wrote about Greenwich Village during the early 1920s in his famous autobiographical book, *Exile's Return* (1934). Like the Beats, he also rejected the dull conformity of American life, 'joy and colourless, universally standardised, tawdry, uncreative, given over to the worship of wealth and machinery' (Cowley 1964: 77). The Village embodied two kinds of bohemian 'revolt' against this, sexual and political – 'the revolt against puritanism and the revolt against capitalism' (66) – although the latter seemed to have died away by the 1920s, which meant that Cowley's account of the Village's radicalism was by this time a nostalgic one. Even so, the sense that a bohemian existence *ought* to reject capitalism (if only by name or in part) was important to Cowley, who invoked the older image of Grub Street to make his point:

> Grub Street develops in the metropolis of any country or culture as soon as men are able to earn a precarious living with pen or pencil; bohemia is a revolt against certain features of industrial capitalism and can exist only in a capitalist society. Grub Street is a way of life unwillingly followed by the intellectual proletariat; bohemia attracts its citizens from all economic classes: there are not a few bohemian millionaires, but they are expected to imitate the customs of penniless artists. Bohemia is Grub Street romanticized, doctrinalized, and rendered self-conscious; it is Grub Street on parade.
>
> (55)

These fascinating remarks distinguish between two kinds of literary or artistic subcultures: the romantic and the unromantic, the 'self-conscious' and the 'unwilling', those who seem to have transcended class and those who are condemned to remain at the bottom of the class ladder ('the intellectual proletariat'). Cowley's Village is a utopia, but it is a fragile one, coming apart by the beginning of the 1920s to the extent that Cowley, who had moved to Greenwich Village in 1923, already felt alienated from it.

In her important study, *Greenwich Village 1963: Avant-Garde Performance and the Effervescent Body* (1993), Sally Banes puts Cowley's earlier nostalgia into context: 'one of the recurring myths about Greenwich Village is that it always seems to the current generation that the heyday of the Village as bohemia has just ended' (Banes 1993: 29). Banes turns to the Village during the early 1960s, around the time Polsky was chronicling the beat subculture there – and she does so in order to revitalise its critical potential. The key for her lies in a reformulated notion of community. She draws on Michel Foucault's notion of a *heterotopia* to make her point, a term that Foucault coined to describe:

> real places – places that do exist and that are formed in the very founding of society – which are something like counter-sites, a kind of effectively enacted utopia in which the real sites, all the other real sites that can be found within the culture, are simultaneously represented, contested, and inverted. Places of this kind are outside of all places, even though it may be possible to indicate their location in reality.
>
> (Foucault 1986: 24)

A utopia is imagined; a heterotopia is imagined as well, but it also has some kind of realisation, somewhere. For Banes, this is Greenwich Village, a very particular kind of community. Of course, America itself is invested in an idea of community, as Banes notes: 'The myth of the Puritan model of community – small-scale, egalitarian, and tightly bound by common threads of religion, work, and family – is crucial to the American sense of self, despite the fact that most Americans' roots lie elsewhere' (Banes 1993: 37). The fantasy of a *Gemeinschaft* is in many respects a mainstream one, in other words. But for Banes, Greenwich Village is not the Tonniesian village: it is an *alternative* community, one that in the early 1960s 'looked to folk, popular, and transgressive subcultural styles, as well as to religious ritual, for means to reject the values of both the previous generation of artists and the socio-political establishment' (9). The Village offers a sense of community to those who have *left* their homes, and their small towns, precisely because 'there was, in fact… no gemeinschaft at home' (38). The kind of bohemian community created at the Village may indeed only be possible in the city, in the midst of *Gesellschaft*: offering an urban vision, rather than a pastoral one (39). Its sensibilities are not local and in this sense it is quite different to the Italian and other immigrant communities there – which it also displaces, a point Polsky had made in his essay on the Village beats. It is instead eclectic, hybridising (think of Kerouac's Buddhism and the Beats' fascination with the East), 'plugged into what Marshall McLuhan termed the "global village" being created by the electronic mass media' (80). One of the defining features of the Village at this time, for Banes, is that it seemed to be a place where whites and African-Americans 'could mingle socially' (146). She seems to agree with Mailer, that hipsters and the Beat writers 'appropriated elements of black cultural style, from marijuana to sexual freedom to jazz prosody' (146). In mainstream America, whites and black Americans were generally segregated, socially and culturally – occupying, among other things, 'separate aesthetic domains'

(146). In Greenwich Village, however, whites and black Americans were proximate, even 'integrated', at least for the moment – a point which in turn indicated just how segregated the Village was from the rest of America. This is what characterises the Village as a *heterotopia*, although Polsky's much less romantic view of the white beat subculture's relations to African-Americans might mean that Banes's account itself has something heterotopic about it, just as much imagined or imaginary as it is real.

Chapter 5

SUBCULTURES AND CULTURAL STUDIES
Community, class and style at Birmingham and beyond

Working-class community and the problem of subculture

S UBCULTURAL STUDIES GAINED some clarity and definition in the early 1970s through graduate student research into British subcultures at the University of Birmingham's Centre for Contemporary Cultural Studies (CCCS) and the subsequent publication of two remarkably influential books: Stuart Hall and Tony Jefferson's edited collection, *Resistance Through Rituals: Youth Subcultures in Post-War Britain* (1975), and Dick Hebdige's *Subculture: The Meaning of Style* (1979). The CCCS was established in 1964 under the directorship of Richard Hoggart, with money from Sir Allen Lane of Penguin Books; and it is where British Cultural Studies is also generally said to have formally begun. Cultural Studies has written and rewritten its own history as a discipline over and over – compulsively, it can sometimes seem – and this is not the place to rehearse that history all over again. My focus, however, is on *subcultural* studies, which means this chapter's approach to CCCS commentaries will be a little different. The key to British Cultural Studies in the 1970s is *class*, and specifically the working class or proletariat; but as we have seen, subcultures are often positioned *outside* of class, closer in kind to Marx's *lumpenproletariat*, lacking class consciousness, self-absorbed or self-interested, at a distance from organised or sanctioned forms of labour, and so on. Subcultures were therefore a problem for British Cultural Studies, but also a kind of symptom, an effect. The focus on class both caused that problem, and seemed to help explain it.

The two most influential, foundational texts for British Cultural Studies are usually taken (e.g. in During 1993: 3–4) to be Richard Hoggart's *The Uses of Literacy* (1957) and the literary scholar Raymond Williams's *Culture and*

Society 1780–1950 (1958) – both published more or less around the same time, in fact, as Norman Mailer's 'The White Negro' and Jack Kerouac's Beat novel *On the Road*, although their interests could not have been more different. I shall talk about Hoggart and Williams's texts in a moment because they are important to subcultural studies, too. But a third foundational text must be added here, published a few years later, just before the establishment of Birmingham's CCCS: E.P. Thompson's classic historical study, *The Making of the English Working Class* (1963). Thompson was a literary scholar as well as an historian, the early chapters of his book invoking the writers John Bunyan and William Blake as central to the traditions of English Dissent that he charted, covering the period from the 1780s to the early 1830s. This book is important to subcultural studies for three reasons. First, it did indeed characterise the English working class in terms of dissent, defining them through their nonconformity. The opening pages describe the soon-to-be-outlawed London Corresponding Society, with its 1792 edict, 'That the numbers of our members be unlimited' – a clubbish expression of inclusiveness in one sense, and defiance in another. The English working class comes into being through its opposition to the propertied classes, 'their rulers and employers' (Thompson 1986: 11). They are thus defined primarily through conflict, as Dick Hebdige noted later on when he cited Thompson approvingly in the early pages of *Subculture: The Meaning of Style* (Hebdige 1988: 10). Class is thus relational, a matter of 'action and reaction' – or, as Thompson put it in a kind of unexpectedly hip 1960s way, class 'is not a thing, it is a happening' (Thompson 1986: 939). Class was also a matter of organisation. Thompson thus distinguished working-class dissent from the 'Mob' (24), since the embryonic proletariat could not also be *lumpenproletariat*: the former had to be conscious, self-aware, articulate, responsible. To underscore the point he devoted a chapter to mob uprisings during the 1780s and 1790s, structuring them as a sort of pre-Oedipal moment of wild, dumb unconsciousness, prior to the birth of the English working class as an organised, articulate phenomenon. Here, he gives the working class a 'sub-political' (59) prehistory that also leads him back to accounts of thieves, harlots, gamblers and vagrants in London at the time: subcultures that his chapter characterised, melodramatically, as 'Satan's Strongholds'.

Second, Thompson also defined the English working class culturally rather than, say, economically, that is, in terms of their shared rituals and traditions. It helped that his focus was on the working class at a pre-industrial historical moment, when working-class occupations were primarily defined in terms of craft. 'I am seeking', he wrote, 'to rescue the poor stockinger, the Luddite cropper, the "obsolete" hand-loom weaver, the "utopian" artisan…from the enormous condescension of posterity' (12). The pre-industrial identity of these craft-based occupations meant that – at the moment of the birth of the English working class – their traditions and rituals were already dying away. Thompson's account is therefore necessarily soaked with nostalgia. The third reason why his book is important to subcultural studies adds to this felt nostalgia: namely, that Thompson saw the early English working class as a community, or a set of communities: as a *Gemeinschaft*. The Friendly Societies he describes, with their 'simple cellular structure' (462), are forerunners of industrialised unions, and yet radically different from them. His work turns to a moment prior to industrialisation, a moment, we might say, before alienation, before *Gesellschaft*. It looks at a self-made kind of sociality cohering through dissent and defined by shared rituals and traditions, but it also places limits on its future. The English working class in this account is literally anachronistic, a notion I shall return to in Chapter 7. In terms of method, Thompson recovers these 'obsolete' figures through a process he famously referred to as 'history from below', the title of an essay published in the *Times Literary Supplement* in April 1966. The phrase expresses the kind of history written by and/or about subordinated, ordinary people, distinguishing this from 'top down', conventional historical work (what Thompson called 'English History Proper'). This, too, has been important for subcultural studies, and we have of course already seen examples of subcultural histories-from-below in previous chapters. We see it again in CCCS commentaries: for example, Angela McRobbie's 'Second-Hand Dresses and the Role of the Ragmarket' (1989), which contrasts the 'unofficial' world of ragmarket street fashion with corporate designer fashion and argues that changes in the fashion system come 'from below', i.e. from the former, not the latter (McRobbie 1994: 153). McRobbie's account of London's itinerant street trade, incidentally, is also very much in the tradition of Henry Mayhew – who was of much interest to Thompson as well (see Thompson and Yeo 1971).

Raymond Williams's earlier study, *Culture and Society*, began its historical account around the same time as *The Making of the English Working Class*, in the 1780s – but unlike Thompson, it stretched its focus into the present day, having something to say about modern conditions in the late 1950s as a kind of epilogue to its survey of the historical past. Whereas industrialisation was not a structural feature of Thompson's work, for Williams it was an originating keyword. *Culture and Society* is also about the English working class and working-class culture, wondering as Thompson did about how to represent a particular 'way of life' in the fullest sense. *Industry* was an important keyword, but *culture* was the primary one, defined here in terms of the ways in which ordinary people – the working class, in this case – collectively make their lives meaningful. The problem for Williams, however, was that industrialisation seemed to fragment traditional working-class cultural forms rather than cohere them. His own time only seemed to make things worse, with mass communication and mass culture (television, mass media, and so on: 'low in taste and habit') continuing to wreak havoc on the shared traditions of working-class life. The last part of Williams's book is a rather long-winded meditation on the modern predicament of the working class. It understands working-class culture as an expression of sociality, of *community* – as opposed to 'bourgeois culture' which is underpinned by a 'basic individualist idea' (Williams 1984: 313). But it also worries about the problem of having too much 'solidarity' here, wanting instead to keep the idea of the social relatively open and progressive. The entire mode of expression in Williams's study is designed to unify, built as it is upon the un-self-reflexive use of the second-person plural ('we', 'our'). It aims to draw people together, stretching his sense of community across class and beyond, effectively reproducing the edict of Thompson's London Corresponding Society, noted above. *Culture and Society* is not about distinction, difference, or deviance. Quite the opposite in fact, and this is its problem. It heavily invests in a sense of community (rather like Chris Jenks's 'strong sense of the "together"') that it already knows is no longer realisable, which means its tone is both utopian and elegiac. Tying community so intimately to the English working class, Williams ensures that it has no future other than an imaginary one (and indeed, his book is primarily a study of literary writers). Anything less than this community/working class nexus, however – like a subculture – is condemned to be defined only by what it lacks.

We can see exactly this predicament at work in the third – or I should say, the first – of these three foundational Cultural Studies texts, Hoggart's *The Uses of Literacy*. Already defensive about his project – 'It is often said that there are no working-classes in England now...' (Hoggart 1990: 13) – Hoggart nevertheless sketches out an entire *Gemeinschaft* of working-class life in England, characterised by its oral traditions, its sense of neighbourhood and family affiliations (in a section rather coyly titled, 'There's No Place Like Home'). There are even descriptions of the generic working-class Mum and Dad, the latter of whom 'often seems to me almost physically recognisable' (53): such is the imaginary investment here. Hoggart's account is quite different in kind to Thompson's sense of working-class dissent, even though he offers up (a fairly quietist) 'them' and 'us' model. Sameness is the cultural key: the 'strong sense of the group among working-class people', he writes, 'can express itself as a demand for conformity' (178). He faces the same problem as Williams, however, since *too much* conformity runs the risk of ossifying the working class, flattening out its capacity to adapt to new pressures. But Hoggart is more nostalgic than Williams, and more or less entirely seals the working class off from its modern circumstances. Mass communication and mass culture ('the newer mass arts', popular radio, magazines, forms of entertainment, and so on) are again the enemy of this class-based *Gemeinschaft*, and much of Hoggart's anger is directed towards this 'candy-floss world' – expressed in a manner that recalls the diatribes a few years earlier against mass entertainment and the 'culture industry' by the German Frankfurt School critic, Theodor Adorno (see Adorno 2001). But Hoggart was most scathing about those who seemed to *leave* the working-class *Gemeinschaft*, abandoning its conformist way of life. The 'scholar-ship boy' is one representative example, someone who leaves the community and moves upwards, socially speaking, rather than downwards: making the opposite kind of 'self-adjustment' (291) to the one we had seen with Albert K. Cohen's description of the delinquent in Chapter 2. A second example, however, is subcultural. The 'juke-box boys', for Hoggart, are 'symptomatic of the general trend', utterly under the influence of mass cultural forms, spend-ing their evenings 'listening in harshly lighted milk-bars to the "nickelodeons"' (247). The following description of those modern nickelodeon-cafés captures Hoggart's nostalgia for the homeliness of the working-class *Gemeinschaft* and his contempt for those who deviate from it:

> the nastiness of their modernistic knick-knacks, their glaring showiness, [demonstrates] an aesthetic breakdown so complete that, in comparison with them, the layout of the living-rooms in some of the poor houses from which the customers come seems to speak of a tradition as bal-anced and civilised as an eighteenth-century town house.
>
> (247–48)

The juke-box boys are indeed deviants here, rejecting community for subculture: literally leaving the home. But they are cast in the opposite way to the 'schol-arship boy', sliding downwards, not upwards: moving *below* class, we might say, rather than above it. Having invested so much in his notion of working-class community, Hoggart can therefore only regard them negatively: not as the pro-letariat, but as the *lumpenproletariat*. 'They form a depressing group', he writes, 'and one by no means typical of working-class people; perhaps most of them are rather less intelligent than the average, and are therefore even more exposed than others to the debilitating mass-trends of the day' (248–49).

Resistance through rituals: from content to style

Hoggart, Williams and Thompson provided a set of positions or perspec-tives upon which researchers at the CCCS during the 1970s drew in order to understand the phenomenon of subcultures. First, their focus was on the English working class, understood as a *Gemeinschaft*, a community bound to a neighbourhood and tied together by family. Second, these prehistories of the English working class established a 'them' and 'us' binary with varying degrees of dissent, as well as a programme for writing 'history from below'. Third, the emphasis was cultural: on rituals, traditions and practices, and the meanings they conveyed. Fourth, contemporary life, defined through mass communication, mass cultural forms, entertainment and consumerism, was seen as a threat to all this and therefore viewed negatively: dispersing and dumbing down those who fell under its influence – a younger generation especially – enough to characterise them as the new *lumpenproletariat* (and in fact, Williams had explicitly compared mass cultural effects to that of the late eighteenth-century mob: as if it amounted to a step backwards, socially and psychologically). Subcultures were filtered through these four things, which significantly coloured the CCCS's perception of them. We can see the effects of this by turning to an early, influential essay from Birmingham, Phil Cohen's 'Sub-Cultural Conflict and Working Class Community', first published in 1972 in the CCCS's *Working Papers in Cultural Studies*. Cohen turned to the working-class community in London's East End, the focus of much sociological and anthropological (as well as literary) interest over many years. Cohen conventionally defines this community through its stability, its kinship networks, its local economy, its shared sense of neighbourhood and 'neighbouring', its shared sense of traditions, and so on: that is, it is a *Gemeinschaft*. But he then traces the fragmentation and displacement of that community as urban planners modernise the area and new immigrants move in. The focus here, as in all of the subcultural work at the CCCS, is on working-class *youth*: how are they affected by all this? Their family and neighbourhood – what he calls their 'parent culture' – pulls them one way, constraining them, returning them to the home and neighbourhood; but the result is 'generational conflict' (Cohen 1972: 22). The 'them' and 'us' in this model, then, is working-class parents and their children. Modernisation and 'the new consumer society' that accompanies it pulls youth in another direction, however, much less constraining, more tied to mobility, leisure and enjoyment. Working-class youth thus seem to live out the break-up of their community.

Far from being alienated by this, however, these young people 'solve' their problem when they leave their community precisely by becoming *subcultural*. London's subcultures, Cohen writes,

> can thus all be considered as so many variations on a central theme – the contradiction, at an ideological level, between traditional working class puritanism, and the new hedonism of consumption; at an economic level between a future as part of the socially mobile elite, or as part of the new lumpen. Mods, Parkers, skinheads, crombies, all represent, in their different ways, an attempt to retrieve some of the socially cohesive elements destroyed in their parent culture, and to combine these with elements selected from other class fractions…
>
> (23)

The two options here recall Hoggart's 'scholarship boy' (becoming 'part of the socially mobile elite') and the juke-box boys ('part of the new lumpen'): where one moves either above the working class or below it. Either way, these various subcultures leave their community: they are in this sense *devi-*

ant, nonconformist, less constrained than their parents were. The solution is also a social one. But for Cohen, it is 'magical' as well (23): a solution that seems more imaginary than real. Phil Cohen's essay might once again recall the work of his namesake, Albert K. Cohen, since they both look at subcultural identity as a matter of (re)adjustment, moving out of one social group and into another. But while the latter had seen this as a social/psychological issue, Phil Cohen sees it structurally and ideologically. His analysis moves away from Raymond Williams's insistence on the full register of a community's 'way of life': what came to be called the *culturalist* approach. Instead, Cohen's approach is essentially a *structuralist* one, attuned to meaning-making or signification. Subcultures, he controversially writes, 'are symbolic structures, and must not be confused with the actual kids who are their bearers and supports' (23) – a perspective that could not be further away from the Chicago School's empirical, ethnographically researched 'real-life stories'. The shift in emphasis is important to register. Subcultures at the CCCS are no longer social worlds to be described through their sociality – even though the working-class communities from which they emerged had been described in exactly this way. They are taken, instead, as a symptom of a particular kind of predicament, caught somewhere in between an older notion of community and modern, consumer society, liminal in this sense. And they are read for the ways in which they *signify* that predicament: which meant that, as we see in Cohen's essay as well as in all the subcultural work at Birmingham's CCCS, researchers paid especial attention to style.

Phil Cohen's long essay heavily influenced an even longer essay about subcultures which introduced the 1975 *Resistance Through Rituals* collection: John Clarke, Stuart Hall (who became director of the CCCS in 1968), Tony Jefferson and Brian Roberts' 'Subcultures, Cultures and Class'. By this time, Cultural Studies at the CCCS had become neo-Marxist and Continental, turning to the work of the French structuralist/Marxist Louis Althusser and the Italian Marxist Antonio Gramsci, as well as the early work of the French cultural and literary critic, Roland Barthes: the father of modern semiotics, the study of signs and signification. 'Subcultures, Cultures and Class' elaborated most of Cohen's points, but emphasised the continuing importance of class and its 'stubborn refusal... to disappear' (Clarke *et al.* 1993: 25). They took up Cohen's notion that subcultures provide an 'imaginary' solution to the predicament of working-class youth, broadening it by drawing on Althusser's notion of ideological subject formation: which is imaginary (that is, one inevitably imagines one's relations to the real) for *everyone*, not just working-class subcultures. So how are subcultures special here? The authors solved their own problem by turning to Gramsci's concept of hegemony, which returns a certain amount of 'materiality' to unequal relations between people. Hegemony 'works through ideology, but it does not consist of false ideas, perceptions, definitions' (39). It looks instead at how subordinate classes *remain* subordinate: this happens because the classes that rule them do so not just through coercion but also, and in many ways more importantly, by securing the subordinated classes' actual *consent* (39). This rather depressing view is a long way from E.P. Thompson's account of a fundamentally *dissenting* English working class. But it allows for some oppositional force when it suggests that subordinated people can never be 'wholly and absolutely' absorbed by hegemony (41). There is always some scope for 'resistance', for 'winning space' back from the ruling classes. As with Cohen, subcultures were seen to do this in two main ways: territorially, by winning or claiming their own 'space' (as distinct from owning property) and investing it with 'subcultural value'; and in terms of style, by using commodities, the signs of 'dominant culture', differently.

The problem for CCCS commentators was that this was not enough to warrant crediting subcultures with any real, progressive political force. As I have noted, having so strongly registered the loss of a sense of working-class community – with its capacity for political dissent, for organisation, for self-awareness, class consciousness, and so on – the subcultures which emerged and deviated from them could then only be seen in terms of *lack*. Thus Paul Corrigan's essay in *Resistance Through Rituals*, 'Doing Nothing', suggests that 'the main action of British subculture' is indeed to hang out on street corners and 'do nothing' (Corrigan 1993: 103) – as if subcultures are now entirely emptied of motive and content. John Clarke's essay, 'The Skinheads & The Magical Recovery of Community', reduces skinheads to a *lumpenproletariat* condition defined precisely by their apparently deluded attempt not just to re-create but to *dumb down* a community to which they no longer belong: 'We would argue that the Skinhead style represents an attempt to re-create through the "mob" the traditional working class community as a substitution of the real decline of the latter' (Clarke 1993a: 99). The image of the mob haunts these accounts of contemporary subcultures; so does the sense that they are not-quite-in-touch-with-reality. The turn to style didn't help matters, since the view of subcultures as primarily aesthetic once again lifted them out of the real to emphasise instead their imaginative potential. Clarke's essay, 'Style', looks at the way youth subcultures alter the meanings of the commodities they take up, and it introduces the notion of *bricolage*, taken from the work of the structural anthropologist, Claude Levi-Strauss: a term that expresses the alternative and often improvisational uses to which commodities are put by certain groups. Subcultures, Clarke suggests, attempt to solve 'problems arising from class contradictions' as they slide from a disappearing working-class community to the class-less realm of consumer culture and mass communication. But they 'do not mount their solutions on the *real* terrain where the contradictions themselves arise' (Clarke 1993b: 189).

This sense that subcultures are somehow less 'real' – of less political significance, less socially dissident, less *realistic* – than anyone else pervaded CCCS analyses. Clarke emphasises the 'limits of working class subcultures' and seems instead to admire hippies for at least attempting to 'create alternatives over a wider range of life-areas' (191). Because of their interest in working-class subcultures, CCCS researchers had paid little attention to hippies who mostly seemed to come from the middle classes. An exception is the work of Paul Willis, an ethnographer who gained his Ph.D. at Birmingham's CCCS in 1972. Ethnography was rarely undertaken at the CCCS and, indeed, the *Resistance Through Rituals* volume begins by distancing itself from ethnographic work elsewhere – such as that of Howard Becker in his book, *Outsiders*, which the general introduction to *Resistance Through Rituals* dismisses. Willis's *Profane Culture* (1978), however, is an ethnographic study of two quite different subcultures during the late 1960s, hippies and bikers: one from the middle classes, the other working class. For Willis, hippies were certainly nonconformists, who had a shared 'sense of community' – but it was 'informal' and disorganised, with 'no political analysis behind the radical life-style' (Willis 1978: 125). The English 'motor-bike boys' Willis interviewed were also nonconformist, even 'lawless' ('profane') – although less confronting, and less iconic, than the American bikers that Hunter S. Thompson had notoriously detailed not long before in his remarkable book, *Hell's Angels* (1966). Thompson's Angels enjoyed LSD and other illicit narcotics; Willis's English bikers, on the other hand, steadfastly rejected drugs. In this and in other ways, they thus seemed both lawless and disconcertingly conservative. Like the hippies, Willis finds the motor-bike boys challenging only to a certain extent, and politically impotent. More importantly, though, he casts them as *lumpenproletariat*, like Clarke's skinheads: enclosed in their club-like world, with their 'simple, unreflective morality' (Willis 1978: 43), their sense of going 'nowhere in particular' (78), and their 'limited…ability to imaginatively explore other possibilities for organizing the world' (49).

Dick Hebdige had published two essays in the *Resistance Through Rituals* collection. 'The Meaning of Mod' took the late 1960s English mod as a social aspirant, someone who wanted to rise above his working-class origins: rather like Hoggart's 'scholarship boy' but without the scholarship. For Hebdige, this was mostly therefore a matter of imaginative fantasy. The mods enjoyed a 'certain exquisiteness of dress' and took up the Italian scooter as a 'symbol of solidarity' (Hebdige 1993a: 91, 93). But recalling the boys in Thrasher's study of Chicago gangs (see Chapter 2), they also lived vicariously through American gangster movies and drugs, avoiding a 'less glamorous reality' around them. Theirs was a 'romantic victory, a victory of the imagination' (94); but this only made them all the more vulnerable, and in fact Hebdige's essay is about the *end* of the mods, their re-absorption back into 'dominant culture'. Like other CCCS researchers, Hebdige takes the mod as a particular social type (*the* mod) and in this respect he shares the typology of Chicago School sociologists (*the* hobo, *the* Italian, etc.). He also shared with the Chicago School an interest in race and ethnicity, although this became increasingly important to the CCCS, too, through the influence of Stuart Hall. The mod, for Hebdige, 'was the first all-British White Negro of Mailer's essay', utterly hedonistic and sensual, characterised 'by a fierce devotion to leisure' (94). His second essay, 'Reggae, Rastas & Rudies', is the only essay that actually deals directly with racial issues in *Resistance Through Rituals*. It looks at the 'rude boy' subculture, originating in Kingston, Jamaica, but spreading to England as Jamaican families emigrated there in the 1960s. Hebdige is attracted to the 'subversive' power of Jamaican ska and reggae music and Rastafarian subcultural styles, a topic later developed by Paul Gilroy in his book, *There Ain't No Black in the Union Jack* (1987) where – through reggae and its sound systems, along with Rastafarianism's commitment to solidarity and emancipation – Jamaica is cast as a potent, globalising 'subcultural resource'. But Hebdige also looks at cross-cultural influences. He turns to the English skinheads, casting them (against the grain of conventional representations of them as racist, etc.) as intrigued by the rude boys, their music and their culture. But the skinhead was condemned to remain the CCCS's favourite *lumpenproletariat* figure. As the rude boys or rudies consolidated their subcultural identity in England and 'closed their ranks', Hebdige writes, the 'bewildered skinhead' was locked out: 'the rude boys had come of age' but the skinheads 'were sentenced to perpetual adolescence' (Hebdige 1993b: 150, 152). A more successful example of a white English subculture linking cross-culturally to Jamaican rudies and reggae music was found instead in *punk*, the primary subject of Hebdige's enormously influential study – and still a key text for Cultural Studies, thirty years later – *Subculture: The Meaning of Style*.

Punk and semiotics

Hebdige responded enthusiastically to late-1970s English punk subculture, for two primary reasons. First, as I have noted, he wanted to argue that punk was ethnically 'open', willingly affiliating itself cross-culturally to immigrant Jamaican subcultural forms. Class remains an issue in his study – punks are still seen (rightly or wrongly) as a working-class subculture, or at least, as the *performance* of a working-class subculture – but race is the dominant sociological category. Unlike other CCCS commentators, Hebdige drew on American work for his study including, once again, Mailer's 'White Negro' essay. One of the chapters in his book even begins with an epigraph from Kerouac's *On the Road* – the passage where the narrator finds himself 'wishing I were a Negro'. Mods, skinheads and Teds are all positioned in relation to black British subcultural identity and found wanting: hostile, racist, retreating back into their working-class whiteness. But English punk seems to bear out Mailer's view of the American hipster or beat: an example of 'a white "translation" of black "ethnicity"', or more simply put, 'white ethnicity' (Hebdige 1988: 64), where punk engages sympathetically with reggae forms and seems even to be con-

nected to them 'at a deep structural level' (29). The extent of punk's 'open
identification' with black and Caribbean British subcultures ebbs and flows
in his book, however, partly because the emphasis on race over class remains
unstable (with race in fact disappearing as a topic about half-way through)
– and partly because, as the book unfolds, it increasingly refuses an easy syn-
thesis of the two, allowing them to be proximate at one point (we might think
of the Clash here, for example) and then utterly segregated at another. By the
end of the first part of his book, in fact, punk seems as stranded as any other
white, English subculture, with its 'dead white face', its 'curiously petrified
quality, its paralysed look, [and] its "dumbness" which found a silent voice in
the smooth moulded surfaces of rubber and plastic…' (64, 69). As we shall
see, the 'dumbness' of punk haunts this otherwise spirited and sympathetic
account, rather like the way the image of the *lumpenproletariat* haunts CCCS
accounts of subcultures broadly speaking – unsettling Hebdige's enthusiasm
for the subculture, and worrying at the investment he makes in its promise
and potential.

Second, Hebdige turned to punk as an expressive subculture that could be
defined first and foremost through its styles and 'posture'. What made punk subcultural, and special, was that its styles were nonconformist, confrontingly so.
'No subculture', Hebdige wrote, 'has sought with more grim determination than
the punks to detach itself from the taken-for-granted landscape of normalised
forms' (19). His account of punk drew on Althusser (for ideology) and Gramsci
(for hegemony), consistent with other CCCS researchers. But it also departed
from this convention, taking subcultural studies in an entirely new direction:
away from the earlier sociological and criminological interests of Phil Cohen
and Paul Willis, and towards a much more aesthetically focused approach, more
akin to literary criticism. Hebdige's study of punk was in fact influenced by con-
current developments in Continental structuralist and post-structuralist literary
theory – the work of Roland Barthes on 'mythologies', for example, and Julia
Kristeva – as well as modernist and avant garde literary practice. It begins by
invoking the French writer, vagabond, petty thief and radical political activist,
Jean Genet, the son of a prostitute. CCCS commentators (and we might say the
same thing about Hoggart, Williams and E.P. Thompson) seemed flatly uninter-
ested in issues to do with sexuality, and certainly homosexuality was something
that seemed to pass them by unnoticed. Genet's homosexuality (so important
to Genet's self-fashioning as a writer and dissident figure) is only of incidental
interest to Hebdige, a means to a broader end: of demonstrating the 'subversive'
power of subcultural signs, their 'profanity', their capacity to go against 'nature',
to challenge (in Kristevan terms) the 'symbolic order'. Like John Clarke,
Hebdige turned to the idea of *bricolage* – the way punks, in this case, reconfig-
ured or cut up conventional signs (the Union Jack, the face of the Queen), thus
erasing or 'de-naturalising' their 'original straight meanings' (104). Drawing on
a phrase from the Italian novelist and semiotician, Umberto Eco, Hebdige called

this 'semiotic guerrilla warfare' (105) and gave it a genealogy that traced it back to the Continental avant garde projects of Surrealism and Dada. For Chicago School sociologists, the analytical relationship had been between subculture and ethnographer; for Hebdige, it is now between text and (a potentially disoriented) reader. One reads a subculture for the meanings it throws up and/or dismantles, for the way it *signifies*. Subcultural semiotic 'warfare' thus takes place not so much in the street here, as in language. Drawing on Barthes, Hebdige writes, 'Our recognition of the operation performed within the text at the level of signifier can help us to understand the way in which certain subcultural styles seem to work against the reader and to resist any authoritative interpretation' (126). This is Hebdige's poststructualism, tied to a sense that subcultural style (at its most progressive, at least) is textually anti-authoritarian, a kind of semiotic (rather than sexual) queering of the linguistic pitch. Ultimately, it is less about 'warfare' and more to do with 'play' (126).

Punk for Hebdige may have 'signified chaos at every level', but it could also be read or understood as a 'meaningful whole' (113). He drew on the term *homology* to express this, a term used earlier on by Paul Willis but again derived, like *bricolage*, from the anthropology of Claude Levi-Strauss. Homology tied the signs of a subculture to its group-ness, to its 'collective self-image' (114). A subculture's clothes, music, attitude, behaviour: all of these signifiers could be understood as being consistent or homologous with one another, expressing the punkness of punk, for example. For Hebdige, however, they were also vulnerable to 'incorporation' back into the dominant system of values and meanings, typified by the mass media. The 'symbolic challenges' issued by a nonconformist subculture might be trivialised, for example; or, having made themselves stylistically spectacular, they might then be reduced to a 'mere' spectacle; or, they might be used to inflame a sense of 'moral panic' in society, to recall Stanley Cohen's phrase. Worse, punk styles can also be normalised or made fashionable and 'chic', their deviance – Hebdige used the more fashionable term, *otherness* – minimised. The 'original innovations' of punk are inevitably turned into commodities and marketed, produced 'on a mass scale' (96) and so becoming conventional: which marks the death of the subculture. Like Hoggart and Williams before him, Hebdige understood mass culture and mass media negatively, as a kind of dumbing down of an original and originating popular consciousness. But this came not from an investment in an idealised sense of working-class community. Quite the opposite: it came instead out of his affiliation with the avant garde and high literary traditions of modernism. Perhaps surprisingly, Hebdige ended his book by invoking *three* writers who have 'presided over our study throughout': not only Jean Genet, but also Roland Barthes and the profoundly conservative modernist poet, T.S. Eliot. The comments on Eliot are brief and just a little jarring. Eliot gives Hebdige his 'primary definition of culture', a version of Williams's notion of culture as a 'way of life'; but he also bestows on him the high modernist sense of a 'tradition which he is pledged to defend against the vulgar inroads of mass culture: the trashy films, the comics, the mean emotions and petty lives of all the faithless "hollow men"' (136). This remarkably elitist, bitter comment is inexplicably left hanging. But it does exactly what Williams and Hoggart had done before (like Eliot himself): that is, it sees mass culture and the *lumpenproletariat* as pretty much one and the same thing.

Punk becomes the last stand against 'the vulgar inroads of mass culture' in this book, an attempt to keep the *lumpenproletariat* at bay. But in another sense, it already seems to have arrived. As Hebdige's close textual reading of punk goes on, it becomes less and less clear about its conclusions. If punk represents 'noise' (90) and signifies 'chaos', then what meanings can be drawn from it? Hebdige asks exactly this question about one of the punk signs, the swastika. It seems doubtful that the punk swastika signified Nazism, although it may have crystallised an anti-English or anti-authoritarian position. Outside of its shock value, however, Hebdige has no other explanation. The swastika seems to have been 'exploited as an empty effect', without any identifiable values at all. 'Ultimately', he concludes, 'the symbol was as "Dumb" as the rage it provoked. The key to punk style remains elusive' (117). As we saw above, E.P. Thompson had invested in the articulateness and self-awareness of the English working class – and Hebdige had similarly invested in punk, taking it as a self-aware, even 'ironic', subculture. With the swastika, however, something changes: sense-making meets senselessness: what was supposed to be articulate is now 'dumb'. Hebdige continues to wonder, right to the end of his book, how much sense a reader can actually glean from punk, even though he had insisted all along that subcultures are 'expressive forms' (132). A kind of melancholy overtakes this otherwise exhilarating semiotic study as a result. It concludes with a grim expression of its own failure, finally registering nothing less than its alienation from the subculture – and the reality – it had tried so hard to understand:

> The study of subcultural style which seemed at the outset to draw us back towards the real world, to reunite us with 'the people', ends by merely confirming the distance between the reader and the 'text', between everyday life and the 'mythologist' whom it surrounds, fascinates, and finally excludes. It would seem that we are still, like Barthes…condemned for some time yet to speak *excessively* about 'reality'.
>
> (140)

This abject final paragraph raises a set of methodological questions about subcultural studies that are indeed difficult to answer. How 'textual' or aesthetic can subcultural studies afford to be? Are aesthetically-oriented, semiotic interpretations of subcultures destined always to be less 'real', less *realistic* – a kind of mirror-image of the CCCS's view of subcultures themselves? In subcultural studies, is it *either* the text *or* the 'real world'? Literature *or* sociology? And who, incidentally, is producing the *excess* here: the subculture, or the person who reads that subculture and accounts for it? It is certainly disconcerting to see the key study of subcultures in Britain during the 1970s end by registering its alienation from its subject-matter. But maybe the problem lies with imagining at the outset that the study of a subculture might reunite both the subculture and the sociologist who studies it with 'the people'. We could ask how possible, or desirable, what Noel King has called Hebdige's 'strange form of democratic narcissism or narcissistic democracy' (King 1991: 83) might actually be. But, having presumably departed from 'the people' in the first place, perhaps subcultural studies should come to terms with its own deviant trajectory.

Girls at home and elsewhere

Although feminism had already generated a lot of academic and social interest by the time of *Resistance Through Rituals* and Hebdige's *Subculture* book – Kate Millet's ground-breaking *Sexual Politics* had been published back in 1970, for example – CCCS commentators nevertheless had almost nothing to say about gender. The exception was Angela McRobbie, who had published an influential essay with Jenny Garber, 'Girls and Subcultures', in the *Resistance Through Rituals* collection: the only essay there which actually looked at this topic. For McRobbie and Garber, the term *subculture* had acquired 'strong masculine overtones', not least because most of the sociological and criminological work on the subject was performed by men. Its association with 'resistance' and the tendency to locate subcultural activity on the 'street' consolidated *subculture*'s unconsciously accumulated masculinisation (McRobbie and Garber 1991: 3). McRobbie and Garber responded to the 'invisibility' of girls in this paradigm in two main ways. First, they turned back to the home, looking at spaces inside the home that are particular to girls: like the bedroom. And second, they read girls primarily through their relationship to commercial or mass culture. Girls and women, they note, 'have always been located nearer to the point of consumerism than to the "ritual of resistance"' (8). The problem here, however, is that it isn't clear whether this point is made critically or affirmatively. Their essay looks briefly at some subcultural girl representations – the 'biker girl', the 'mod girl', the 'hippy girl' – but it doesn't develop any of these enough to suggest a distinctive female subcultural identity. (The 'mod girl', for example, seems to resemble mod boys, just as fussy about clothes and appearance and equally vulnerable to disenchantment over 'social expectations' [10]). The essay then turns to 'teenyboppers', pre-teen girls whose cultural tastes seem in most respects to be conformist, tied to mainstream (and usually male) pop stars, girls' pop magazines, and so on. Are teenyboppers subcultural? Probably not in this account, since there is little evidence of nonconformity or non-normativity here. Social distinction is mostly a matter of age demographics: teenyboppers represent a phase of mass consumption that simply distinguishes them from 'both their younger and their older counterparts' (14). But in fact McRobbie and Garber don't convey any sense of actualised teenybopper sociality. (In this respect, they are typical of the CCCS, which more or less ignored the subcultural *experience* of sociality altogether.) Pre-teen girls are spoken for in the plural here, but this seems to be because they are all cast as equally enthralled by a 'totally packaged cultural commodity' (11) – a point which results not in a history written 'from below' but rather, yet another example of the standardising and homogenising effects of one of Adorno's top-down 'culture industries'. The girls' bedrooms are sites of uncomplicated consumption: no *bricolage* or 'semiotic guerrilla warfare' here, so it would seem. And there is no rebellion against their 'parent culture', either, no deviance from the sanctuary of the home and the safety of the bedroom. The enclosed world of the pre-teen girl offers 'few personal risks' because it remains so *close* to the parent culture (13). Indeed, this account emphasises the role of the parent as the teenybopper's sexual protector: 'parents tend to be more protective of their daughters', McRobbie and Garber write, 'than they are of their sons' (12).

McRobbie's sustained focus on girls makes her own work distinctive in the context of the CCCS, although her emphasis on *working-class* girls is more representative. She agrees with Hebdige that subcultures are 'aesthetic movements' (McRobbie 1991: xv) – rather than, say, social groups – but she comes at them from the other end of the cultural spectrum, as it were. 'It is not necessary to have an education in the avant garde or to know the history of surrealism', McRobbie writes at the beginning of *Feminism and Youth Culture* (1991), 'to enjoy the Sex Pistols' (xv). In contrast to Hebdige – as well as the American rock historian Greil Marcus (1989), who had also linked punk and the Sex Pistols to the French avant garde – McRobbie associates subcultures not with high culture, but with mass culture: what she calls 'the popular mass media' (McRobbie 1991: xv). They are therefore accessible and open, rather than exclusive and elitist. Her view of subcultures-as-enjoyment on the one hand, and subcultures as subjected to 'popular mass media' influences on the other can, however, seem contradictory. She has described her own subcultural activity while growing up in the West Midlands as a kind of exhilarating escape from reality: something 'so forceful and so captivating that it gathered people up in an endless whirl of events, which blocked out the depressed economic present by creating a local utopia, a Birmingham bohemia' (xvi). But her account of working-class girls is a good deal less enthusiastic. Against the grain of much CCCS commentary, which had seen working-class youth subcultures as a deviation from working-class traditions precisely *because* they involved themselves in modern-day consumer culture, McRobbie sees consumer culture as the reason why working-class girls remain working class. Girls' popular magazines such as *Jackie*, for example, seem 'to secure girls even tighter to an unchanging message', that is, of getting a boy-friend or a husband, having babies, etc. (xvii–xviii). Working-class girls seem to be condemned to conformity here, locked out of the utopian/escapist pleasures that Birmingham's subcultures had seemed to offer.

McRobbie's view of the bedroom as a place where girls are protected from risk, sexual risk especially – unlike the street – only fixes working-class girls as homebound, passive, and conformist: so that her account of them in these early essays is not really subcultural at all. But other commentaries on pre-teen and teenage girls give very different kinds of perspectives. Barbara Ehrenreich, Elizabeth Hess and Gloria Jacobs have written about teen and pre-teen girls' behaviour during the 'Beatlemania' craze of the mid-1960s. The bedroom here is not a refuge but a point of departure: far from remaining in its confines and conforming to the prevailing models of sexual restraint, teen and pre-teen girls went out into the streets and concert halls to express their sexuality as a matter of sheer *excess*. For Ehrenreich *et al.*, Beatlemania turned the teenybopper adulation of male pop stars inside out. Girls may well have found themselves under the influence of a pre-packaged, top-down cultural commodity, but they responded in an unconventional way, actively asserting and expressing their sexuality in public places *without* tying their identity to marriage, babies, and so on. 'It was, in its own unformulated, dizzy way', the authors suggest, 'revolutionary' (Ehrenreich *et al.* 1992: 90). Elsewhere, Helena Wulff has written about the 'excitement' – 'a positive experience of states of heightened pleasure' – early teenage girls can gain from actually being out *on* the street, socialising with each other and meeting (as well as avoid-ing) boys (Wulff 1988: 34). Hers is an ethnographic study of twenty girls in Southwick, London: some white, and some black, from Jamaican and African immigrant families. She looks at the girls' domestic lives at home, following up McRobbie's call for subcultural studies to examine what happens 'around the breakfast table' (McRobbie 1991: 32). But she also looks at their lives on the street and at the local girls' club – the former especially being less subject to adult rules and protection. Wulff regards the term *subculture* as a useful way of depicting 'relatively distinctive organizations of meaning and their expres-sions' among social groups (Wulff 1988: 22). But she prefers the more fluid term *microculture*, which seems to capture a more contingent sense of shared experiences, tastes and so on across 'personalities, localities, and events' (26) – things that are not so obviously determined and stabilised by, say, class back-ground. Naturally enough, race (which was missing from McRobbie's work) is an important factor in Wulff's study: the popular girls' magazine *Jackie*, she notes, is read 'only by white girls' (43).

A pre-teen girl's bedroom can also be understood as a creative site, not just a place of consumption – and even a *clandestine* site, a place of 'dark play' that can evade the parent's supervisory gaze (Baker 2004). Later work in subcultural studies has developed the sense that a girl's bedroom can in fact host a good deal of *non*conformist activity. The Cultural Studies turn in the mid-1990s to a post-feminist valorisation of 'girl power' helped the formation of an academic subdiscipline of 'girl studies' (e.g. Driscoll 2002). One striking subcultural expression of 'girl power' was found in the riot grrrls, emerging from the US post-punk music scene in the early 1990s and defined by 'attitude' and critical, sometimes radical, social commentary. Marion Leonard has discussed the role of the underground fanzine or 'zine' in the riot grrrl subculture, usually a self-published, inexpensive set of stapled sheets: a 'low production' text through which contributors 'reflect their thought and experiences' (Leonard 1998: 105). Zines are not created on the street; they are most often put together in and around the bedroom, which becomes (at least for the moment) a kind of improvised, amateur publishing house. As the zine moves onto the internet – to become an e-zine – networks of producers and readers are usually widened, even as they remain physically within the 'safe space' of the bedroom. Hebdige had talked about punk fanzines, with their 'typing errors and grammatical mistakes, misspellings and jumbled pagination' – all of which he took as another performance of 'working-class' identity (Hebdige 1988: 111). For Leonard, however, riot grrrl zines and e-zines are determined more by gender than class; their issues are girls' and young women's issues, built around expressions of intimacy created *through* the bedroom and a yearning for 'community' that can stretch far *beyond* it.

For McRobbie, the girl's bedroom is protected, sealed off from the more precarious world of the street. For Anita Harris, on the other hand, 'girl power' has increasingly cast girls as 'risk-takers'. Harris has also looked at grrrl and gURL online zine cultures, seeing the internet as a mechanism for crossing the private (bedroom)/public ('street') divide – thus enabling young women to carve out 'a space to themselves in a time when young people's public and private space is either limited or over-managed' (Harris 2003: 48). But the girl-as-risk-taker is also an image exploited by policy makers, state bureaucracies and corporate advertisers/marketeers, all of whom can happily accommodate – and regulate – 'girl power' as yet another way of re-energising capitalist consumer culture. McRobbie makes a similar point in her own later work: that, having moved out of the bedroom, girls then find that 'their bodies, their labour power and their social behaviour are now the subject of governmentality to an unprecedented degree' (cited Harris 2003: 40). For Harris, girls' zines provide a counter-hegemonic response to all this – and in fact, her account is pretty much consistent with the more optimistic CCCS notion that subcultures can 'win space' back from the ruling classes. She agrees with McRobbie's representation of girls as 'consumer citizens', closely tied to 'the popular mass media' and routinely regulated, governed, and supervised: licensed at one level, but constrained at another. The solution seems to be a utopian one, unfolding outside and inside the bedroom simultaneously –

hence the need amongst young women 'for both a public forum and a haven' (Harris 2004: 170). The kinds of sociality forged by these girl zine networks turn inward and outward at the same time; subculturally speaking, they represent 'an urgent need on the part of young women to express themselves outside of the spaces currently available to them' (170).

After/beyond/post subcultures

It seems as if every academic commentator on subcultural issues has – right to the present day – returned almost obsessively to the work of CCCS commentators during the 1970s, Dick Hebdige's especially, as if it constitutes a kind of ur-text that has cast its shadow over everything that follows. Since the responses are usually critical, perhaps we can put this another way: that is, it is as if the CCCS is like a (usually, bad) father with whom subsequent researchers are condemned to play out some sort of defiant Oedipal struggle. In Britain over the last decade or so, sociologists have distinguished themselves from the CCCS's work on subcultures through a variety of prefixes: 'post-subculture' (Muggleton and Weinzierl 2003), 'after subculture' (Bennett and Kahn-Harris 2004) and 'beyond subculture' (Huq 2006). David Muggleton's book, *Inside Subculture: The Postmodern Meaning of Style* (2000), intentionally echoes Hebdige's title, *Subculture: The Meaning of Style* – but only in order to mark out its utter rejection of the CCCS 'approach', which 'falls into the trap of reifying the concept of subculture' and is 'not equipped to provide an analysis at the individual level' (Muggleton 2000: 23). Muggleton's dispute with CCCS approaches (sometimes he pluralises this, sometimes not) stems from the development of his own 'postmodern' perspective, to which I shall shortly return. One of the earliest and most persuasive criticisms of Hebdige and the CCCS, however, was in fact an essay by one of the CCCS's own researchers: Gary Clarke's 'Defending Ski-Jumpers: A Critique of Theories of Youth Subcultures' (1981). The objection here was an important one that subsequent commentators, including Muggleton, continue to reproduce: namely, that the CCCS and Hebdige especially had over-emphasised subcultural *difference*, and in doing so ignored the more mundane features of people's everyday lives. Clarke brought the perspective of Raymond Williams to bear on the CCCS, arguing that – by focusing on the extra-ordinary aspects of subcultures, especially in terms of style, symbols and signs – Hebdige and others turned their backs on 'ordinary life'. But he also mounted a defence of mass culture, which Hebdige especially had so disdained. The 'ski-jumper' (a cheap, mass-produced, acrylic sweater) was mass culture's fashion statement here, a defiantly ordinary, 'straight', working-class garment. Clarke spoke up for the ordinariness of mass cultural styles but he also argued against Hebdige's view – that culture, and subcultures, must 'defend against the vulgar inroads of mass culture' – by suggesting that mass cultural and subcultural styles are much more (and already, i.e. before 'incorporation') entangled or enmeshed. He concluded that 'the absolute distinction between subcultures and "straights" is increasingly difficult to maintain: the current diversity of styles makes a mockery of subcultural analysis as it stands' (Clarke 2005: 174).

This withering final assessment in fact returns us to the kind of cultural pluralism we had seen in the work of John Irwin towards the end of Chapter 2 – whose book *Scenes* was more or less contemporary with CCCS commentaries. Although none of the more recent British commentators listed above seem aware of Irwin's study, it nevertheless helps – along with Clarke's essay – to set up some key points of departure from Hebdige and other CCCS work. In particular, Irwin's emphasis on consumer choice and 'lifestyle', as well as his sense that subcultural identities can be 'casual' and contingent (or *fluid*, to recall the terminologies discussed in Chapter 3), are reproduced in the British 'post-subculture' commentaries. I want to list three main points of departure from CCCS work here, each of which arguably carries with it some gains, and some losses. The first returns to Gary Clarke and is to do with the way CCCS commentaries appear remote from ordinary life. Sometimes, it can seem as if this is a recent observation. The popular music sociologist Simon Frith makes it, for example, at the end of Bennett and Kahn-Harris's collection, *After Subculture* (2004), when he writes that 'the sociology of culture is turning at present from attempts to "decode" or "decipher" texts or cultural objects towards a concern with the ways in which they are used by real people in real situations' (Frith 2004: 173). But the same point had in fact been made more than twenty years earlier by the British sociologist, Stanley Cohen, in the introduction to the second edition of his important study, *Folk Devils and Moral Panics* (1980). Here, Cohen returns us to the issue I had flagged above, to do with the apparently irreconcilable differences between semiotic and sociological – aesthetic and 'real', theoretically-informed and empirical – approaches to subcultures. As a sociologist, Cohen is naturally impatient with Hebdige's Continental-influenced 'decoding' of punk: 'This is, to be sure, an imaginative way of reading the style; but how can we be sure that it is not also imaginary?' (Cohen 1980: xv). He wants the analysis of subordinated social groups to leave the 'forest of symbols' and return to more 'mundane' sociological matters, those found in 'the daily round of...life'. The imperative to become empirical, to return to the ordinary and the everyday – the 'real' – is, of course, central to the discipline of sociology itself, as I have already noted; and we see it again in Muggleton's *Inside Subculture*. But we have also seen in previous chapters that subcultures do indeed get imagined by others – coded, symbolised, and so on – as a matter of course. As we saw with Thrasher's gangs in Chapter 2 or with the Grub Street scribblers in Chapter 4, subcultures can lend an imaginary gloss to their *own* predicament, too –

although it doesn't follow, as some CCCS commentators would have it, that they are therefore less 'realistic' than other people. A semiotic approach to subcultures might very well *over*-interpret, casting a subculture as a kind of excess of signification. A sociological approach, however, may err in the opposite direction by reifying the ordinary just as much as Hebdige (recalling Muggleton's remark, above) had reified *subculture*: by being just a little too literal-minded.

In its dogged return to the 'ordinary', sociology can therefore often seem flatly unromantic about subcultures. One of the complaints about Hebdige is that his own work was *too* romantic, a criticism he had in fact already anticipated (Hebdige 1988: 138). His romanticism made it seem appropriate to invest in punk as a spectacular, excessive subculture. But it may be difficult for some subcultures *not* to be rendered in an excessive, even spectacular, way. Keith Kahn-Harris's chapter in *After Subculture* is titled 'Unspectacular Subculture? Transgression and Mundanity in the Global Extreme Metal Scene'. One might expect that a subculture built around extreme metal music would indeed have something spectacular about it. Kahn-Harris thus notes that extreme metal fans and musicians do 'dress in an identifiably spectacular way', sometimes 'espouse extremist views' and engage in 'deviant' and occasionally unlawful activity (Kahn-Harris 2004: 108–09). But he rejects the view of subcultures associated with Hebdige, which sees them as spectacular per se and then casts this as a matter of cultural transgression. Instead, he tries to look at the way extreme metal fans and participants simultaneously engage with what he calls *mundanity*. The extreme metal scene can be shocking at first, even overwhelming; one might therefore respond by trying to 'normalise' it, reducing its shock effects. For example, one might build mundane practices such as record collecting into one's scene involvement (114). For Kahn-Harris, extreme metal scene participants both produce their own spectacularity (which is an imaginative, performative act) and then 'normalise' this in a 'non-scenic' way (112–13). The problem here is that Kahn-Harris finally finds himself closer to Hebdige than his chapter might otherwise suggest. Participants in the extreme metal scene 'are deeply committed' to it (117) and relish their differences in musical taste, style, etc. which they may very well play up, or talk up. It bothers Kahn-Harris that some extreme metal participants seem involved in their scene to the point of 'solipsism' (113–14), almost to the point of disengaging themselves from the 'non-scenic' world, i.e. from ordinary life, altogether. As with Hebdige's obscure punks, this makes them difficult to read. They especially lie outside of the 'balance' Kahn-Harris is striving for with extreme metal participants, which wants to locate them somewhere *in between* the spectacular and the mundane. In one sense, these 'solipsistic' and self-absorbed participants therefore seem to be *too* subcultural; we might say that they slip outside of the 'post-subcultural' paradigm by not being 'casual' or 'fluid' *enough*, by *remaining* in some way remote from the ordinariness of daily life. Kahn-Harris's chapter recognises that it too is caught in an in-between position, still tied to CCCS perspectives (emphasising the spectacular, the transgressive) even as it wants to become 'post-subcultural' (turning to the mundane, the ordinary) – so that it is, finally, neither one thing nor the other. Perhaps unsurprisingly, he is therefore equivocal, even contradictory, about the use of the term *subculture* itself: 'Although I would argue that subculture is an inappropriate concept to use in the analysis of contemporary cultural practice, it none the less illuminates some of the more difficult problematics of creating youth culture' (118). The term *subculture* is both 'inappropriate' and 'illuminating' here: maybe that's about as much as we can ask of any descriptive social category.

The second point of departure stems from the CCCS's emphasis on class – and in particular, the working class – as the determining category for subcultures. It has often been noted that punk subculture was more middle class than working class, coming not out of working-class communities at all but contrived instead out of a 'bohemian' English art school scene (e.g. Frith 1978). In fact, Hebdige had already recognised this and talked instead about the way punk *performed* its 'working-classness' as a kind of signifier. But the focus on working-class-derived subcultures meant that the perspectives of CCCS researchers were limited: for example (with the exception of Hebdige), regarding them as the outcome of local pressures on working-class communities rather than, say, as transnationally or globally influenced. The emphasis on working-class origins also meant that they inevitably saw their subcultures in masculinist terms (as boys 'doing nothing', or with some potential for winning back 'space', for 'resistance', etc.). Some contemporary sociological commentators can tend to reject this older emphasis on class outright. For Sarah Thornton, 'class is wilfully obfuscated by subcultural distinctions' and, indeed, the London clubbers she describes seem to play out a 'fantasy of *classlessness*' (Thornton 1995: 12; my italics): quite the opposite to Hebdige's punks. The Marxist perspectives of the CCCS don't seem especially relevant to Thornton's study, which instead emphasises gender, subcultural relations to media and internal issues of subcultural taste, status and knowledge in the dance club scene. On the other hand, an essay by Susan Willis on the hardcore music subculture in America (following groups such as Black Flag) wants to *recover* class as a category for thinking about the predicament of contemporary American youth. Willis is much more sympathetic to Hebdige and the CCCS, which helps her to read hardcore not simply in terms of internal features (tastes, styles, status, etc.) but also structurally in terms of its material relations to capitalism. Hardcore youth may not be working class, but their predicament can nevertheless be understood in relation to the labour they undertake as America puts them to work under a logic of *under*-employment (rather than simply, unemployment). Willis suggests that an exploitative labour market built around the service industries 'has created a *lumpen* class distinct from the traditional working class. This is a dispersed work force, a transitory work force, and, sometimes, an occasional work force that has no consciousness of itself as a class…' (Willis 1993: 377). Her study doesn't look at the hardcore subculture in the way Hebdige had looked at punk, i.e. as a relatively autonomous (anti-)consumer culture. Rather, she suggests that the ways in which hardcore youth actually *do* consume are tied to the way they work or produce: expressing 'the contradiction of a system that degrades them as workers and flaunts them as consumers' (381).

Willis atypically returns to CCCS perspectives which had seen subcultures as both a deviation from working-class origins and a rejection of the monotony (or, the *mundanity*) of the workplace: for example, Hebdige on the mod. As we have seen, CCCS commentators had therefore often cast subcultures as a kind of *lumpenproletariat* that lived out its transgressions in a restricted cultural field, through styles, while at leisure, and so on. For Willis, however, American hardcore participants are already cast as *lumpen* in the workplace itself, which makes her account grimmer than even the most negative of the CCCS writings discussed above. In the wake of all this, some of the 'post-subcultural' commentators have complained about the 'seriousness' of CCCS approaches to subcultures. 'The issue of young people playing their "subcultural" roles for "fun" is never really considered by the CCCS', Bennett and Kahn-Harris suggest (2004: 8). Post-subcultural commentary is a bit more celebratory as a consequence, perhaps naively so in some respects. It unhooks subcultures from class, releasing them from all the traditions and rituals and theoretical baggage that accompanied this kind of identification, and undoing the implied association of *subculture* and *lumpenproletariat* in the process. CCCS commentators had thought that one's entry into consumer culture resulted in a dumbing down, a loss not just of class consciousness but of self-consciousness. Post-subcultural commentators read this entry into consumer culture much more positively, however. Rupa Huq's *Beyond Subculture* (2006) is a kind of benign, postcolonial celebration of 'multi-ethnic' diversity and consumer creativity: fairly typical of the upbeat approach to consumer culture found in much contemporary work in Cultural Studies and in the kind of postcolonial cultural commentaries that put their faith in 'hybridity'. Bennett and Kahn-Harris support the view 'that post-war style offered young people an opportunity to construct new identities not bound by tradition or habit…but rather by a newly experienced consumer reflexivity…' (Bennett and Kahn-Harris 2004: 7). It might be difficult to find examples of transgression or 'resistance' here, which is also the point of post-subcultural commentaries; but it remains celebratory all the same. The emphasis on 'consumer reflexivity' is the key that distinguishes the post-subcultural subject from the CCCS's position, and this is where we find their third point of departure. Whereas for CCCS commentators post-war youth subcultures didn't really seem to know what they were doing, for post-subcultural commentators youth subcultures in fact make conscious, and self-conscious, choices. The shift in focus here – which is why John Irwin's earlier work is so relevant – is precisely from *sub-culture* to *lifestyle*.

Post-subcultural approaches turn away from the modernism of CCCS commentaries to *post*modernism; and they do so in order to break down late modernity's conventional cultural divisions. From this perspective, for example, subcultures are no longer able to be distinguished from, or opposed to, mass culture: the kind of view we have already seen in Gary Clarke's early essay. There may also no longer be, as Muggleton puts it, 'a coherent dominant culture against which a subculture can express its resistance' (Muggleton 2000: 48). For Hebdige, English punk had been a kind of authentic, original and originating movement, a grass-roots 'refusal' of dominant paradigms. For post-subculturalists, however, no single mode of cultural expression is any more authentic – or inauthentic – than any other. Muggleton gives this relativistic, pluralist view of the world expression when he writes that post-subcultural 'ideology' values 'the individual over the collective' and 'elevates difference and heterogeneity over collectivism and conformity' (49). It isn't as if post-subcultural commentators don't value nonconformity: they *do*. Muggleton's *Inside Subculture* is in part an ethnographic study in which he interviewed fifty-seven young English people in the mid-1990s, selecting them 'on the basis of what I regarded as their unconventional appearance' (171). What this principle of selection might mean isn't exactly clear, but nevertheless there is at least a gesture here towards nonconformity even if the study itself works against this through its relentless cultural relativism. Many of his interviewees, interestingly enough, have a kind of *lumpen* social identity, being unemployed or casually employed. But their social predicament – and indeed, their sociality – is of little interest to Muggleton, who instead devolves one's participation in consumer culture down to a matter of sheer individuality. Like Huq's *Beyond Subculture*, his book celebrates 'self-expression, individual autonomy and cultural diversity' (167): pretty much all the things we find celebrated in any benign, pluralist social-liberal democracy.

The term *subculture* becomes fragile here, losing its connotations of sociality even though this can still haunt post-subcultural commentaries – with Muggleton's study concluding, against the grain of his criticisms of the CCCS, that his interviewees 'have an elective affinity with bohemian values' and are therefore similar in kind to punks, as well as beats, mods and so on (167). We have seen in previous chapters that the 'social worlds' of subcultures are a response to the individualisation and alienation of modern life. In post-subcultural commentary, however, individualisation is modern life's logical and desirable conclusion. David Chaney, who has written a book about 'lifestyle' (1996), has an essay in *After Subculture* titled, 'Fragmented Culture and Subcultures'. For Chaney, what was once called 'dominant culture' has now 'fragmented into a plurality of lifestyle sensibilities and preferences' (Chaney

2004: 47). 'Lifestyle sensibilities' here might seem to be something rather like John Irwin's much earlier definition of *scenes*, outlined in Chapter 2 – and Irwin, of course, had also emphasised consumer choice and cultural plurality, as I've noted. But he had also described *scenes* as sites through which sociality – in an increasingly fragmented and alienated world – could be recovered and put to use. Chaney, on the other hand, tells us that 'any confidence in a shared space with commonly recognised features has…evaporated' (48): a view that makes him suggest that the term *subculture* is therefore now 'redundant'. His blithely postmodern (or perhaps post-Thatcherite) world is now so fragmented that any sense of shared social experience has all but dissolved away. Such a view gives us the dark side of the post-subcultural trend in Britain, which can be so culturally relativistic that it refuses to see sociality – sites of shared experiences, expressions of social distinction – anywhere. The CCCS almost certainly overstated the discreteness and distinctiveness of their subcultures. But post-subcultural commentators run the risk of doing away with sociality and social distinctions altogether. Their subcultural participants may be under-stood as more self-reflexive and diverse than they were for the CCCS, but that's where distinction begins and ends. All that this post-subcultural picture of heterogeneity is left with here is a benign and docile expression of capital-ism's primary ideological fantasy, the 'individual's freedom of choice'.

Chapter 6

SUBCULTURE, MUSIC, NATION
Jazz and hip hop

Bebop, race and jazz aesthetics

IN 1963, TWO IMPORTANT BOOKS were published about jazz: Howard Becker's *Outsiders*, and LeRoi Jones's *Blues People: Negro Music in White America*. But these books could not have been more different. Becker's study was consistent with Chicago School sociological methods, a work of participant ethnography which cast jazz musicians as a socially 'deviant' group. Their deviance was defined primarily through their rejection of 'conventional' musical tastes and the pressures to 'go commercial' – imperatives they associated with 'squares'. The jazz musicians wanted to find a space (or a place) to play in that was free of these things, allowing them to lay claim to their rightful autonomy as 'artists'. Their preferred drug was marijuana, which helped to consolidate their sense of sharing an identity and of being different. On the other hand, these jazz musicians were by no means an underclass. They were gifted, mostly privileged, older men and they were also white, or as Becker put it, 'fully assimilated' (Becker 1963: 98). Their social difference and their sense of social 'isolation' was not imposed on them by others, which is how deviance is so often understood in Chicago School sociology; it was instead a matter of choice and disposition. They practised what Becker therefore described as 'self-segregation'. For LeRoi Jones, however, jazz was all about being African-American, being *black*. The antagonistic relationship with commercial pressure and the 'mainstream' was still a primary defining feature of jazz. But this relationship was at the same time cast in racial terms, since commercial success in jazz seemed in this account to be tied explicitly to the fact of being white. For black jazz musicians, segregation was not a matter of choice and disposition: it was, and still is in so many respects, a structural feature of modern American life.

LeRoi Jones had moved to Greenwich Village in 1954, where he co-founded the influential Beat journal *Yugen* as well as Totem Press, which published the Beat writers Jack Kerouac and Ginsberg. But he also became increasingly involved with political activism and especially with black nationalist cultural politics, moving to Harlem later in the 1960s, opening the Black Arts Repertory Theatre/School, and adopting the Arabic name, Amiri Baraka. Jones's role as an artist at this time – he was a successful poet and playwright – folded into his investment in black cultural nationalism to make his account of jazz both essentialist and ambivalent. *Blues People* was the first book to suggest that jazz was in essence African-American, tying it to a black tradition of the blues, that is, to a conception of African-American musical practices already distinguished from mainstream, white America. Black jazz musicians were thus cultural representatives, the individual musician transmitting, as well as standing for, an explicitly African-American cultural system; a 'machine inside the machine', in the black novelist Ralph Ellison's words (cited in Dinerstein 2003: 128). But jazz was also an open, mutable form. Sometimes, it seemed to deviate from black musical traditions altogether, which is the view Jones presents of the big-band 'swing' phase of the 1930s, for example. 'Swing', Jones writes, 'had no meaning for blues people' (Jones 1963: 181). Despite the prominence of black musicians such as Duke Ellington and Count Basie, it seemed like an 'assimilated' form, its audiences as well as its best-paid stars (like Benny Goodman) being white. A newer jazz form seemed more promising, however. Bebop emerged in the mid-1940s, identified with jazz musicians such as Charlie Parker, Dizzy Gillespie and Thelonious Monk: all African-Americans. It was played by smaller ensembles in smaller nightclubs, like Minton's Playhouse which opened on New York's 118th Street in 1938 with a house band that featured Thelonious Monk on piano. For Jones, bebop produced a 'wilfully harsh, *anti-assimilationist* sound' that helped to return jazz 'to its original separateness, to drag it outside the mainstream of American culture again' (181, 182). It 're-established blues as the most important Afro-American form in Negro music' (194) and it also appeared to turn away from commercialising imperatives. White jazz critics didn't seem to understand it: Jones quotes the jazz broadcaster and ragtime enthusiast Rudi Blesh, for example, who wrote that bebop 'comes perilously close to complete nonsense as a musical expression…exploiting the most fantastic rhythms and unrelated harmonies that it would seem possible to conceive' (cited 190): rather like ranting, we might say. Bebop provides a perfect example here of the way in which black cultural nationalism expresses itself *subculturally*, as socially distinctive and nonconformist. But the subcultural characteristics of bebop make this particular jazz movement no less open and mutable. 'Socially', Jones writes, 'the term bebop…came to denote some kind of social nonconformity attributable to the general American scene, and not merely to the Negro' (190). For all its pathologisations, Norman Mailer's essay on the 'white Negro'

– discussed in Chapter 4 – had at least noted the openness of the bebop sub-culture to whites as well as African-Americans. 'Self-segregating' whites may well have come to identify with the 'anti-assimilationist' world of bebop, but as Jones suggests (in a way that puts Becker's point into its racialised context), the conditions of that identification are different:

> The white beboppers of the forties were as removed from society as Negroes, but as a matter of choice. The important idea here is that the white musicians and other young whites who associated themselves with this Negro music identified the Negro with this separation, this noncon-formity, though, of course, the Negro himself had no choice.
>
> (187–88)

The racialising of jazz – especially the emphasis on its difference from the (white) American mainstream – has ebbed and flowed in jazz criticism, and caused its share of anxiety amongst commentators, especially and unsurpris-ingly the white ones. But it has also led to powerful articulations of social, as well as musical, distinction. The jazz keyboardist, composer and producer Ben Sidran's *Black Talk* (1981) extended the African-American's claim on jazz as subcultural, noting that 'simply being a Negro in America' was enough 'grounds for nonconformity' (Sidran 1981: 80). The fact that some white jazz critics were perplexed by bebop seemed to help tie racial difference to dif-ferences in musical form: 'The "white" jazz became more formalised, more precision-oriented (more Western in general), and the "black" jazz became once again improvisational, casual, and heavily blues orientated' (82). Like Jones, Sidran also notes that white hipsters or beboppers gravitated to the bebop 'scene', which became 'increasingly multiracial in membership'. But 'the shadow of the racial barrier' (110) lay across bebop, dividing whites from blacks even though they may have shared similar subcultural predic-aments and sensibilities. For Sidran, black jazz musicians in fact worked to *preserve* their 'ethnic singularity', staying one step ahead of white hipster audi-ences who (unlike the 'squares' in Becker's study) were so closely affiliated to them. The musicians' 'jargon' or slang provided one way of doing this: 'when a facet or phrase of black, or hip, jargon gained too much currency within the white world, it was summarily dropped by blacks' (110–11). This is where Sidran's notion of jazz as a form of 'black talk' is literalised; but his point is consistent with a powerful binary that is often invoked in commentaries to do with cross-cultural musical influence, where African-American music is seen as 'original' and 'innovative', in relation to which white music is cast as 'imitative' (see, for example, Paul Gilroy's account of reggae in the UK in *There Ain't No Black in the Union Jack* [1987]). Jazz here becomes an 'under-ground' language, racially as well as formally/stylistically segregated from white America. For Sidran, black bebop musicians reflected, or embodied, this kind of segregation in two ways. The first was through their 'cool' pose and demeanour: their aesthetics of 'cool'. In recordings such as Charlie Parker's *Cool Blues* (1947) or Miles Davis's *Birth of the Cool* (1957), this kind of aesthetics is written into black jazz music as a definitive condition. In terms of pose or demeanour, being 'cool' conventionally means being relaxed and calm, being composed or 'together'. But Sidran also suggests that 'cool' was a subcultural way-of-being-in-the-world, a pose that gave a kind of otherworldly expression to the real predicament of African-Americans:

> Audiences, critics, and even musicians outside the [bebop] movement assumed that because the black musician turned his back on an audience or because he wore a look of boredom, he actually felt detached. The style of the bop musicians, however, grew out of great inner turmoil. The 'cool' posture was not a reflection of passivity but, rather, of actionality turned inward: the active repression of very basic emotional turbulence for fear it would turn outward to mainstream America and invite retribution.
>
> (Sidran 1981: 111)

This remarkable claim sees 'cool' as a repressive, rather than expressive, phenomenon: a kind of survival strategy that makes bebop performance possible by preventing the black jazz musician from becoming militant (a point that recalls Eric Lott's claim about bebop, that it 'was intimately if indirectly related to the militancy of its moment' [cited in DeVeaux 1997: 25]). 'Cool' is all about *restraint* here: one plays out – and tolerates – one's segregated role by keeping one's 'inner turmoil' under strict control. The second way in which black jazz musicians embodied their segregation seemed to help this along. Unlike the marijuana-smoking jazz musicians Howard Becker had studied in Chicago, 'hipster' bebop musicians used heroin. The 'supreme hipster' Charlie Parker was a heroin user by his early teens. For Sidran, heroin 'spoke kindly to the "cool" style of the hipster for three reasons: it suppresses emotional excess; it establishes an in-group of users and dealers; and it eases anxieties not directly concerned with procuring it' (113). So bebop, for black jazz musicians at least, is *not* a subculture defined by excess: quite the opposite. The 'cool' posture, helped along by heroin use, is a kind of subcultural solution to the problem of racial segregation; lifting black jazz musicians away from the gaze of mainstream, white America and thus enabling them to perform bebop pretty much on their own terms.

These accounts of bebop and black bebop musicians allow us to think about subcultures here in relation to American, and in particular, African-American predicaments. Did bebop really signify African-American-ness? Some commentators have complained about the exclusivity of this perspective and about the limits of thinking only in black-or-white terms. For David Ake in *Jazz*

Cultures (2002), 'black jazz is most typically seen as an expression of a unified community ("the people")', while 'white jazz is often understood as the creation of a rag-tag group of outsiders' (Ake 2002: 11). Ake returns to New Orleans to look at French-American Creole traditions in jazz in an attempt to get around the prevailing black-and white division. Other commentators have complained about the 'imitative', secondary roles attributed to whites in African-American jazz histories. Charley Gerard's *Jazz in Black and White* (1998) is critical of those 'proponents of the black music ideology' who 'have written a revisionist history of jazz that overstates the impact of racism on African-American musicians and minimized the influence of whites' (Gerard 1998: 31). But he also recognises that jazz has indeed been 'closely linked to the ways in which African Americans have adopted different strategies of achieving sociopolitical goals' (xix). Bebop, he writes, was 'the first jazz style in which African Americans got the credit for being the leaders and creators of the music' (23). But he adds that black audiences for bebop were smaller than they had previously been during the swing era, another feature that helped to cast bebop as a jazz subculture rather than as a popular musical form. Bebop embodies African-American-ness, but it also deviates from it, cutting its ties with 'the people' as it consolidates its identity as a subculture. This is a point Burton W. Peretti makes in *The Creation of Jazz* (1994): black jazz musicians, he writes,

> dispensed with some rich elements in African-American music – such as the rural traditions of song and dance – and...Europeanized their music and worldviews in some pronounced ways. This may explain why jazz declined as a popular black music after 1940 and why later jazz players formed an insular, deviant subculture cut off from the white – and black – mainstream.
>
> (Peretti 1994: 215)

We can probably best think of bebop as an insular-yet-open subculture, attracting – as we have seen – devotees, as well as musicians, who were *not* African-American and who may very well have therefore found themselves in a secondary, imitative relationship to it. From a white perspective, however, bebop didn't so much seem to stand for the prevailing realities of segregation; rather, it evoked an existential condition: not segregation, but *alienation*. This is the account that Jerry Gafio Watts gives in his book on Amiri Baraka/LeRoi Jones: 'In the eyes of many of the disaffiliated whites drawn to the Village bohemian scene', he writes, 'jazz musicians were the quintessential alienated artists' (Watts 2001: 30). To those around him, Charlie Parker's drug habit thus 'signalled his alienation from the mundanities of bourgeois life in 1950s America' (30). It might have worked to suppress his own emotional reaction to the fact of being segregated as an African-American, but it also radiated out to non-blacks as an already recognisable expression of nonconformity. Howard Becker's 1963 study had captured jazz's alienated, anti-social sensibility, but this structural feature had also been discussed a few years before in an important article by the American ethnomusicologists Alan P. Merriam and Raymond W. Mack, 'The Jazz Community' (1960). These authors note that jazz had mostly been written about either though close analyses of the music itself, or through biographies of great musicians. Their study, however, looks at the 'attitudes' of jazz musicians, their values and 'ideologies': the things that appear to define them collectively. In fact, jazz musicians do indeed seem anti-social. Their isolation from 'society at large' is their most striking feature. For Merriam and Mack, there are three main reasons for this. First, jazz's association with African-American culture (the 'Negro') and its links to 'protest and revolt' (Merriam and Mack 1960: 216) make the majority of white Americans reject it. Its audiences are taken from particular demographics, African-Americans, 'intellectuals' and 'adolescents', each of which is understood here to have some sympathetic relationship to protest and nonconformity. Second, the jazz musician's profession makes him mostly nocturnal and itinerant and removes him from conventional forms of education, work, and daily life. Third, the jazz community has a particular kind of investment in his music as an art form, which – whether the musician is African-American or not – also works to contribute to its segregated position.

Is jazz a community or a scene? Is it defined by its shared internal values, or by its openness to others? The eminent historian Eric Hobsbawm (under the pseudonym 'Francis Newton') wrote a book called *The Jazz Scene* in 1959, although this term had been used in relation to jazz much earlier on. Perhaps *scene* is more open or 'fluid' than *community*, as we saw with John Irwin's use of the term in Chapter 2. But it can also connote exclusivity. The jazz promoter Norman Granz released a limited edition box set of jazz recordings, also titled *The Jazz Scene*, in 1949: ten years before Hobsbawm's book. These recordings sold for US$25.00 each, a great deal of money at the time, and quickly became connoisseur-collectors' items. As Paul Lopes explains in his study, *The Rise of a Jazz Art World* (2002), Granz had tapped into a growing jazz market served mostly by small independent record labels designed to preserve jazz's identity as an aesthetically distinctive musical practice. Elaborating the points already made by Merriam and Mack, as well as Becker, Lopes notes that professional jazz musicians aspired to be artists in a heavily commercialised marketplace increasingly oriented towards popular and mass musical forms. He thus talks not about *scene* or *community*, but about the 'jazz art world': a world distinguishing itself in aesthetic terms first and foremost rather than, say, racially or socially. 'While professional musicians were refashioning jazz music', Lopes writes, 'a jazz art world of magazines, books, clubs, and concerts developed to support this music. This art world provided the organisation, production, criticism and audiences to make jazz a distinct genre and specialised market in

American music' (4). On the other hand, these aesthetic distinctions are consistent with what LeRoi Jones and Ben Sidran have to say about bebop and African-American-ness in relation to a marketplace codified as white. The 'art world' of bebop is racially inflected, with racial identity and aesthetics/style mutually informing each other: both of which are characterised by segregation, or 'self-segregation'. Eric Porter has noted this in his comments on the 'renegade style' of bebop, where black jazz musicians asserted their aesthetic *and* racial difference by challenging:

> the banality of popular swing music, the complacency of older musicians, and a system of economic exploitation and cultural expropriation by whites in the music business. In doing so, they helped to forge a subculture that distanced itself from and confronted the mainstream.
>
> (Porter 2002: 55–56)

Improvisation was the key, distinguishing bebop from the more standardised, regulated and danceable world of swing. The virtuosity of the soloist became paramount, a feature that only increased the sense of bebop's remoteness from the integrated sound of mainstream swing and restricted performances to a select and closely bonded group of skilled musicians practised enough to be able to react 'instinctively' to each other's movements. In his book on improvisation, Daniel Belgrad suggests that some reviewers therefore regarded bebop as 'solipsistic', a description we saw in Chapter 5 in relation to extreme metal enthusiasts. Bebop jazz was an especial challenge to the audience: 'Listeners trying to track the "thread" of the solos…had to pitch their attention at a high level of nervous excitement' (Belgrad 1998: 187).

The anti-commercial values of bebop musicians and devotees make bebop a modernist art form, rather like 1970s punk as Dick Hebdige had described it. It invests in its own autonomy, moving away from the overt commercialism of swing to find what Scott DeVeaux calls 'a new point of engagement' with the marketplace, one more in tune with the exclusivity of its relatively sophisticated aesthetics (DeVeaux 1997: 17). DeVeaux's important study, *The Birth of Bebop*, draws together some of the aspects of this jazz subculture that I have outlined above. Bebop is 'rooted deeply in the uncomfortable realities of race in America' (169), he writes. But the racialised narrative of bebop is simultaneously a story about aesthetics, pose and style. Its 'anticommercial stance' distinguishes it from other kinds of jazz which are tied more overtly to the corporate interests of the 'culture industries' and informs its bohemian, alienated condition: something whites can identify with, too. Its investment in virtuosity also leaves it open to the admiration of outsiders and, DeVeaux suggests, 'musicians of both races quickly mastered the style' (19). Bebop, then, is both a racially and aesthetically exclusive subculture; but it is also a 'fluid' one, open to others. It can therefore be cast as fragile and vulnerable by those commentators who invest in its (racial, anti-commercial and aesthetic) purity. An example is Mark Anthony Neal's account in *What the Music Said: Black Popular Music and Black Public Culture* (1999) which briefly charts the rise of bebop's black, anti-commercial identity and then suggests that the 'recording' and 'subsequent commodification' of bebop allowed it to be 'appropriated by an emerging post-World War II middle class', so that by the early 1950s 'bebop patronage was largely in the province of the young white artists and intellectuals of the liberal and radical left' (Neal 1999: 22). This is a version of a now-familiar narrative of a subculture's blossoming and decline, not unlike John Irwin's account of hippies and surfers described in Chapter 2, or Hebdige's account of the 'incorporation' of punks. The difference is that for bebop, this is also necessarily a narrative about race: with African-American origins and a white destination.

Hip hop, rap and vernacular nations

Although it emerges some thirty years later, the explanatory narratives that build up around hip hop share many of the features we have seen with bebop and jazz. Most obviously, hip hop is primarily an urban African-American musical culture, structurally linked in this case to America's 'post-civil rights era' (George 1999: viii) but also reflecting a much longer history of black segregation and impoverishment. Hip hop is a visual and highly visible musical culture, finding expression through breakdancing, graffiti and fashion, as well as the musical genre of rap, another, often rather elaborate example of 'black talk'. It is routinely defined in terms of its relations to 'the street' and the 'hood or neighbourhood – and both of these features help it to be identified subculturally. But hip hop is also credited with national, or even nationalist, significance: as in the phrase often used about it in public culture, 'hip hop nation'. The award-winning African-American writer and novelist Nelson George's chronicle of hip hop's recent history, *Hip Hop America* (1999), is an influential example of this kind of designation, beginning as it does with a quote from President John F. Kennedy ('We would like to live as we once lived, but history will not permit it'). George inscribes hip hop with two related narratives that are worth mentioning here. The first recalls Neal's point above, about bebop's origins and destination. For George, hip hop – like America itself – had its 'founding fathers', 'a loose community of energetic, creative, and rather naive young people from the Bronx and upper Manhattan who reached adolescence in the '70s' (George 1999: 20). As with bebop, the narrative of origins here is a romantic, albeit endearing, one, almost prelapsarian in its evocation of hip hop's foundational moment of innocence: 'Naive is the key and perhaps unexpected adjective in describing this crew, yet I think it is essential. I'm not simply saying they were naive about money…By naive, I mean the spirit of openhearted innocence that created hip hop culture' (20). Such a narrative is destined to go in only one direction, however, as hip hop finds itself falling into a kind of Blakean realm of experience, cynicism, commercialism and whiteness. In fact, George actually *opens* his book with an account of hip hop's final destination, offering up a desolate 'tragically-comic' image of hip hop performing its stereotypes of African-American hyper-masculinity 'for the pleasure of predominantly white spectators worldwide' (vii): losing its original innocence, as well as its localness, in the process. But the second narrative gives quite a different account of hip hop's transition from local origins to worldwide interest. 'There is a reluctance on the part of many hip hop-generation performers to leave the USA', George writes,

> a manifestation of some weird extension of the ghettocentricity that informs the culture. It sounds juvenile (and it is) but many rap stars are reluctant to leave their hotel rooms or tour buses when overseas, complaining about the food, weather, etc., instead of enjoying the chance to explore other cultures.
>
> (207)

The localness of hip hop culture – its foundational 'innocence' – returns here as a criticism: hip hop is not cosmopolitan. It may now have a worldwide following, George notes, 'but to date its own narrow-mindedness has limited its international clout' (207). Earlier on, George had paid tribute to hip hop's youthful innocence, but now he chastises it for not growing up, for remaining 'juvenile'. These two narratives give us an instability that we often see in commentaries on hip hop culture: where the romantic investment in hip hop-as-nation can indeed flip over into an account of hip hop as tied too much to the 'hood, as 'ghettocentric' or parochial, inward-looking rather than engaged with the wider world.

Most commentators agree that the cultural and racial origins of hip hop and rap are mixed. For Cheryl L. Keyes in her study *Rap Music and Street Consciousness* (2002), Afrika Bambaataa and the Zulu Nation is a potent early source, but this, too, is linked to other influences from elsewhere and is also a matter of self-fashioning and performativity:

> Using the rhetoric of the Nation of Islam, Rastafarianism, the styles and expressions of Black Panthers and Black nationalist poets of the 1960s, and the wearing of African garb, nation-conscious rappers address the political and economic disenfranchisement of black people in mainstream America.
>
> (Keyes 2002: 158)

115

The Universal Zulu Nation's official website in fact lists the 'father of hip hop' as the Jamaican immigrant, Kool DJ Herc, who worked his sound system at block parties in the Bronx from 1969 onwards, 'adapting pieces of Funk, Soul, Jazz and other musics into the melting pot' <http://www.zulunation.com/hip_hop_history_2.htm>. Even singled-out sources for hip hop can be culturally split. For Imani Perry in *Prophets of the Hood* (2004), the boxer Muhammad Ali was another of hip hop's founding fathers:

> Countless...references to Ali exist in hip hop. He was one of the fore-runners of hip hop, with his introduction of black oral rhyming into the mainstream. Hip hop uses Ali's style – whether referring to his Cassius Clay bragging or his Nation of Islam-inspired conversion into an outspoken nationalist athlete.
>
> (Perry 2004: 58)

We can see already in these various comments a subdued tension between recognising a mixture of sources for hip hop and rap, and the ways in which those sources are then invested with 'black nationalist' identities. Houston A. Baker's *Black Studies, Rap and the Academy* (1993) was a notable defence of rap as an authentically black and potentially subversive musical form, and it also wanted to use rap as a way of invigorating African-American Studies in American universities, bringing the 'outside' and the 'inside' together (in theory, at least). But even here, there were disputes and divisions: most controversially, perhaps, between Baker and another prominent black literary academic and advocate for a distinct African-American cultural tradition, Henry Louis Gates Jr, over the worth and value of rap group 2 Live Crew's album, *As Nasty as They Wanna Be* (1989), the subject of a prosecution case for obscenity in Florida in 1990. Hip hop has itself been cast as an invigorating black American cultural practice – a form of 'black urban renewal' – by Tricia Rose, although she also notes its 'Afro-diasporic' cultural identity (Rose 1994: 71, 85). Even so, its black autonomy is preserved by her account of it as 'a style nobody can deal with', a point also made by Baker who noted that rap – although it may take its samples and influences from a variety of sources, musical and otherwise – could nevertheless not actually be *covered* by white musicians (even though white performers may very well be able to 'do' rap, to mimic or imitate it: think of Eminem).

Jeffrey Louis Decker is one amongst many commentators who has been critical of 'hip hop nationalists', however, and his account of their 'Afrocentricity', with its parochialism and racial essentialism, compares with Nelson George's sense of hip hop's 'ghettocentricity' (Decker 1994). Paul Gilroy is another, emphasising in *The Black Atlantic* (1994) the ways in which African-American and Afro-Caribbean cultural practices do indeed have cosmopolitan features, confidently travelling outwards rather than stubbornly remaining attached to an often-mythical point of origin called home: emphasising destination over origins. *The Black Atlantic* is a critique of Afrocentrism and black nationalism, paying tribute to African-American cultural hybridity. Gilroy therefore asks (a little ingenuously since he probably knows the answer), 'what is it about black America's writing elite which means that they need to claim this diasporic cultural form in such an assertively nationalist way?' (34). His question does at least draw attention to the way in which a subculture can be invested with value and force by those who claim it and comment on it: in this case, those who have tied hip hop to a racialised conception of the nation. On the other hand, hip hop has also been understood through its links to homeliness, local territory, neighbourhood and kinship: the things that might therefore allow us to describe hip hop culture as a *Gemeinschaft*. Murray Forman has talked about hip hop and rap not in national terms but as increasingly regional and localised phenomena, spread across American cities from New Orleans to Seattle, each scene distinguishing itself from the others – as the West Coast had distinguished itself from the East Coast a few years earlier (and more audibly). Rap music is consequently associated with 'smaller-scale, more narrowly defined and highly detailed places' (Forman 2000: 66), with the nation thus subdivided into a plethora of 'hoods. Cities may themselves host a number of them: Forman looks at Compton, for example, one 'hood amongst several others in Los Angeles. Together, these sites work to give America a hip hop subcultural geography, something rap itself directly articulates: constructing the 'hood through its lyrical content, invoking and imagining it, and mapping its co-ordinates. Forman speaks about rap's 'spatial discourse' in these terms: 'It is precisely through these detailed image constructions that the abstract spaces of the ghetto are transformed into the more proximate sites of significance or places of the 'hood' (88). Rap music's relationship to the 'hood is also defined in collective terms, rather like the older logics of the 'gangland', discussed in Chapter 2. In his book, *The 'Hood Comes First* (2002), Forman remarks that collective identities 'are evident as a nascent reference through rap history', most obviously in group names such as 2 Live Crew and the Sugarhill Gang (Forman 2002: 177). *Posse* is a key term here, 'the fundamental social unit binding a rap act and its production crew together, creating a collective identity that is rooted in place and within which the creative process unfolds' (Forman 2000: 71). Even record labels can be defined in terms of posses. The term may well evoke 'notions of lawlessness and frontier justice' (Forman 2002: 177), again rather like earlier urban gangland identities – and we might also think of hip hop 'face offs' and 'feuds' here, like the one involving rapper Lil' Kim's posse and a rival crew outside the WQHT-FM Hot 97 station in Greenwich Village in 2001, an event which saw her lie to protect her posse and gain a subsequent conviction for perjury. The posse is like a kind of alternative family, an expression of kinship and, through the 'hood, of belonging and homeliness. 'Those who stay in the 'hood', Forman suggests, 'generally do so to be closer to friends and family, closer to the posse' (Forman 2000: 71).

The double invocation of the 'hood and 'the street' in hip hop culture gives us a sense of hip hop as an expression of being *at* home and *away* from home at the same time. The latter image – of hip hop as a kind of street culture – lends itself as much to romanticism as it does to a sense that hip hop artists are indeed 'street-wise' and thus speak from their direct experience. Rap music in particular has a strong 'experiential' imperative, usually expressed precisely through narratives about being out there 'on the street'. Keith Negus has also talked about rap music in terms of 'street marketing' – taking rap events to the streets, literally, through word-of-mouth, local radio, and so on – and 'street intelligence' (Negus 1999: 92–93). Negus's account of 'the business of rap' is in one sense anti-romantic, however, reminding us that rap performers are by no means naive about money (to recall George's comments above) since they often operate successfully in corporate, commercial music industries. On the other hand, rap's reliance on 'cliques, collectivities, affiliations and group and label identities' (93) means that business has been done a little differently. Because of its 'street-wise' self-definition, rap 'has… been able to generate alternative resources, and through these the genre has continually reinvented itself in those spaces and places designated (for want of terminology rather than as a transparent description of "reality") as "underground"' (102). This is now a romantic account, but the inverted commas around *underground* suggest that Negus is also wary of romanticising rap too much: something that is difficult not to do since the discourse of 'the street' is so pervasive across this subculture.

Perhaps rap attracts romantic and anti-romantic investments simultaneously. Its most notorious off-shoot, gangsta rap, may provide a good example of this. As Eithne Quinn has noted, the prevailing view of gangsta rap in what he calls Black Cultural Studies (like Houston A. Baker's work) is indeed an 'experiential' one. Gangsta rap conventionally reflects 'a dire and depressing underclass reality', 'documenting the perilous predicaments of an oppressed community', and so on (Quinn 2005: 19). Yet – and perhaps this is more anti-romantic still – there are those who think that gangsta rap isn't a 'reflection of life' at all: that it is purely commercial, cynical in its outlook, 'damaging and fake' (19–20). Quinn's own perspective also seems anti-romantic, as it shears gangsta rap away from the African-American 'community' and its modern tradition of protest and dissent. He writes, 'gangsta's very real political energies lay in the struggle to come to terms with an age in which there was a dramatic decline in popular protest politics, precisely for a community that had a vital protest history' (30). Gangsta rappers, by contrast, can seem self-interested and self-indulgent: features we have often seen attributed to subcultures. They may very well reject political projects altogether ('I ain't no political muthafucka'), replacing the national project of black protest with a narrative built around self-preservation and libertarianism. This 'post-protest' position can still reflect the shared predicament of young (male) African-Americans, however. Racism and police harassment are common themes, and gangsta's embracing of the term *Nigga* as a 'badge of honour' helps to demonstrate that racial discrimination remains a fact of American daily life. Gangsta is also cast as a 'career' for young black men: Quinn turns to Niggaz With Attitude's Dr Dre as an example, for whom gangsta is represented 'as a kind of hustle, in opposition to respectable occupations' (37). 'The embodiment of the "nigga" persona for profit and power and in the face of heartfelt objection', Quinn writes, 'crystallises this bird-in-the-hand, hustling image and its all-important ghetto-centric legitimacy' (37). A term of racial abuse is now inverted as well as 'embodied', and made parochial. But it is also *performed*. We had seen that for bebop, *cool* had been understood in terms of restraint. Gangsta, on the other hand, is defined by excess. Its particular brand of 'black talk' is driven by hyperbole, increasingly sliding into self-parody, exaggeration and surreal humour. For Quinn, this may be the thing that links gangsta back to African-American cultural traditions: the thing that allows it finally to be romanticised. Those traditions are *vernacular*, a word derived from the Latin *vernaculus*, 'domestic, native', and *verna*, 'home-born slave'. Vernacular language is tied to localness and pitched against 'official', national languages; it is improvisatory rather than formal, which makes the 'black talk' of bebop a kind of vernacular, too. But we can especially think of hip hop slang along these lines, since it plays around with language and expression in often remarkably elaborate ways – and also improvises through 'freestyle'. Its linguistic focus is perhaps well illustrated by the way *cool* (the condition, the way of being) is signified by nothing less than the word *word* – which, incidentally, is the last word in Nelson George's book on hip hop. Henry Louis Gates Jr has been perhaps the most important commentator on the African-American vernacular tradition, tracing it back to African slaves' refusal to learn their white slave owners' language. In his influential study, *The Signifying Monkey: Towards a Theory of Afro-American Literary Criticism* (1989), Gates sees parody, verbal play and hyperbole as central to black American vernacular expression. His defense of 2 Live Crew against their obscenity charge in 1990 appealed precisely to this tradition, arguing that their otherwise inflationary and hyper-sexist lyrics should be seen in the context of the humour and boisterousness and hyperbole of the African-American vernacular: a judgement Houston A. Baker had dismissed as 'hyperbole' in its turn, making a not-very-good album signify far too much (Baker 1993: 57).

Interestingly, the notion of hip hop/rap as a vernacular language has been developed more persuasively *outside* of the United States, precisely in those places at which touring American rap performers, as Nelson George had suggested, might stay indoors and complain about the food. From a black nationalist perspective, rap is distinctly African-American and whites are unable to cover it – so that the 'white rapper', rather like the white bebop musician, is condemned always to appear to be inauthentic. From a 'global' perspective, on the other hand, it can sometimes seem as if pretty much anyone can do it. Tony Mitchell has been critical of black American commentators who celebrate hip hop 'as an essentialist and monocultural expression of African-American culture' and refuse – rather like George's touring rap performers – 'to look outside the parochial, provincial and increasingly atrophied and brutalising parameters of US hip hop, at ways in which it has been increasingly appropriated, indigenised and re-territorialised all over the world' (Mitchell 1999: 127). Mitchell has written about hip hop in France, Italy, Aotearoa/New Zealand and Australia, among other places, and his investment in its global reach makes him cast African-American hip hop culture, in contrast, as stale and moribund. The 'ghetto vernacular practiced by many African-American rappers has become so atrophied and ossified in its relentless repetition of a severely limited range of expletives that any claims for "resistance" have long passed their use-by date' (Mitchell 2003: 3). Italian hip hop, on the other hand, can speak directly to political agendas and – while gangsta rap in the United States seems self-absorbed and self-indulgent – it also makes a claim on *community*. In his article 'Questions of Style: Notes on Italian Hip Hop', Mitchell describes a 'rap night' in the southern Italian town of Cisternino, and quotes from the festival programme:

> rap…is and has always been the sound of the social centres, of festivals in remote provincial towns, of programmes on tiny private radio stations. It is a public, collective, noisy language of social commitment, which needs to unravel itself in real time, in full view of everyone.
>
> (cited in Mitchell 1995: 34)

Mitchell emphasises the importance of doing rap in one's 'native language', and doing it in outlying, provincial regions as well as metropolitan centres. Rap is made 'indigenous' here, and is understood as instrumental in the reinvigoration of local indigenous cultures such as that of the Maori in New Zealand. He therefore talks about '*resistance* vernaculars', retaining the latter term from its earlier African-American context but inscribing it with some extra countercultural energy. The problem here is that although it unfolds in outlying places, well away from the metropolitan centres of the United States, Mitchell's notion of a vernacular hip hop ends up being just as parochial and romantic as the black nationalists'. Maori hip hop in New Zealand, for example, 'is an act of cultural resistance and preservation of ethnic autonomy, and as such, it is a choice that overrides any global or commercial concerns' (Mitchell 2003: 16). This conflation of the local, the ethnically autonomous and the anti-commercial recalls George's image of American hip hop's earliest days, with its 'loose community' of creative but 'innocent' young African-Americans in the Bronx who were 'naive about money'. It is a conflation that may well be necessary to foundational images for hip hop culture anywhere in the world. But it also means that hip hop is destined to remain 'ghettocentric', no matter where it might be.

Australian hip hop gives us an example of this recast kind of ghettocentric logic. Although there are some Aboriginal as well as Pacific-Australian hip hop performers in this country, by far the best known Australian rappers are white: like the Hilltop Hoods. Ian Maxwell's anthropological study of the hip hop scene in Sydney's underprivileged western suburbs sees it distinguishing itself from African-American hip hop precisely along these lines: hip hop in Australia, he writes, 'is not a *black* thing' (Maxwell 2001: 259; see also Maxwell 2003). Indeed, white Australian rappers are often at pains to distance themselves from African-American hip hop, not least by emphasising their local accents. For the Hilltop Hoods, this also means distinguishing themselves from New Zealand/ Maori performers, who they regard as far too willing to be under African-American hip hop's influence. 'We do rap in an Australian accent and we embrace our local culture so much it can be hard for people to swallow when they're used to hearing American accents', one member says. 'In the New Zealand Hip Hop scene they actually strongly mimic anything that's happening in America so their stuff gets lapped up by major labels…I think that's the main reason why New Zealand Hip Hop is doing so well commercially' (Perera 2006: 63). This view of New Zealand/Maori rappers as commercially successful imitators is quite different to Mitchell's account of them, above. On the other hand, that account can now explain the predicament of the Hilltop Hoods, who also conflate their local-ness with an anti-commercial imperative (or at least, a sense of not being *able* to be commercially successful). For Ian Maxwell, Australian hip hop is sufficiently non-African-American for him to suggest that listeners in the United States may 'not even recognise these practices of which I am writing as Hip Hop' (Maxwell 2003: x). He introduces a white, western suburbs Sydney rapper, Ser Rock, whose cultural investments are entirely local and who also credits himself (as many Australian rappers do) with a socially representative role. 'The constituency for whom he claims to be speaking', Maxwell writes, 'is the social imaginary that sometimes refers to itself as "the Sydney hip-hop community"' (Maxwell 2001: 259). Tony Mitchell has argued that hip hop in places like Australia is a 'glocal' cultural phenomenon, combining African-American influences with 'a dedication to authenticity, roots, place and "keeping it real"' (Mitchell 1999: 139). But this account too easily reconciles the global and the local. As we have seen, white Australian hip hop can unhook itself from African-American influences – rhetorically, at least – in an attempt to talk up its local-ness and claim a relation to place that is indeed *imagined* as 'real'. White hip hop can be just as 'ghettocentric' in this respect as any other kind.

Chapter 7

ANACHRONISTIC SELF-FASHIONING
Dandyism, tattoo communities and leatherfolk

Dandies, zoot-suiters and Teds

THIS CHAPTER LOOKS AT three very different examples of self-fashioning – that is, the ways in which people 'create' their bodies and their dress, representing themselves to others around them – that we can claim as subcultural. Of course, people fashion themselves in one way or another as a matter of routine. Dressing for work in overalls or a suit or a uniform of some sort provides an example of everyday self-fashioning, and so does dressing up (or down) for various leisure pursuits. The act of preparing the body for public display involves a set of rituals – cleansing, grooming, applying make-up, dressing, decorating in various ways – which are designed to help people to conform to the conventions of the places they go into, or alternatively, to 'stand out', to look and be different. These rituals, in other words, can either normalise the subject or produce non-normativity, depending on the case. In 1904 the German sociologist Georg Simmel, whose work had influenced Robert E. Park, published his famous essay, 'Fashion', making exactly this point. Simmel was a sociologist of modern life, focusing especially on the European metropolis. Responding to Tonnies' notion of the *Gesellschaft*, Simmel saw that urban society was neither stable nor 'total' but, rather, was fluid and fragmentary. Social formations in the modern city reflected this, resulting in increased levels of differentiation – something Simmel associated with civilised life, as Park was to do later on. He talked about *Vergesellschaftung* or forms of 'sociation', accounting for the ways in which individuals do indeed continue to socialise together in the *Gesellschaft* – and providing a useful term for subcultural studies. No form of sociation was too minor or insignificant for Simmel. The minimum number of people needed here was three: not so much a crowd, as the basic building-block for social interaction. His essay 'Fashion' took what seemed to be a proliferation of different clothing styles at the time as a kind of symptom of modern metropolitan capitalism and the human imperatives to socialise: to conform in some respects but to stand out in others. Fashion, he wrote, 'is the imitation of a given pattern and thus satisfies the need for social adaptation...At the same time, and to no less a degree, it satisfies the need for distinction, the tendency towards differentiation, change and individual contrast' (cited in Frisby and Featherstone 1997: 189). Simmel's notion that fashion answers two conflicting impulses – for 'imitation' and for 'differentiation' – provides an important cultural logic that we often see played out in subcultures, both internally (since subcultures can have their own conventions, norms and so on, even as distinctions are drawn here between those who 'imitate' and those who are more authentic or originating, the 'fluid' and the 'persistent' etc.) and externally in relation to others around them (where subcultures can indeed be differentiated in some respects, but can 'blend in' in others, as I noted about 'cruising' in Chapter 1).

For Simmel, imitation was the result of class distinctions and it moves from the bottom up, as it were, with 'inferior' people imitating their superiors. Fashion was understood as the prerogative of the upper classes, the aristocracy, who – since they are constantly being copied by 'those standing in a lower position' – have to work hard to preserve their own distinction. When the lower orders begin to imitate their fashion styles and thus potentially transgress established class divisions, the upper classes seek out new styles in order to differentiate themselves from the lower orders all over again. 'And thus', Simmel remarks, 'the game goes merrily on' (cited 190). Upper class and aristocratic fashion styles may have their own logics of conformity, however, and are by no means necessarily subcultural – especially if one thinks of the imperative to write subcultural histories 'from below'. On the other hand, we can certainly understand some aristocratic fashion styles and movements as dissenting and non-normative. The Macaronis were aristocratic young men around London just after the mid-eighteenth century, influenced by Italian styles, who dressed extravagantly, wearing high, curled wigs and feathered hats, nosegays of flowers, coats with huge buttons on them, and long, thin shoes. The name of this style was invoked not least to distinguish younger men from their older counterparts – but it also became a term of abuse, linking members of the 'Macaroni Tribe' to foppishness, foreign influence, narcissism, homosexuality and what Miles Ogborn calls 'luxurious effeminacy' (Ogborn 1998: 457). Macaronis were a highly visible aristocratic subculture, defined perhaps unsurprisingly by excess and what Thorstein Veblen much later on, in his *The Theory of the Leisure Class* (1899), came to call 'conspicuous consumption'. We might think of the Macaroni as a kind of *dandy*, a much more commonplace word describing aristocratic foppishness. But in fact the dandy and 'dandyism' emerged a few years after the Macaronis and embodied quite a different sort of cultural – or subcultural – logic. The first dandy to be 'celebrated specifically as such' (Garelick 1998: 6) was, of course, George 'Beau' Brummell (1778–1840): not an aristocrat at all by birth, but certainly someone who was soon able to make himself a familiar and significant figure at court. Brummell's fashionability was of quite a different order to that of the earlier Macaronis, however, and with quite different connotations. Ellen Moers notes that the Macaronis 'had sponsored a cult of slovenliness and disarray to counter their reputation for affectations and effeminacy in dress'. Brummell, on the other hand, advocated 'the principles of restraint, naturalness and simplicity' (Moers 1978: 33). He was obsessed with bodily cleanliness, soaping and washing himself for several hours at a time. Moers tells us that he 'did not need perfume: he did not smell' (32). We might have commonly assumed that the dandy would signify effeminacy. For Moers, however, the unperfumed body of the dandy combined with the 'dignified simplicity' of his costume to produce a persona that was 'indubitably masculine' (36). Unlike that of the Macaronis, however, the dandy's costume was designed *not* to attract public attention. It was designed purely to be registered by his inner circle, as a kind of fashion ideal: an act, we might say, of *inconspicuous* consumption. 'The dandy's distinction', Moers writes, 'was to be apparent only to the initiate' (35).

The dandy's restraint in terms of dress and bodily presentation was nevertheless offset by a certain mode of performativity: the cultivation of a frivolous, witty persona, for example, or an air of boredom or ennui. The prevailing academic view of the dandy is that he did not quite fit into even his inner circle, more the result of an ethic of non-participation and abstinence than actual dissent. The dandy – if we think of Brummell again – did not work. Nor was he a libertine. Rhonda K. Garelick writes about the 'essential uselessness' of women to the dandy (Garelick 1998: 25), and Brummell himself was also not homosexual. Dandyism, she notes, is a matter of 'negating the body altogether', replacing the 'corporeal' with the 'cultural': whereby the dandy exists solely for his 'social effect' (23). This negation of the physical body casts the dandy not as an extravagant or excessive figure, but as something close to an ascetic in what is essentially an ongoing act of bodily self-denial. In his eulogy to the dandy in *Le Peintre de la vie moderne* (1863), the French poet Charles Baudelaire wrote: 'Contrary to what a lot of thoughtless people seem to believe, dandyism is not…an excessive delight in clothes and material elegance' (Baudelaire 1972: 420). Some time earlier, Thomas Carlyle had scathingly caricatured the figure of the dandy as a man who 'lives to dress' in *Sartor Resartus* (1833), a commentary built around an imaginary German philosopher and author of a book called 'Clothes: their origin and influence'. But Carlyle, as James Eli Adams has argued, was himself invested in 'ascetic self-presentation' in relation to his reading public, as a particularly austere kind of English writer and intellectual (Adams 1995: 12). Serious Victorian writers like Carlyle turned their intellectual labour into an 'elaborately artic-ulated program of self-discipline'; and it is here, rather than, say, through their erotic or libidinal identities, that such writers located (and defended) their masculinity. This is again a kind of self-fashioning, but it rests on a belief in work as an act of self-discipline and self-denial and is tied to the Carlylean notion of the 'hero-prophet', the isolated, suffering, but self-forgetting artist. The dandy, by contrast, is satirised as 'self-absorbed' and 'parasitic' on the economy (21): recognisable subcultural features, but quite the opposite figure to the romantic Carlylean hero. Even so, Adams suggests that in spite of their radical differences (seriousness as opposed to frivolity, labour as opposed to ennui, etc.) both cultural types have a meticulously fashioned programme of self-discipline in common. In particular, they both turn away from the cor-poreal and the libidinal: so that even though dandyism does in some ways connote excess and exaggeration, Adams can still characterise it by its 'exem-plary asceticism' (35).

Perhaps what is often referred to as *dandyism* is more of a genre than a sub-culture. The French novelist Jules-Amédée Barbey d'Aurevilly wrote the first 'treatise' about dandies, *On Dandyism and George Brummell* (1843), claiming that Brummell was 'unique' even though, as Garelick notes, there were 'genera-tions of dandies' to follow (Garelick 1998: 6). Blending biographical fact with fiction, d'Aurevilly effectively transformed Brummell's life into a work of art. There had already been novels about dandies, such as the Conservative Prime Minister Benjamin Disraeli's *Vivian Grey* (1827) – Disraeli was himself a dandy, as have been a number of prominent Tories ever since (most recently, George Walden) – and Edward Bulwer-Lytton's *Pelham* (1828). The French novelist and royalist Honoree de Balzac had also written a treatise on the dandy, and they often featured in his novels. In England, novels about dandified gentle-men in the Regency period were called 'silver forks', a derisive term coined by William Hazlitt in an essay on 'The Dandy School' (1827) which wanted to reassure its readers that England is 'not a nation of dandies' (Hazlitt 1934: 147). The dandy in fact lasted as a fictionalised social type for some consider-able time. But a narrative of decline and ruin was written into the dandy's life story, again with Brummell – who went into exile to escape his debts and died in squalor – as the model. For Baudelaire in the early 1860s, dandyism was an attempt to create a new kind of aristocratic, aesthetic sensibility, thus ensuring its own inevitable failure. 'Dandyism is a setting sun', he famously wrote,

> like the declining star, without heat and full of melancholy. But alas! the rising tide of democracy, which spreads everywhere and reduces every-thing to the same level, is daily carrying away these last champions of human pride, and submerging, in the waters of oblivion, the last traces of these remarkable myrmidons.

(Baudelaire 1972: 421–22)

In this account, the dandy is left behind by modernity itself, smothered (or drowned, to preserve the metaphor) by the homogenising forces of what later on came to be called mass culture. As Christopher Lane has put it, the dandy is therefore in a certain sense an 'anachronism', not just an 'exile from the social body' but also out of place, and out of step with his times (Lane 1994: 36).

This could very well be a useful way of understanding dandyism: as an anachronism that refuses to go away, as a mode of fashionability that survives against the odds and makes a *point* of being out of step with its context. In early June 1943, when the United States was at war, white American servicemen clashed with Mexican-American 'zoot-suiters' in Los Angeles, beating them and stripping them of their clothes: a series of events which became known as the Zoot-Suit Riots. Mexico was a war ally, but Mexican-Americans were routinely discriminated against and had been represented as a major social problem: the 'Pachuco' problem. Mexican-American youth were especially a target, seen as 'juvenile delinquents in their failure to conform to American social standards' (Pagan 2003: 7). But it was their dress that particularly bothered American servicemen. The zoot suit was fashionable amongst Mexican-American youth – as well as some younger African-Americans in northern cities, particularly amongst the jazz community. The word *zoot* meant 'something done or worn in an exaggerated style' (White and White 1998: 254) and the zoot suit, a combination of long coat and ultra-high waisted trousers with pegged cuffs around the ankles, along with heavy shoes and a wide-brimmed hat, certainly bore this meaning out. The problem was that the zoot suit violated wartime rationing laws which placed severe limits on the amount of fabric to be used for civilian clothing. It didn't help that the wearers were already from a vilified ethnic minority. What disturbed white Americans and especially those white servicemen drafted into inner Los Angeles, as Shane and Graham White note in their book *Stylin'* (1998), was the way in which 'a significant number of young men from the non-white underclasses thumbed their noses at their country's patriotic demands' (249) precisely by wearing these extravagant suits. For Mauricio Mazon, the zoot-suiter 'was the antithesis of the serviceman' and contravened 'all of the taboos of homefront America' (Mazon 2002: 7, 14): this was its anachronism. For the eminent American journalist and editor Carey McWilliams – who had written an influential study of immigrant farm workers in America, *Factories in the Field* (1939) – the zoot suit was 'a badge of defiance by the rejected against the outside world and, at the same time, a symbol of belonging to the inner group...a sign of rebellion and a mark of belonging' (McWilliams 2001: 190). Stuart Cosgrove repeats the point in his article, 'The Zoot-Suit and Style Warfare' (1984), which – also recalling Dick Hebdige's study of English punks a few years earlier – sees the zoot suit as a 'refusal', signifying 'anything from unconscious dandyism to conscious "political" engagement' (Cosgrove 1984:

89). The issue of how conscious or otherwise subcultures might be of what they do and wear, and what effects these things might have on others, is probably an impossible one to resolve. We have seen commentators go either way in this book: casting subcultures as 'self-knowing' (e.g. Hebdige's 'ironic' punk) or dismissing them as unaware of their own predicament, out of touch with their 'reality', and so on. George Lipsitz has been on the former side, stressing agency and selfhood much in the contemporary traditions of Cultural Studies, and understanding minority cultural practices as both progressive and of national significance. The zoot suit, he writes, 'conveyed a bold sense of self-assertion that reflected the social struggles waged for equal rights and fair employment practices. The zoot suit made a virtue out of being different: it flaunted, celebrated, and exaggerated those things which prevailing social norms condemned. It brought to male dress an ornamentation traditionally associated only with women's clothing...' (Lipsitz 1994: 84).

We have seen Georg Simmel's view of fashionability as a process of influence that works from the top down, from the restricted world of the upper classes (who originate fashion styles) to the more widespread lower classes (who imitate them). For Lipsitz, however, the zoot suit 'originated with poor people and made no attempt to copy the dress of the rich' (84): a seemingly autonomous example of fashion excess 'from below'. He lends his support to a New York Times article from 11 June 1943, written in the midst of the Zoot Suit Riots, which claimed that the zoot suit was invented in 1940 by Clyde Duncan, an African-American busboy from Gainesville, Georgia, who got his local clothing store to order a suit made to his own extravagant specifications. The tailor then photographed Duncan in his new suit and sent the picture to a fashion magazine, Men's Apparel Reporter, after which the style gained publicity and, surprisingly enough, caught on. But Shane and Graham White also note that the New York Times article suggests another source for the zoot suit: Clark Gable's character, Rhett Butler, in the blockbuster film Gone With the Wind (1939), which had opened in Georgia a few months before. There is a 'deep irony' in this claim since the film perpetuated racist stereotypes of African-Americans and, of course, Butler was white and well-to-do (White and White 1998: 249–50). Shane and Graham White also note an earlier article from the African-American newspaper, Amsterdam News, where the first 'zoot-suiter' is identified as the Duke of Windsor, courtesy of exclusive English tailoring. George Washington is nominated as yet another source. 'If the New York Times was propagating a myth of "fashion from below"', the Whites suggest, 'the basis of the [Amsterdam] News's story was a more old-fashioned trickle-down theory of elite influence' (251). If this is true, it makes the underclass dandy all the more anachronistic, living out a kind of aristocratic pose in direct contrast to his own predicament and – in the case of the zoot-suiters – against the grain of national sympathies and affiliations. Even so, the fashion survived, crossing the Atlantic and influencing working-class

English youth, some of whom came to dress just as extravagantly in what was called the 'Teddy boy' style.

A good description of the Teddy boy 'look' can be found in *When the Nightingale Sang* (2004), the memoirs of an English nurse, Cynthia O'Neill, during the 1950s and 1960s:

> The Teddy Boy's exuberant dress code certainly made a marked con-
> trast to the male fashion of the time. The 'Teds' attired themselves in
> patterned silk waistcoats over frilly shirts, over which were worn long,
> colourful, Edwardian style drape jackets with black velvet lapels, cuffs
> and pockets. Around their necks hung a tie – usually of the 'Slim Jim'
> or bootlace variety. Narrow 'drainpipe' trousers, the tighter the better,
> jived the night away as nimble feet dressed in loud fluorescent socks,
> worn under pointed winkle-picker shoes completed the look.
>
> (Franklin and O'Neill 2004: 43)

O'Neill 'steered clear of them, having been warned they were "bad boys"' (43). The Teds were in fact notorious for acts of hooliganism and violence and were conspicuously involved in the racist Notting Hill and Nottingham riots of 1958 which saw white youths attacking blacks and their property. The British journalist and editor T.R. Fyvel described the Teddy boys at some length in his remarkable book, *The Insecure Offenders: Rebellious Youth in the Welfare State* (1961). Teds may have derived their costumes from older 'Edwardian' styles – hence their anachronism – but they turned to Europe for their influences, too, rather like the Macaronis all over again. Fyvel thus grudgingly admires them for breaking away from their otherwise inwardly turned working-class backgrounds:

> given the ingrown conservatism of any English working-class commu-
> nity and its opposition to dandyism or any hint of effeminacy, it must
> have taken a special boldness for the first Teddy boys of South London to
> swagger along their drab streets in their exaggerated outfits.
>
> (Fyvel 1961: 51)

The 'proletarian' faces and 'dandified clothes' seem incongruous to Fyvel, who represents the Teddy boys as local grotesques. But he charts their sub-culture – their dress, their behaviour, the places they hang out in, like the dance halls, juke-box cafes and expresso bars – with much more care and sympathy than, say, Richard Hoggart (see Chapter 5), even though he, too, is nostalgic for the older securities of working-class communities, especially church and home. These are boys who refuse these older securities, however, preferring to go out to the cinema rather than stay home to watch televi-sion, which is 'boring'. The American gangster film seems to be 'tailored for them' (107), just like their extravagant suits. Fyvel sees the Teddy boys as anti-authoritarian, 'rootless and neurotic' (25), 'shiftless' and *'primitive'*, a key adjective for the Teds that he often repeats. These are the characteristics that define them as subcultural and crystallise their 'anachronism'. But Fyvel sees them as modern, too, participating in a newer, cosmopolitan kind of world that is no longer so 'ingrown' and home-bound. The English playwright Steven Berkoff has spoken about his own experiences as a Teddy boy, relishing the 'dandified costume' for the sense of release it offered, and the way it helped to open up a range of previously unavailable 'performance strategies': 'you were who you wished to be', he writes, 'warrior, lover, Jimmy Cagney, Tony Curtis, villain, spiv, leader, loner, heavy, Beau Brummel [*sic*]' (cited in Cross 2004: 36). For Robert Cross, there is a natural and inevitable connection between Berkoff's early subcultural career as a Ted and his evolution into a tough-guy actor and theatrical iconoclast, the 'Ted routine' linking him to a set of imaginative postures and providing an early way of 'achieving self-definition through adversity' (36).

Tattoo histories and 'modern primitives'

We can pursue the notion of anachronistic self-fashioning through the phenomenon of tattooing and what we might call 'tattoo communities' – following Margo DeMello's account of the 'modern tattoo community' in her book, *Bodies of Inscription* (2000) – or perhaps just 'tattoo enthusiasts', to draw on the terminology Michael Atkinson uses in his very different study, *Tattooed* (2003). The anachronism of the tattoo is usually registered in terms of its origins, which for some commentators are always present in the tattoo even if tattoo enthusiasts themselves can sometimes seem to be unaware of them. More importantly, those origins are of a particular kind: usually non-western, and in fact commonly derived from 'uncivilised', indigenous cultures in remote places. The prevailing view is that the tattoo's origins are Polynesian or Oceanic, introduced to the West during Captain James Cook's voyages into the South Seas in the late eighteenth century – where, for example, the appearance in England of a tattooed Tahitian man known as Omai 'sparked a tattooing vogue among the English aristocracy' (Fleming 2000: 67). For the anthropologist Nicholas Thomas, the contemporary, western tattoo always carries this history along with it, which therefore makes those enthusiasts who wear them on their bodies not only anachronistic but *inauthentic*. Their modern 'pseudo-Oceanic' designs, he dourly suggests, 'are influenced by naive and one-dimensional New Age romanticizations of indigenous culture and spirituality' and 'appropriate elements of living indigenous cultures, ignorant and indifferent to indigenous notions of cultural property' (Thomas 2005: 29).

Of course, it may well be that anthropologists are more invested in notions of cultural authenticity than most other people, and therefore more alert to (and disapproving of) contemporary acts of cross-cultural 'appropriation'. Because of its anthropological affiliations, Thomas's co-edited book, *Tattoo* (2005), arguably overburdens the contemporary tattoo with its historical Polynesian origins, and thus over-emphasises the naivety (and homogeneity) of contemporary tattoo enthusiasts. On the other hand, contemporary tattoo enthusiasts have from time to time themselves invested in the 'otherness' of their tattoos, valuing them precisely *because* of their non-western significance. The anachronism of being in the contemporary western world and adorning oneself with body art attributed to non-western indigenous cultures from the sometimes distant past is well expressed by the term *modern primitives*. This term is supposed to have been coined by the celebrated American body modifier, Fakir Musafar (Roland Loomis), in 1979. In a later, influential anthology of examples of extreme body modification, *Modern Primitives* (1989), editors V. Vale and Andrea Juno note that it is in fact 'impossible to return to an authentic "primitive" society'; even so, they invoke the 'primitive' as a romantic trope, using it in much the same way as Baudelaire had used the dandy, that is, as a way of providing a countercultural, sensual alternative to the homogenising forces of mass culture. Modern society is colonised by 'millions of mass-produced images', designed to elicit 'spurious memories and experiences'. The tattoo, on the other hand, 'is a true poetic creation and is always more than meets the eye', expressive and 'unique' (Vale and Juno 1989: 5). Far from being inauthentic, the tattoo in this account is one of the few authentic expressions left in contemporary society – precisely *because* of its anachronistic, 'primitive' features. But *Modern Primitives* wasn't the first book to celebrate the 'primitiveness' of the tattoo. Albert Parry's *Tattoo: Secrets of a Strange Art*, was published back in 1933 and identified itself as the first such study of this form of body adornment. Here, the tattoo is tied to a 'primitive desire for an exaggerated exterior' and is characterised as an 'atavism', a throwback (Parry 2006: 1–2). Parry was influenced by Freud and suggested that tattooing amounted to 'the recording of dreams, whether or not the tattooed are aware of it' (2). He also linked tattooing to one's sexual awakening, noting that tattoo images were often erotic, that getting tattooed was often a rite of passage for young people and combined 'pleasure and pain', and that tattoos were often placed on the 'intimate' parts of one's body. But Parry was also alert to different kinds of tattoo communities, that is, social and occupational groups for whom tattoos were a shared phenomenon. He discussed sailors, prostitutes, criminals and circus folk. But he also noted the flow of tattoos into other, often more respectable areas of society: doctors and lawyers, for example, and other examples of the 'ruling classes'. We have already seen that tattooing was a 'vogue' among the English aristocracy in the late eighteenth century, influenced by exoticised indigenous figures from other places. For

Parry, however, wealthy social groups around the end of the nineteenth century and early twentieth century drew their influences from the *lower* orders, thus reversing Simmel's notion of the top-down or 'trickle-down' flow of fashionability. 'When the ruling classes go in for tattooing', he wrote,

> they are perfectly aware of the fact that slum-dwellers, toughs, sailors and other plebs constitute the majority of the tattoo-fans in all the civilised countries. But they are not at all repulsed by this consideration. On the contrary, it is the subconscious desire of the upper class to borrow the primitive strength of the lower class.
>
> (92)

Here, of course, the location of the 'primitive' is shifted, from non-western indigenous culture to the West's own underclasses – both of whom are taken as the authentic, originating site of the tattoo, which others duly imitate.

For Margo DeMello, the contemporary tattoo community 'is now largely defined by elite tattooists and tattoo magazine publishers who are primarily from the middle class' (DeMello 2000: 3). Her study is critical of this newer kind of community (partly built around the various tattoo conventions and publications, and partly 'imagined') precisely because it no longer seems to owe very much to the tattoo's 'authentic' underclass origins. Indeed, she suggests that it 'has been…sanitized or stripped of its working-class roots, in order to ensure that the tattoo is now fit for middle-class consumption' (4): a version, perhaps, of Dick Hebdige's notion of the 'incorporation' of authentic subcultural practices by the dominant culture. The contemporary tattoo's 'exotic, primitive flavour' is consciously inscribed into it, part of a middle-class tattoo aesthetic which likes its tattoos to be 'custom-designed' rather than 'formulaic' (4). It might be worth noting that tattoos are probably no more or less formulaic in their design than they ever were. But the broader point – that tattoos once had authentic 'working-class' origins which are now corrupted – is also reductive. Different communities clearly used tattoos in different ways and for different purposes. A sailor's tattoo arguably first and foremost signified his 'line of work', for example (Rediker 1989: 12) – and, incidentally, there is some doubt over whether sailors were influenced by Polynesian tattooing practices. For criminal gangs in late seventeenth-century Osaka in Japan, tattoos were transformed into a mark of social distinction, designed by highly skilled specialists (Leupp 1999: 130). Juliet Fleming notes that it was fairly common for British pilgrims to Jerusalem in the fifteenth, sixteenth and seventeenth centuries to get themselves tattooed there: long before Polynesian tattoos came into vogue (Fleming 2000: 79–80). DeMello's suggestion that the contemporary tattoo is 'sanitized' for 'middle-class consumption' may also only be a partial view, since tattoos have probably been tradeable and consumable commodities for some time now. For James Bradley, the 'tattoo craze' in Britain and the United States in 1899 interestingly coincided with the publication of Thorstein Veblen's *The Theory of the Leisure Class*, which I mentioned above in relation to the Macaronis. Veblen had viewed fashion as a wasteful form of conspicuous consumption, but he had nothing to say about tattoos – perhaps because, as Bradley suggests, they were often literally a form of *inconspicuous* consumption since they could be hidden by clothes (Bradley 2000: 153). Even so, they still reflected 'luxurious' tastes, with skilled tattoo artists even reproducing notable works of art on people's bodies. Tattoos may well reflect class differences, differences in tastes, self-image and occupation. But, Bradley writes, we 'should avoid the romantic and essentializing impulse to interpret working-class tattoos…as somehow more authentic than their bourgeois counterparts' (154).

The commentaries on tattooing oscillate between those who see tattoos as a specific expression of social distinction – a social *act* – and those who see it as a diverse, widespread and individualised phenomenon. The American sociologist Clinton R. Sanders' ethnographic study, *Customizing the Body* (1989), is an important example of the former, regarding tattooed people as subcultural not least because of the way the tattoo had for so long been pathologised and associated with deviance (for example, with sexual promiscuity or criminality). 'Wearing a tattoo', he writes, 'connected the person to significant others who were similarly marked, [making] one unique by separating him or her from those who were too convention-bound to so alter their bodies' (Sanders 1989: 45). We might think, for example, of bikers and their often elaborate and extensive tattoos in this context. For Michael Atkinson, however, the meanings attached to getting tattooed are too varied to warrant characterising this act as subcultural – even though he, too, recognises the often-striking unconventionality of heavily tattooed bodies. 'Tattoo enthusiasts do share common understandings of tattoos', he suggests, 'but not to the extent that one could decipher a specific subcultural perspective about the practice' (Atkinson 2003: 96). However, Atkinson does at least preserve the social features involved in one's commitment to getting (heavily) tattooed. For others, however, the contemporary western world is too fractured and atomised – too postmodern – to allow tattoo enthusiasts any kind of social affiliation (real or imagined) at all. The eminent sociologist Bryan S. Turner's essay, 'The Possibility of Primitiveness: Towards a Sociology of Body Marks in Cool Societies', was published in a special issue of the journal *Body and Society* (1999) devoted to body modification. Turner's essay returns to the sense that the contemporary tattoo is an anachronistic fashion style, drawing a distinction between tattoos as they once were (or might have been) and tattoos as they seem to be now. Once, in pre-literate indigenous cultures, he tells us, tattoos had been 'permanent, collective and largely obligatory'. But these days tattoos are 'optional, playful, ironic': no longer 'serious' and no longer authentic

(Turner 1999: 40–41). This is what Turner means by 'cool': not the jazz community's sense of the term as described in Chapter 6, but a much more generalised notion that expresses postmodern society's distance from the 'real'. The modern or postmodern tattoo is thus 'merely a cliché, borrowing from and adapting Polynesian patterns, Japanese motifs and Chinese military emblems' (49), cut adrift from traditional indigenous spiritual practices and connected instead 'to the commercial exploitation of sexual themes in popular culture' (40). This remote, disapproving essay has little to do with the actualities of tattooing and the social worlds – however they might be construed – of tattoo enthusiasts. Instead, it plays out a version of Tonnies' distinction between *Gemeinschaft* and *Gesellschaft*, seeing the former in terms of the social solidarity and originality of 'primitive' cultures and the latter in terms of a contemporary society understood as inauthentic in some quite essential, definitive way: condemned only to be able to imitate a 'primitive' culture's originality, showing off its forms but emptying it of content. Class is also important to Turner's argument. The tattoos of working-class men, he suggests, once indicated 'membership of a male culture of work and hardship' – whereas nowadays, the 'discrete and aesthetic butterflies and flowers on the shoulders and backs of fashion models and middle-class professional women are sexual consumer images', mere 'surface indicators of identity and attachment' (49).

We can think about the stark gendering of Turner's class distinction here, where the 'hot' associations of masculinity/solidarity/work are contrasted with the 'cool' shallowness of femininity/fashion/consumerism. We can also think about the nostalgia that underwrites this distinction, for a time when the tattoo seemed to directly convey the significance of its immediate context (the working class, 'primitive' cultures, etc.): a time when it seemed to be 'serious'. Turner's perspective recalls Nicholas Thomas's view of tattooing noted above, through its shared investment in the authenticity of the 'primitive' tattoo and disapproval of the inauthenticity of contemporary tattoo designs – as (to recall Thomas, above) 'pseudo-Oceanic' etc. But perhaps the modern primitive *also* shares this investment. In the same special issue of *Body and Society*, Christian Klesse argues that this particular subculture is indeed serious about its spiritual practices and communal identity, all *too* serious. For Klesse, modern primitives live out a kind of unreflective romantic *Gemeinschaft* in the midst of the *Gesellschaft*: primitivism in the midst of postmodernity. They do this by invoking exactly the same binary we see in the essays from Thomas and Bryan Turner, appearing to draw a radical distinction between 'primitive' cultures (as authentic, communal, original etc.) and modern society (as inauthentic, fractured, merely imitating). Indeed, for Klesse modern primitives reproduce this binary wholesale, living it out through their rituals, their fascination with shamanism, their unconventional and often extreme body practices, and so on. The problem is that modern primitives invoke this binary only to *refuse* it, as if it is indeed perfectly possible to be 'primitive', or 'primitivist', right in the midst of the contemporary western world: so much so that those taken-for-granted differences between the authentic and the inauthentic can now be difficult to sustain. The modern primitive, in other words, can appear to be here-and-now and in some other time and place simultaneously. The next section will look more closely at this anachronistic predicament, beginning with some comments on the work of the great early sociologist, Emile Durkheim, on religion and 'the lower societies'.

Tribes and leatherfolk

Durkheim is an important sociologist for subcultural studies, not least because of the way he prioritised the social over the individual. The more social one becomes, the less individualised one is; moreover, the achievement of a social identity was understood as the gaining of something extra, that thing that individualism cannot possess: collective consciousness, which Durkheim also referred to as *solidarity*. In his classic study, *The Elementary Forms of the Religious Life* (1915), Durkheim looked at religion to make his case, arguing that religion is first and foremost 'something eminently social' (Durkheim 1976: 10). In order to best understand the 'elementary' characteristics of religion, however, Durkheim turned back to 'the lower societies', so-called 'primitive' groups of people such as the Australian Aboriginals who at the time were being closely studied by colonial anthropologists. The key to these 'lower societies', so it seemed, was the apparent absence of any notion of individualism. The 'primitive' group, Durkheim writes,

> has an intellectual and moral conformity of which we find but rare examples in the more advanced societies. Everything is common to all. Movements are stereotyped; everybody performs the same ones in the same circumstances, and this conformity of conduct only translates the conformity of thought.
>
> (5–6)

We can note in passing just how close this account of 'primitive' groups is to later commentaries on mass culture which equally emphasise 'conformity of thought', stereotypes, etc.: as if this particular distinction between the 'primitive' and modernity is already compromised. (We might also recall Simmel on modern fashion and the need to 'imitate' others.) But there is another reason why Durkheim turns back to the 'lower societies' for his analysis of religion. So-called 'primitive' groups *reveal* rather than conceal, a view that was necessary and important to the scrutinising project of colonial anthropology. They are in a certain quite literal sense, Durkheim suggests, unadorned; and as a consequence, their religious characteristics 'are shown in all their nudity' (6). This is why they seem 'elemental'. A distinction is then drawn between the unclothed, primary nature of 'lower societies' (their nudity is why the analysis of them can lead to 'revelations') and the attired, secondary nature of modern society (which is therefore harder to read, more veiled and obscure). Durkheim expresses the predicament of the 'lower societies' in this way: 'That which is accessory or secondary, the development of luxury, has not yet come to hide the principal elements' (6). The perhaps surprising remark is in fact close in kind to Veblen's notion of fashion as 'conspicuous consumption', except that Durkheim doesn't actually seem to be talking about fashion. Nevertheless, he does seem to suggest that modern society has 'luxury' – adornments, accessories – but 'lower societies' don't. And yet even this distinction is compromised with an afterthought: 'But that is not equivalent to saying that all luxury is lacking to the primitive cults…luxury is indispensable to the religious life; it is at its very heart' (6n).

We can think about Durkheim's attempt to distinguish the 'primitive' from the modern, especially in terms of these unstable binaries of conformity/individualism, primary/secondary, elementary/luxury, nudity/accessories, and so on: binaries which also evoke the restraint/excess distinction I have been working with throughout this book. But the 'primitive' and the modern fold into each other in various ways here, too, and soon become difficult to properly tell apart (they both have 'luxury', for example). Of course, Durkheim's study is built around the idea that the 'primitive' will *reveal* something about the modern, as if the latter is really just a less transparent and harder-to-read version of it. Modern religion can thus be understood by looking at 'the primitive cults': the two, it seems, are therefore closer in kind than we might first expect. We might think that studies emphasising the proximity of the 'primitive' and the modern are now pretty much a thing of the past, associated mostly with social anthropology from the late nineteenth and early twentieth centuries: like Thrasher's account of Chicago gangs in the 1920s, for example (see Chapter 2) or Minehan's account of child tramps in the 1930s (Chapter 1). But contemporary, neo-Durkheimian sociology has brought this back to us all over again, most notably through the work of another Frenchman, Michel Maffesoli. Maffesoli's *The Time of the Tribes: The Decline of Individualism in Mass Society* (1988; trans. 1996) has been remarkably influential in some aspects of subcultural studies. It turns to what it calls 'dionysiac values': the passions and emotions that bind social groups – 'emotional communities' – together in a modern world otherwise given over to massification and dehumanisation. But these passions and emotions have something religious about them, too. Maffesoli draws on Durkheim's notion of the 'social divine' to explain the irrational or super-natural connections that bind social groups together. Sociality here is close to a state of transcendence, and tied to ritual practices. An 'emotional community' has to develop a set of rituals through which it defines itself *as* a community, repeating them over and over. The 'sole function' of community rituals, Maffesoli writes, 'is to confirm a group's view of itself' (Maffesoli 1996: 17). Durkheim had also noted that the rituals of 'primitive' religious cults strengthen socialisation (Durkheim 1976: 63). And in fact, Maffesoli gives his modern examples of 'emotional communities' – anything from sports associations to the Mafia – exactly this kind of designation. In spite (or perhaps because) of their modernity, they retain something 'primitive' in their socialisation. He refers to them as *tribus* or 'tribes'; 'religiosity', he says, 'is an essential ingredient' (Maffesoli 1996: 3) in modern tribalism; and they share all the features ascribed to religious cults. It can consequently often seem as if Maffesoli isn't really talking about the modern world at all. His account is an ultra-romantic one, juxtaposing the Dionysian vitalism of modern 'tribes' with the secular rationalism of modern society. In this respect it is essentially a newer version of the Tonniesian distinction between *Gemeinschaft* and *Gesellscahft*: distinguishing the vitalist, expressive and 'enchanting' social world of the tribe from the 'sanitized' (99), repressed and generally disenchanting realms of modern society, even as these two things are exactly concomitant with one another.

It may be that Maffesoli's work is best suited precisely to the sort of 'anachronistic' modern subcultural identities which *themselves* invoke a sense of the 'primitive', the cultish, and the religious and 'divine'. Of course, religious communities are by no means necessarily subcultural; to be so, they would need to be understood as in some way non-normative or unconventional, like the Ranters described in Chapter 4. Over the last 20 years, much attention has been given to what have been broadly referred to as 'neo-Pagans', people who live out anachronistic predicaments by bringing pre-Christian religious beliefs and rituals into modern life. Wicca or witches are a good example. Unlike the established Church, wicca have no public place of worship, remaining instead relatively hidden from public view. Their socialisation is partly built around the coven and the various rituals attached to this, which are often highly exclusive and hierarchical and a matter of esoteric knowledge. In *The Triumph of the Moon* (1999), Ronald Hutton sees British wicca as dedicated to their 'craft', disciplined in their rituals, but also actively engaged with the world around them, especially ecologically through their often elaborate relations to Nature: something that mainstream Christianity has had little interest in. Lynne Hume's study, *Witchcraft and Paganism in Australia* (1997), similarly situates wicca in the context of ecological movements and increasing concerns about environmental 'balance', which helps to identify them as modern. But wicca – even in a place like Australia – is also 'old', drawing on 'ancient magical and shamanistic practices' (Hume 1997: 228). Forms of wicca socialisation can vary, from festivals and conferences attached to large-scale 'federations' to the casual and fairly ordinary gatherings Susan Greenwood describes in her account of 'the magical subculture in London' (Greenwood 2000: 3–8). It might be worth recalling that Durkheim had also talked about magic in *The Elementary Forms of the Religious Life*, distinguishing it from religion because it seems much more 'reclusive', much less a matter of community-like 'association'. '*There is*', he insisted, '*no Church of magic*' (Durkheim 1976: 44). The various accounts of modern-day wicca, however – in wicca newsletters and publications like *Pagan Dawn* or *The Cauldron*, as well as in academic studies – emphasise the bonds between participants and seem to demonstrate that community-based forms of association occur here as a matter of necessity and routine.

The wicca 'revival' is part of a broader, renewed interest in neo-Pagan activities in the modern world: in 'Heathenry', 'Druidry', and especially in what Hume had called 'shamanistic practices'. There has been much interest in modern shamanism or neo-shamanism in recent years, especially from anthropologists who have emphasised the combination of modern predicaments and ancient or 'primitive' interests and practices, understanding the shaman as a kind of healer, a mediator between humans and the natural world, as well as the 'otherworld' (Harvey 2003; Wallis 2003). But the fascination with modern shamanism goes back a little earlier and returns us to the anachronism of the 'modern primitive', discussed above, as well as to issues to do with subcultural self-fashioning. In 1984, Geoff Mains published an important book called *Urban Aboriginals: A Celebration of Leather Sexuality*. This book in fact had nothing to do with Aboriginal people at all, but it claimed the designation and attached it instead to a metropolitan subculture in the United States which drew its inspiration from leather attire. Leather had gained its subcultural, and its sexual, associations through various biker organisations in post-Second World War America, gaining iconic status as an erotic *macho* fashion accessory in Laslo Benedek's film, *The Wild One* (1953), starring Marlon Brando as a biker gang leader: the first 'biker outlaw' movie. The interest in 'leather sexuality', however, is differently conceived. For one thing, it is usually tied to S/M (sado-masochistic) sexual practices and an extensive S/M scene. For another, its practitioners are primarily although not exclusively gay men, tracing a lineage back through gay bikers' groups such as the Los Angeles-based Satyrs Motorcycle Club, founded in 1954, the longest, continuously running gay organisation in the United States and the first motorcycle club founded by and for gay men (see http://www.satyrsmc.org/). The 'primitive' features of leather (as 'raw', a 'second skin', etc.) are no doubt important to the 'leather sexuality' subculture's understanding of itself as a *tribe*: as 'urban Aboriginals'. But for Geoff Mains, who was himself a leatherman, 'leather tribalism' also provides an 'identity' for its practitioners and a 'network within which its members can focus those relationships that are face-to-face, personal and intimate.... In contrast, the relationships of leathermen with the outside world are largely secondary – impersonal and at arm's length' (Mains 2002: 26).

This account exactly recalls Durkheim's primary/secondary distinction above, as well as Tonnies' distinction between *Gemeinschaft* and *Gesellschaft*. The outside world is alienating and disenchanting; the world of leather tribalism, on the other hand, works to *re-enchant*, to re-acquaint its members with spirituality and optimism, as well as intimacy. 'As a sub-culture', Mains writes,

> leather refracts the values of western society to create its own vision. It takes images of masculinity, the use and abuse of power, and the values of creativity.... It creates from all of this an experience that is cathartic, ecstatic and spiritual. In turn, this revelation provides further strength to the tribal identity.
>
> (27)

Leather is like religion itself here, as Durkheim had defined it: 'something eminently social'. Or rather, it is like the 'social divine'. Mains insists on precisely this connection between the material (literally) and the spiritual: 'leather is no affectation; it is an expression of the soul' (27).

In a later anthology, *Leatherfolk* (1991) – partly devoted to shamanism – Guy Baldwin ties leather and S/M sexuality to 'the achievement of ecstasy, bonding, altered states of consciousness, and a deep meditation.... It is little wonder that we sometimes refer to them as religious experiences' (Baldwin 1991: 171–72). For Stuart Norman, a 'leatherfaerie shaman', leather is indeed 'deep in my soul', a 'second skin and a sacred garment'. But it is also 'my shaman's garb' (Norman 1991: 276). Investing in a more playful kind of leather identity, however, Norman associates leather spirituality with magic rather than with religion. The S/M associated with this subculture is also 'magical practice' (281): sado-masochism as 'sex magic'. It is cast here in terms of fantasy and enchantment, and imbued with utopian potential; indeed, its shamanistic task is to do nothing less than heal the 'sickness' of society and 'remake the world' (283). What we might call the *rhetoric* of leather sexuality intentionally works against the grain of conventional or mainstream (i.e. usually disapproving) views of sado-masochistic sex. Leathermen even distinguish themselves from mainstream gay culture in this respect (Thompson 1991: xii), just as *leatherdykes*, that is, lesbian leatherwomen, have similarly distinguished themselves from many lesbian feminists. Gayle Rubin has written about Samois, probably the first organised group devoted to lesbian sado-masochism, founded in San Francisco in June 1978. The increased visibility and vocality of S/M women 'sparked a barrage of condemnation asserting fundamental incompatibilities between lesbian feminists and S/M'. But Samois's 'greatest notoriety', she suggests, 'came from its role in the feminist sex wars', especially its battles with the powerful lobby group, Women against Violence in Pornography and Media (Rubin 2004: n.p.). Leatherfolk certainly relish their 'kinkiness' and complain about those afflicted with what Guy Baldwin has called 'kink-o-phobia' (Baldwin 1991: 176). But they also represent S/M leather sexuality as a practice underwritten by techniques of self-discipline and – perhaps surprisingly to those who might regard it as a sexually *excessive* subculture – self- and mutual restraint. S/M, writes Stuart Norman, 'requires discipline, close attention, and concentration, as well as trust and respect between partners' (Norman 1991: 280). It is a matter of education or pedagogy, where one goes through an apprenticeship, carefully guided by more experienced members, those already in the know. Inauthenticity is banished from the leatherfolk world – leather cannot connote inauthenticity – even though S/M sex acts may well involve the staging of fantasies and performance. 'Do not try to bluff your way into an SM or leather scene', advises Joseph W. Bean in his book, *Leathersex: A Guide for the Curious Outsider and the Serious Player* (1994).

> No pretending. About *anything*. Tell the man or men you are with that you are a novice. Tell him (them) what you think you want, and what you are sure you do not want to try.... This sort of conversation in which you spell out your level of experience, your tastes, and your limits is called 'negotiation'.
>
> (1)

Face-to-face contact is especially important here and, as I have noted, the leathersex scene seems to place special emphasis on intimacy and trust. This is where the utopian possibilities of leathersex can be found. In Gayle Rubin's history of the Catacombs, a 'fist-fucking' and leather club which opened in San Francisco in 1975, intimacy, self-discipline and safety are emphasised to the extent that this otherwise perverse sexual practice in fact becomes an exemplary form of 'safe sex' (Rubin 1991: 136). S/M leathersex play, Mark Thompson suggests, 'is about healing the wounds that keep us from fully living' (Thompson 1991: xvii): this is its shamanistic role. By comparison, normative sexual practices are lacking or incomplete; without the 'primal' energies attached to leather, they can in fact seem positively unenlightened. With leatherfolk, we therefore have a specifically subcultural phenomenon. Their sociality or 'sociation', to recall Simmel's term, is built around a fetishised material that works to make them distinctive. It helps them to infuse their subcultural practices with utopian aspirations (to 'remake the world') even as the emphasis on intimacy, personal development and sexuality means they also remain self-absorbed and self-centred.

Chapter 8

FANS, NETWORKS, PIRATES
Virtual and media subcultures

RPGs, MMORPGs and immersed communities

THE LAST CHAPTER ENDED with an example of a subculture that emphasises local face-to-face intimacy. But in many contemporary subcultures, participants might never see or meet each other. Nancy MacDonald describes the urban graffiti subculture in this way, for example. 'When you step into this subculture', she writes, 'you are expected to leave all traces of "real life" on its doorstep' (MacDonald 2001: 192). In this account the graffiti subculture is a kind of home-away-from-home, but it is also a place where a graffiti artist or tagger's 'personal and physical' self no longer seems to matter. Graffiti tags convey 'attitudes' rather than the reality of one's identity, usually tied (since MacDonald mostly looks at male taggers) to inflated or excessive masculine narratives of 'strength, power and control' (214). They are a kind of fantasised performance, a combination of style and content that may very well bear little or no connection to the actuality of the taggers themselves. As one tagger says, 'you are what you write' (216) – and, since taggers are usually nocturnal and difficult to see, what they write is usually all there is. For MacDonald, this amounts to an expression of 'the "virtual" self': 'Having a virtual identity leaves one's "real life" or physical persona very much in the shadows.... Even one's sex, the most prominent feature of one's self, is obscured' (196).

We have already seen subcultures accounted for precisely in terms of their combination of imaginative effects and 'real life stories', as well as in terms of performance and role playing where one's real identity can indeed remain 'obscured'. In those subcultures where play itself is definitional – that is, where play provides a subculture's structural logic – we might expect these features to be still more prominent. An obvious example is the subculture built around role-playing games (RPGs) which developed during the 1970s, especially through the influential RPG, *Dungeons and Dragons*, derived from wargame scenarios and fantasy literature and first released in 1974. Gary Alan Fine's *Shared Fantasy: Role-Playing Games as Social Worlds* (1983) was an early academic study of modern 'fantasy gamers', something that Fine himself, as a sociologist in the Chicago School tradition, was a little apologetic about. 'By any standards', he wrote, 'fantasy gaming…is a rather small, perhaps trivial, social world' (Fine 1983: 1). By the end of the 1970s, Fine estimated, *Dungeons and Dragons* was selling at the rate of around 7000 per month, usually to young adult middle-class men. Two aspects of this RPG gave it subcultural definition for Fine. First, it was an 'avocation'; that is, it called its players into an occupation of sorts and even lent them a kind of 'career' as they progressed and developed, but it had nothing to do with *work*. Quite the opposite, since it was of course built around play. Second, this particular game required a player's full commitment: what Fine called *engrossment*. 'For the game to work as an aesthetic experience', he wrote, 'players must be willing to "bracket" their "natural" selves and enact a fantasy self. They must lose themselves to the game' (4). *Engrossment* is understood as a social act here, with the RPGs providing 'a structure for making friends and finding a sense of community' (59). But playing an RPG also meant abandoning 'real life', something that became a matter of concern for parents, teachers and employers as their children, students and employees were increasingly drawn into its realms (sometimes for very long periods of time). The world of an RPG is a fantasy one, not a real one; when they enter it, players take on fantasy identities. For Fine, RPGs – rather like graffiti tagging for MacDonald – in fact serve a kind of Walter Mitty purpose, enabling players to endow themselves with attributes that in reality they don't possess: 'strength, social poise, rugged good looks, wisdom, and chivalric skills' (60). They also provide the kind of support and 'protection' that players may not be able to get in the real world.

The prevailing view of *online* RPGs – multiplayer online roleplaying games (MORPGs) or 'massively multiplayer online roleplaying games' (MMORPGs) – seems to be similar in kind. The unusually named LambdaMOO (a MOO is an 'object-oriented' multi-user domain or MUD) is one of these, founded in 1990 by Pavel Curtis and operated entirely on a volunteer basis. This game in fact offers an entire fantasy world administered by 'wizards', and players constitute its 'population' although numbers have been in decline for some years. It is now commonplace in the sociology of 'gamers' to talk of 'game *communities*', that is, to account for game-playing as a social act – even if the identities of players are entirely fabricated. Leo Sang-Min Whang has looked at the extremely popular Korean medieval fantasy MMORPG, *Lineage*, noting that the game promotes clan-like affiliations among players that enable them to 'exercise and express a sense of loyalty' to particular groups (Whang 2003: 32). P. David Marshall has suggested that MMORPGs enable players to build 'social networks' precisely *because* they are able to live out shared, esoteric 'rituals' and develop 'their own argot and acronyms'. Game players, in other words, can 'make their culture' (Marshall 2004: 74). Edward Castronova's study, *Synthetic Worlds: The Business and Culture of Online Games* (2005), recalls Fine's earlier work (although it never mentions it) through its apologetic opening pages, repeatedly describing the social worlds of online gamers as 'strange'. Since a typical user spends 20 to 30 hours per week on MMORPGs, Castronova suggests, 'something quite bizarre must be going on' (Castronova 2005: 2). It isn't always clear *why* these game worlds are strange and bizarre, but Castronova rightly notes that they have generated their own levels of moral panic with parents banning their use, laws passed against some of them, anxieties expressed about game 'addiction', and a general 'anti-gamer sentiment' (277) intensifying in a society that continues to invest in productive labour and remains suspicious of 'excessive' forms of fantasy play. Again, these games are understood as both escapist and reconstructive in terms of identity: 'Whatever you may not like about your body here, it can be undone in the building of a new body there' (78). Castronova takes MMORPGs as simultaneously mass cultural and subcultural. They are mass cultural because they are part of a global entertainment industry and anyone can play, anywhere; Whang estimates that up to ten million players in Korea participate in online role-playing games, for example. But they are subcultural because they provide a site where 'strangers' can become 'friends' through *immersion* – essentially another word for Fine's *engrossment* – which is then understood as an act of nonconformity or even dissent. MMORPGs are where we find the playing-out of radical outsider/insider distinctions: 'every act of gaming is a rebellion', Castronova writes, 'and immersive, life-absorbing game-playing most clearly rebels against the order of affairs on the outside' (277).

Fans as rogues, fanzines as hobos

The sense that people can immerse themselves into fantasy worlds cuts across the kind of distinction I had discussed in Chapter 3, between 'fluid' and 'persistent' subcultural participation. Immersion – or engrossment – is something *more* than persistence. It carries with it a sense that one is now too obsessed with one's subcultural practices, too close to them, too 'solipsistic' (to recall another description used elsewhere in this book): at the expense of a 'balanced' perspective on the 'real world'. Gamers are thus vulnerable to pathologisation. The sociological accounts I have noted above provide a useful counterpoint to this, however, since they map the nonconformist self-absorption of gamers into forms of sociality or community: a good working definition of what subcultures are like, generally speaking. We see the same sort of approach, in commentaries usually associated with Cultural Studies, to fans of particular kinds of popular media. Like gamers, media fans can also easily be patholo-gised: as 'deranged', as stalkers, as having lost touch with reality, and so on. As Henry Jenkins reminds us in his influential study of fans, *Textual Poachers* (1992), the word *fan* comes from the Latin, *fanaticus*, which relates to temple rituals and worship and connotes divine inspiration, even possession by a deity. Fandom is certainly a form of fanaticism, and there can even be something 'religious' about it, as a number of commentators have noted (e.g. Hills 2002; Sandvoss 2005). For Jenkins, fans are routinely cast as excessive, over-enthu-siastic consumers, too heavily identified with and invested in the media texts they build their fandom around: like *Star Trek*, for example, or *The X-Files*. The anti-fan retort, 'Get a Life!' precisely expresses this view that fans don't have enough critical distance, that they are too immersed, too removed from real-ity. But although Jenkins doesn't disagree with this view, he works to create a more positive image for media fan activity. Drawing on the work of Michel de Certeau – which has been influential for contemporary Cultural Studies – he describes fans as 'textual poachers': not so much under the influence of the media they saturate themselves in, as unorthodox *users* of that media, shaping or recasting it to suit their needs. The notion of the fan-as-poacher, however, runs the risk of romanticising fans at the expense of other, more orthodox (but possibly more progressive or critical) readers. 'From the perspective of dominant taste', Jenkins writes, already overstating his case, 'fans appear to be frighteningly out of control, undisciplined and unrepentant, rogue readers' (Jenkins 1992: 18). The view of the fan as a *rogue* takes us back to my account of the Elizabethan underworld in Chapter 1, and in fact Jenkins exactly repro-duces the social logic of the rogue in his description of fans as parasitic, or even as thieves: 'Undaunted by traditional conceptions of literary and intellec-tual property, fans raid mass culture, claiming its materials for their own use' (18). Not owning property themselves, fans are also 'nomadic readers' (27), a notion also lifted from de Certeau but which again recalls a much older subcultural binary which had contrasted sedentary, normative behaviour with vagabonds and itinerant lawlessness. Jenkins's romantic account of fandom as an unorthodox form of 'consumer activism' is typical of the kind of Cultural Studies that developed in the 1990s in Britain and the United States, but for all its problems (its romantic perspective, its generalised and homogeneous view of 'dominant taste', etc.) it did at least turn attention to ways in which mass or popular media use might be understood as subcultural.

Milly Williamson has been critical of Jenkins's study for the way it romanti-cally 'transform[s] the middle-class, white, educated fan into an oppressed rebel, and ignores the elitist distinctions that fans make' (Williamson 2005: 102). Jenkins's work – again not atypically for Cultural Studies at this time – was pop-ulist, reading fandom as a mode of democratic participation in the sense that anyone could do it, at any time. But as we have seen, subcultures can indeed be elitist and excluding, as well as esoteric. It may be relatively normative to be a

Trekker, a committed fan of *Star Trek*. It is less normative, however, to write what is called 'slash' fanfiction around *Star Trek*'s two main characters, Kirk and Spock. K/S or 'slash' fanfiction stages detailed homoerotic relations between these two characters, making it another example of what Jenkins rightly calls 'improper' media use (Jenkins 1992: 187). Unusually, perhaps, it is written by women, even though its protagonists are homosexual men. Jenkins himself sees it as a version of the genre of women's romance fiction through its thematic emphasis on intimacy and commitment, in which case it has some conservative, even mainstream thematic features; but its underground pornographic scenes also make it 'scandalous' and substantially restrict its circulation (202). Constance Penley gives a similar account, distinguishing *Star Trek* fandom – which she sees as inclusive, 'sexually balanced' and attracting 'strong cross-class representation' – from K/S fanfiction which is altogether more narrow in focus and, in some respects, downright perplexing even to the subculture itself. 'The K/Sers', she writes, 'are constantly asking themselves why they are drawn to writing their sexual and social utopian romances across the bodies of two men, and why these two men in particular' (Penley 1991: 153). As well as homosexual intimacy, K/S fanfiction may also evoke 'feelings of solidarity' (157), important to the subculture itself as it carves out an underground readership for its writing. Cornel Sandvoss makes exactly this point, that 'slash' fanfiction 'is accompanied by the establishment of tight social networks' (Sandvoss 2005: 25). If commentators agree on anything about fandom, it is this: that fans create a sense of solidarity amongst themselves, built around their specific interests and practices. In her study of female fans online, *Cyberspaces of Their Own* (2005), Rhiannon Bury concludes that 'fandom is ultimately about relating to other fans', subsuming the adored media text into precisely the sense of solidarity that being a fan can bring with it (Bury 2005: 209). Sandvoss even sees fandom as a kind of *Heimat* or home, what he refers to (perhaps combining *Heimat* with Jenkins's notion of fans as 'nomadic readers') as a 'mobile' home, offering those who migrate into it 'security and emotional warmth' (Sandvoss 2005: 64).

In his essay, 'An American Otaku (or, A Boy's Virtual Life on the Net)', Joseph Tobin describes his son Isaac's involvement with online computer activities as well as the miniature wargame, Warhammer 40K. He calls his son an *otaku*:

> His *otaku* life provides him with a male performative identity, but also, simultaneously, with a way to pursue less macho interests, including art, corresponding, and even interpersonal intimacy.... *Otaku* life is about relating to others while seeming to care only about one's obsession.
>
> (1998: 125)

This remark again gives us an expression of subcultural identity as simultaneously social and self-absorbed. *Otaku* is a Japanese word, however, used to describe a subculture of online game and *manga* or comic and animated art enthusiasts that emerged in Japan during the 1980s. Sharon Kinsella has described the moral panic (she draws on Stanley Cohen's term here) that accompanied the emergence of the *otaku* subculture, especially following a series of murders of young girls in 1988 and 1989 by a young printer's assistant, Miyazaki Tsutomu – where it seemed that young men obsessed with *manga* comic books and online games were capable of playing out their erotic and sadistic fantasies for real. Kinsella notes that *otaku* were then pathologised as too obsessive, too individualistic: cast as antithetical to the normative values of Japanese society, 'family, company, nation'. *Otaku*, she writes, 'came to represent people who lacked any remaining vestiges of social consciousness and were instead entirely preoccupied by their...specialist personal pastimes' (Kinsella 2000: 137). Her own study, however, looks at amateur *manga* enthusiasts as a *social* group, rather than as a ragtag of deviant, disengaged individuals. *Manga* is extremely popular in Japan and is often produced by large publishing companies. Amateur *manga* (*dojinshi*) has developed alongside this, however, produced cheaply through 'mini printing companies' and distributed at first through associations and societies, and then through the various conventions of *Comiket* or the Comic Market – beginning in December 1975 – which brought producers and fans together under one roof. Although participation can be large scale here, Kinsella retains a sense of *dojinshi* production and circulation as subcultural through its amateur status (distinguishing it from professional, mainstream *manga*), its social networks, the level of fans' commitment to it, and their involvement in its often elaborate fantasy worlds.

The idea of the fan as an amateur producer of media has been especially important to accounts of fandom as subcultural. A case in point are zines, potentially the most amateuristically produced forms of micro-media – or what Chris Atton calls 'alternative media' (2002) – of all. Zines can be distinguished from professionalised fanzines or 'prozines', not least because they are generally less obviously devoted to particular mass media texts. Indeed, their interests might primarily be personal and idiosyncratic: in which case they are called 'perzines'. They don't need a publishing house to get produced. They can be put together in someone's bedroom, cutting and pasting, perhaps even writing the text out by hand and then photocopying a few copies for friends and other zine producers – or, as e-zines, they can be cheaply created and circulated on the Internet. As I noted in Chapter 5, Marion Leonard has talked about riot grrrl zine and e-zine production, looking at the way a certain kind of underground female and feminist 'geography' is created through the circulation of 'do-it-yourself' (DIY) amateur texts across a globalised, diffuse subculture, a 'network' of remote but often intimately connected women (Leonard 1998; see also Armstrong 2004). A more elaborate sense of subcultural zine geography, however, is presented in Stephen Duncombe's study of zines in the United States, *Notes from Underground* (1997). For Duncombe, the amateur aspect of zine production is the key to their subcultural status; but they are also social 'institutions', directly engaging with their readerships, soliciting other writers' views, and in particular, speaking about *other* zines. The forerunner to contemporary zine production, Duncombe suggests, is the Amateur Press Association (APA) which emerged in the first decades of the nineteenth century, becoming the National Amateur Press Association in 1876. 'It was in the NAPA', he writes, 'that the tradition of individuals sending their writings to a central mailer, who then collated and redistributed them, was first codified, and the name APA came to stand not only for the organisation that produced the zine but the zine itself' (Duncombe 1997: 50). Duncombe prefers the term *community* to *network* to describe zine production and distribution, however. Zines provide an alternative form of media, radically distinguished from centralised, corporate and metropolitan mass media production. Contrary to the account of the APA above, Duncombe's model of zines is in fact a *decentralised* one, and a celebration of the zine's sheer eccentricity. Influenced in part by Robert E. Park, he turns to the curiosities not of marginal man, but of marginal media. Zines are by no means necessarily politically progressive and zine writers can be well aware of their powerlessness; but they often express dissent and evoke a set of attitudes that Duncombe characterises as 'bohemian'. They may very well participate in a zine community of writers and recipients, but they are not tied to place and, indeed, there seems to be something innately 'homeless' about them. This is where Duncombe's decentralised model manifests itself: in his account of zines in America as a kind of media version of Nels Anderson's hobo, itinerant and property-less, features expressed in the zines themselves which tend to be concerned with 'things they don't own', advocating 'slack ideals' (86) and commonly providing idiosyncratic 'tour guides' and daily schedules (56). Henry Jenkins had seen the media fan as a textual poacher and rogue; Duncombe effectively casts the zine as a kind of vagabond, again taking us back to the themes of Chapter 1. As they flow irregularly across the nation, zines constitute what he calls a 'shadow America', dispersed, nomadic and relatively invisible.

Virtual communities, pirate utopias

The commentaries on Internet or online subcultures discussed so far have tended to emphasise both the lack of face-to-face contact among participants (e.g. gamers, e-zine producers and recipients) and the sense that, despite this, these people are participating in a kind of community where values are shared and socialisation happens even if identities are not always what they seem. From one perspective, of course, there is nothing particularly subcultural about all this. What is now generally called *cyberspace* (a word coined in the early 1980s by the Canadian cyberpunk writer, William Gibson) is itself conventionally understood as a realm that facilitates communication, interaction and social-ity – rather than, say, a place where people remain just as alienated or alone as they ever were. In his important study, *Cyberculture* (2001), Pierre Lévy offers this broad-based but compelling account: 'If the growth of the automobile, which characterises the twentieth century, corresponds primarily to a desire for individual power, the growth of cyberspace corresponds to a desire for reciprocal communication and collective intelligence' (Lévy 2001: 106). For Lévy, one of the key functions of cyberspace is to encourage the development of 'virtual communities', which bring with them 'the general development of contacts and interactions of all kinds. The image of the isolated loner in front of a computer screen is based more on fantasy than on sociological inquiry' (110). The term *virtual community* is lifted from the American cyber-activist and cyber-advocate Howard Rheingold's book, *The Virtual Community: Finding Connection in a Computerized World* (1994), which asserted an essen-tial link between cyberspace and socialisation. We might think that going online is a disembodied and detached affair, signalling the end of community-based identification. But for Rheingold this task has already been performed by modern society *offline*, which has steadily and systematically alienated its subjects from one another. The Internet or Net, on the other hand, offers up a realm where one's yearnings for community can at last find their real-isation. Rheingold's involvement with San Francisco's *Whole Earth* – which becomes the *Whole Earth 'Lectronic Link* (WELL) online – brings a counter-cultural perspective to the Net, juxtaposing it to the mainstream, corporate interests of mass media, rather like Stephen Duncombe's account of zines. For Rheingold, the Net offers the potential for both 'rational discourse' with, and 'emotional attachment' to, others; it is in this sense a fulfilling medium. But it can also, to Rheingold at least, seem strangely *small*: resembling a 'cosy little world', a kind of extended family, a 'virtual village' (Rheingold 1994: 2, 10): what is effectively a computer-age version of Tonnies's folksy *Gemeinschaft*. The metaphors Rheingold uses to describe community-based activity on the Net are in fact often organic – grassroots, plants, ecosystems. These meta-phors underwrite Rheingold's claim that communities online, their virtuality notwithstanding, are *authentic*, an adjective he often repeats. This means that identities online are not seen as fabricated or fantastic; and this in turn means that online communities are really not that different to face-to-face social groups after all. In fact, Rheingold often meets the people he has been talking to online and, although he registers the peculiar sensation of seeing strangers with whom he has been intimate in cyberspace, there appears to be nothing fake about any of them.

Rheingold often refers to his virtual communities as *subcultures* but, as I have often noted in this book, *communities* and *subcultures* are not quite the same things. Some commentators do, however, seem to slide with ease from the one to the other. Luther Elliott's article, 'Goa Trance and the Practice of Community in the Age of the Internet' (2004), turns to the 'Goa trance community', at goa@party.net, which has about 1000 members. Goa or psy (psychedelic) trance is a genre of music, derived from Detroit house and related electronic/techno but specifically associated with residual hippie populations in Goa, a western coastal state of India. It also draws on local sounds and instruments, as well as Hindu and Buddhist iconography and values – so it mixes cultural economies, local and global, South Asian and western. As they debate the nature of the genre and struggle over its role and position in the musical field (is it really 'underground', for example?), its followers, Elliott suggests, participate in the 'preservation of community' (Elliott 2004: 285). Paul Hodkinson's study, *Goth: Identity, Style and Subculture* (2002) includes an account of goth.net activity – the way the British goth subculture communicates with itself online – and similarly suggests that this works to provide goths with a 'strong sense of community'. 'Far from distracting them into other interests or dissolving the boundaries of their subculture', he writes, 'the internet usually functioned, in the same way as goth events, to concentrate their involvement in the goth scene and to reinforce the boundaries of the grouping' (Hodkinson 2002: 176). For the Goa trance community and the British goth subculture, the Net thus helps with communal self-definition and social and generic positioning. Net activity interacts here with real activity: these things are connected, just as they were for Rheingold, the one just as 'authentic' as the other. But as I have noted, the Internet can also seem to encourage fabricated or fantasy identities which work to 'obscure' the identities some participants have in real life. Sometimes, this has been understood positively and enthusiastically, as the means by which – as Tara McPherson puts it – 'new forms appear possible; recombination rules' (McPherson 2006: 205). The MIT clinical psychologist and sociologist Sherry Turkle responds in this way in her influential book, *Life on the Screen: Identity in the Age of the Internet* (1995), a kind of postmodern celebration of identity role play on the Net which saw the creation or invention of 'multiple selves' online as therapeutic and utopian. A more critical approach to what is sometimes called 'passing' online (we could even think of it as a kind of *slumming*) is offered in Lisa Nakamura's *Cybertypes: Race, Ethnicity, and Identity on the Internet* (2002); even so, she still understands the Internet primarily in terms of role playing, as 'a theater of sorts, a theater of performed identities' (Nakamura 2002: 31). But cyber-communities can often remain resolutely tied to real life and real agendas, as McPherson reminds us in a fascinating article about 'cyber-Confederacy' sites online (such as http://www.dixienet.org). Here, 'neo-Confederates' in the United States advance the cause of the Deep South and agitate for the protection of Southern heritages as if the American Civil War was just a kind of momentary aberration. Far from escaping into fabricated, rootless online identities, participants in this cybercommunity resolutely tie themselves to real life and a real location. 'If these virtual rebels are not willing to abandon the physical South in pursuit of virtual glory', McPherson remarks, 'neither do they seem very interested in experimenting with the hybridity of the self' (McPherson 2000: 129).

For David Bell, however, the word *community*, when it is used in relation to the Net, is now 'over-freighted'. In order to distinguish between *community* and *subculture* online, he suggests that *subculture* should be reserved for those groups of people who in fact use cyberspace and computer technologies in ways 'that subvert...dominant social norms or dominant formations' (Bell 2001: 107, 163). On the other hand, he also suggests that the Net *encourages* 'subcultural work' (184), which proliferates online in all sorts of guises: rather like John Irwin's account of the proliferation of scenes in the modern American city, described in Chapter 2. The Net is often taken as a tolerant, liberal realm, the host for all sorts of activity, real and fabricated, visible and sometimes very much 'obscured'. This means it is difficult to regulate and monitor, which for some can be a matter of deep concern. In his book, *The Empire of the Mind: Digital Piracy and the Anti-Capitalist Movement* (2005), Michael Strangelove has noted that – around the time Sherry Turkle was celebrating the possibility of inventing a number of fabricated identities online – others were calling for the Net to 'civilise' itself. Business and social policy interests were especially vocal here: for example, Steven E. Miller's *Civilizing Cyberspace: Policy, Power, and the Information Superhighway* (1995) or Joseph Migga Kizza's *Civilizing the Internet: Global Concerns and Efforts Toward Regulation* (1998). But Strangelove is especially critical of another kind of book, Michael Margolis and David Resnick's *Politics as Usual: The Cyberspace 'Revolution'* (2000), which had suggested that – far from radically altering daily life – the Internet has simply provided a new medium through which conventional and established patterns of social life are reproduced more or less without change: their so-called 'normalisation thesis'. Strangelove, by contrast, speaks up for the 'abnormalisation' of the Internet:

> I maintain that the Internet is developing in precisely the opposite direction to that foreseen by the normalization thesis – its content is beyond control, its audience is extraordinarily active, and its civic life is far from being depoliticised. This 'abnormalization' of the Internet holds dire consequences for an economy that is centred on the management of the consumer's mind through a controlled communication system.
>
> (Strangelove 2005: 96)

One of the ways abnormalisation plays itself out online is through 'culture jamming', a term sometimes attributed to the San Francisco-based experimental music group, Negativeland, who became notorious in the early 1990s for (among other things) their unauthorised use of the Irish rock group U2's name on a record that also parodied one of U2's songs – for which they were duly sued by Island Records for violating trademark and copyright laws. Culture jamming refers to a form of media 'sabotage' that works creatively to alter logos, advertisements, corporate images and so on, sometimes in order to reveal darker corporate realities (e.g. environmental damage, Third World exploitation), and sometimes simply to parody or debunk. Culture jammers (such as the Canadian-based Adbusters network) are often known as 'subvertisers' and they can be openly anti-corporate but they can also work to raise consumer consciousness. Culture jamming can flourish online, of course – as what Strangelove calls 'a direct attack on corporations' claims of sovereignty over the meaning of their intellectual property and cultural products' (105). One aspect of online culture jamming is the illegal use and adaptation/sabotage of corporate-owned material: songs, movies, logos, even web pages themselves. Strangelove calls this 'non-commercial cultural production' because it occurs 'outside of the marketplace' (135). But it also 'capitalizes on the freedom afforded by the Internet' (106), which remains for the most part a relatively unregulated media economy.

We might consider culture jammers – or just jammers – as in effect another kind of 'textual poacher' making 'improper' (or 'abnormal') use of media texts, rather like fans for Henry Jenkins. Strangelove, however, talks about 'digital piracy' in his book, and perhaps *piracy* is a more appropriate – or at least, more commonly used – metaphor here as jammers seize upon corporate cultural property and make it their own in a media realm that may continue to seem *not* to be 'civilised'. The philosopher and linguist Peter Ludlow, who had studied with Noam Chomsky at MIT, has edited a book strikingly titled, *Crypto Anarchy, Cyberstates and Pirate Utopias* (2001). The Net hosts a number of virtual places that experiment with self-governance: like the playful world of LambdaMOO, for example. These autonomous, remote realms can seem like 'islands in the Net', a phrase coined by another North American cyberpunk writer and Net activist, Bruce Sterling. Some of these realms are visible, some not; some are anti-commercial, while others are built around commercial exchange and transactions. Rather like the way fabricated identities online work to 'obscure' real selves, so the Net can work to 'encrypt' transactions to the extent that they are almost impossible to trace. Ludlow gives us a sense of what he means by 'pirate utopias' on the Net when he writes, 'as more and more of our transactions take place behind the veil of encryption, it becomes easier and easier for persons to undertake business relations that escape the purview of traditional nation states' (Ludlow 2001: 4–5). His book includes an important earlier essay by the countercultural American poet and political writer, Hakim Bey (Peter Lamborn Wilson), 'The Temporary Autonomous Zone', first published in 1994. Around the same time, in fact, Bey had also published a book titled *Pirate Utopias: Moorish Corsairs and European Renegades* (1996). The phrase *pirate utopia* refers to the old pirate havens along the Barbary Coast of northern Africa, bases out of which Muslim pirates conducted raids on European ships and coastal towns, capturing large numbers of Christian slaves intermittently over a period of several hundred years. These apparently impossible-to-regulate, hidden-away places provide inspiration for Bey's notion of 'temporary autonomous zones' or TAZs in the Net. He instils them with a kind of mystificatory romance, as fragile, momentary utopias that blossom into being and then – as regulatory economies start to intervene – disappear, leaving behind nothing but 'an empty husk' (Bey 2001: 405). In his later book, *T.A.Z.: The Temporary Autonomous Zone, Ontological Anarchy, Poetic Terrorism* (2004), Bey elaborates his romantic view of these online realms ('like some pagan power-spot at the junction of mysterious key-lines') and develops the notion of a 'shadowy sort of *counter*-Net' lurking pirate-like in cyberspace's high seas (Bey 2004: 107, 110). This 'counter-Net' makes 'clandestine illegal and rebellious use of the Web, including actual digital piracy and other forms of leeching off the Net itself'. It includes 'the marginal zine network, the BBS networks, pirated software, hacking, phone phreaking, [and has] some influence in print and radio and almost none in the big media' (107). Here, the pirate romance of the 'counter-Net' rests on a sense of its 'parasitical' relation to the larger Net economy – a familiar structural position for subcultures, as we have seen.

The heady romance of the 'counter-Net' – those online subcultures that invest in their obscurity, wilfully evading and eluding 'centralised' forms of regulation and control – can, however, have its darker side. Pornography can flourish in an unregulated Net economy, much as it did when censorship laws were liberalised in Restoration England. Online pornography networks are also notoriously difficult to trace, operating – as we saw with the early nineteenth-century pornographer, William Dugdale, in Chapter 4 – under 'a maze of aliases'. In his illuminating book, *Beyond Tolerance: Child Pornography on the Internet* (2003), Philip Jenkins examines perhaps the darkest and most 'obscure' of all the online porn networks. The child porn subculture, he writes, is 'a small but very active underworld' that has 'evolved some remarkably imaginative means for surviving any potential assault by law enforcement' (Jenkins 2003: 51). Working through closed and usually highly concealed electronic networks and newsgroups, online child porn networks are restricted 'to the hardest-core users, usually individuals with highly developed technical abilities' (76). Kenneth Lanning, a former FBI agent, was the first to offer a (rather basic) typology for paedophilic online participants, the 'situational offender' – a dabbler, 'less persistent and predictable' – and the 'preferential offender', who prefers child pornography over other kinds of porn (Lanning 1992: 13). We have here, in fact, a version of the subcultural distinction we saw in Chapter 3, between 'fluid' and 'persistent' affiliations. Jenkins mostly looks at preferential offenders, those in the subculture who are 'driven by the quest for new material, the urge to complete collections' (Jenkins 2003: 105): rather like the pornography collectors and bibliophiles of the nineteenth century. Online child porn networks certainly make 'clandestine illegal' use of the Net, in Bey's terms. But for Jenkins, the Net *already* has 'some degree of tolerance of illegality' (96), a characteristic that complicates the Net/counter-Net distinction Bey draws. 'In many ways', Jenkins writes, 'the seemingly aberrant world of child porn on the Net represents not a total break with approved mainstream ways and mores but their extension into illegality' (96). Bey's them-and-us binary can, however, be deployed by the subculture itself, as it complains about 'witch hunts' and casts Net regulators as the 'enemy' (97, 122). A prevailing view of child pornographers online is that they represent an 'escalation of pre-existing behaviours' (106), an example of *excessive* pornographic tastes: more deviant than they might otherwise be. But child porn networks also enable preferential offenders to feel that they are 'not alone' in their tastes and practices; deviant as they are, they may even feel as if they are 'supported by a new sense of community' (106).

Networks, trolls and hackers

The term *network* is commonly used to describe online interpersonal relations these days, becoming a kind of keyword for our modern, or postmodern, social condition. It signifies what is often taken as a seismic shift in contemporary social relations: the turn from *solidarity* (the old Durkheimian term, with its connotations of social stability and collective consciousness) to *liquidity* (after Zygmunt Bauman's notion of 'liquid modernity', connoting flow, ephemerality and complexity) – a version, more or less, of the distinction between the persistent and the fluid. Manuel Castells's *The Rise of the Network Society* (1996) is the definitive work here, the first in a trilogy of books he has written about the 'Information Age'. For Castells, the organisational, financial and managerial logics of advanced capitalism are now virtual, tied not to place but to space ('the space of flows'), manifesting themselves through communication/media networks that are expansive and flexible. Social movements, which might challenge the ways in which capitalism conducts its business, are networked, too: everybody is, in one way or another. Even so, Castells sees the dynamics of modern society in terms of what he calls 'the bipolar opposition of the Net and the Self', the difference between 'abstract, universal instrumentalism' and 'historically rooted, particularistic identities' (Castells 1996: 3). The Net signifies advanced capitalism's new, spatial, networked forms of organisation; the Self signifies those ways in which people reclaim or recover a more stable sense of identity (through religion, for example, or nationalism). This is not unlike the distinction between liquidity and solidarity, noted above. It might seem as if Castells's account has little to do directly with subcultures, not least because of its focus on networked systems of finance and work and new forms of managerialism: the sorts of things subcultural studies would usually associate with 'dominant culture'. But in fact, one could draw a number of useful connections, some broad, some specific. An example of the latter might come from Castells's account of a new kind of class distinction in advanced capitalism, which sees managerial elites at the top and the 'populace' below. Rather like Georg Simmel's aristocratic fashion trend-setters, discussed in Chapter 7, managerial elites must 'preserve their social cohesion' not least by *distinguishing* themselves from the ordinary people around them (446). To do this, they 'form their own society, and constitute symbolically-secluded communities, retrenched behind the very material barrier of real-estate pricing. They define their community as a spatially bound, inter-personally networked subculture...' (446). This seems to be the only time that Castells uses the term subculture in his book: to describe the 'secluded' social condition of managerial elites. A striking kind of inversion has taken place here, even though – as we have seen – subcultures themselves are indeed often elite and elitist in their social arrangements. For Castells, however, the social organisation of the new managerial elites in advanced capitalism can in fact be secluded enough to resemble something like the ghettoes usually associated with an underclass. 'At the limit', he writes, 'when social tensions rise, and cities decay, elites take refuge behind the walls of "gated communities", a major phenomenon around the world in the late 1990s, from southern California to Cairo and from San Paulo to Bogotá' (447).

Castells also has a sense of what Hakim Bey had called 'counter-Net' activity. He notes that the creation of the Internet was the result not just of managerial and technological elites – 'military strategy, big science cooperation, technological entrepreneurship' – but also of 'countercultural innovation' (45). A footnote here even refers to the contribution of '"hacker" culture' to the Internet. In a later book, *The Internet Galaxy: Reflections on the Internet, Business, and Society* (2003), Castells in fact sees 'hacker culture' as an important contributor to Internet culture generally speaking, especially given the latter's foundational ties to 'open source' software (Castells 2003: 38). A 'principle of freedom' (39) is installed right at the heart of the Internet – quite a different view to Bey's notion that the Net is at the mercy of centralised control and regulation. Open access, the freedom to innovate and 'modify', and even 'the inner joy of creation' (47): these are the qualities of 'hacker culture' for Castells. Hacker culture also shares 'a communal feeling...based on active membership in a community, which is structured around customs and principles of informal social organization' (47–48). We can note here how easily *network* slips back into *community* when things become 'informal'. Indeed, for Castells there can even be something 'primitive' about 'hacker culture', with – for example – the Linux community built around a set of 'tribal elders' (48) who own or maintain particular online projects. Even so, hacker culture is understood, or imagined, here in an important way, as a technological signifier of participatory democracy: 'a culture of technological creativity based on freedom, cooperation, reciprocity, and informality' (50).

Steven Levy had in fact popularised the image of the hacker along exactly these lines almost twenty years earlier in his book, *Hackers: Heroes of the Computer Revolution* (1984), where he outlined a 'hacker ethic' that emphasised the hacker's creative role online and included the tenets, 'All information should be free' and 'Mistrust authority and promote decentralisation' (Levy 1984: 21, 40–45). Levy helped to inaugurate a compelling romance around hacker culture (which Castells has inherited), casting the hacker in a benign and even utopian role: a friendlier sort of pirate, we might say, coming out of the computer labs at MIT, the participant in a subculture which soon developed its own shared argot or slang, detailed in the 'jargon file' begun by Raphael Finkel in 1975, expanded into a book, *The Hacker's Dictionary*, in 1983 and further revised by the 'open source' activist and gun lobbyist Eric S. Raymond as *The New Hacker's Dictionary* in 1991, published perhaps unsurprisingly by MIT Press. Andrew Ross has talked about the hacker as a 'popular folk hero persona', an image helped along by film and television representations of this figure, as well as by the near-future fantasies of the science fiction subgenre, cyberpunk. Hacker culture is not a 'dropout culture', he suggests. Quite the opposite: it 'celebrates high productivity, maverick forms of creative work energy, and an obsessive identification with on-line endurance...all qualities that are valorized by the entrepreneurial codes of silicon futurism' (Ross 1991: 121). Castells, too, had tied the hacker to entrepreneurialism and work ('maverick' as this may be), features that compromise claims about the hacker's countercultural identity – although it is not uncommon to see hackers described in terms of 'fun' and 'play' as well. On the other hand, hackers have also been cast as 'folk devils' and have often been criminalised. To give an example that occurred as I wrote this chapter: young Italian members of the hacker group Hi-tech Hate, who penetrated Pentagon, NASA and a range of other official sites across over sixty countries, were given jail sentences by an Italian court in July 2006. In his book *Hacker Culture* (2002), Douglas Thomas comments on the moral panic over hackers, as 'cybervandals', 'technodelinquents', and so on (Thomas 2002: 205–06). But he also documents some actual cases which saw hackers successfully prosecuted: for example, the American *uberhacker*, Kevin D. Mitnick (197–205). He even gives an account of a 'gang war' – the 'Great Hacker War' – between two rival hacker groups, the older Legion of Doom (named after Lex Luthor's group of supervillains in the *Superman* animated series) and the younger, ethnically mixed Masters of Deception (205–12).

There are now a fair number of manuals written in order to help businesses, administrators and programmers increase security by protecting themselves from online 'intruders' – for example, Kris A. Jamsa and Lars

Klander's *Hacker Proof* (2002) – and regulation and security interests do constantly jostle with the 'hacker ethic' of open access. Bruce Sterling's famous book, *The Hacker Crackdown* (1992), was a sustained complaint about government regulatory control, and in keeping with that 'hacker ethic' it is now freely available online at http://www.mit.edu/hacker/hacker.html. As well as writing cyberpunk fiction, Sterling has been an active member of the Electronic Frontier Foundation (EFF), which was founded in 1990 by activists who met through the WELL, precisely to defend free speech online and 'digital rights'. The commitment to 'open access' and freedom from regulatory (usually, government) interference is what is often referred to in the United States as a *libertarian* (or, a 'civil libertarian') position. In some respects, there is nothing especially progressive about this: Eric S. Raymond's libertarianism allows him to speak up for open access on the one hand, and the right to carry a gun on the other. Chris Hables Gray has provided a rather scathing account of the pro-individualism and 'frantically pro-free market' ideologies of US libertarianism online in his book, *Cyborg Citizen* (2001: 49–52). But the most critical account of hacker libertarianism came a few years earlier in the American cinema studies scholar Vivian Sobchack's article, 'New Age Mutant Ninja Hackers: Reading *Mondo 2000*' (1993). *Mondo 2000* had been one of the hipper, postmodern magazines devoted to cyberspace, celebrating its countercultural potential and singing the praises of cyberpunk and hacker ethics and practices. For Sobchack, however, its prevailing mode is one of 'interactive autism', involving 'electronic, quasi-embodied forms of kinesis ("safe" travel without leaving your desk), interaction ("safe" sociality without having to reveal your identity or "true name"), and eroticism ("safe" sex without risking an exchange of bodily fluids)' (Sobchack 1993: 574). The hacker emerges here as a self-absorbed and partly deluded young, educated, white male (usually). The romance of the hacker – as 'maverick', 'swashbuckling' (574), etc. – also seems mostly to be self-generated, a libertarian fantasy projection which plays itself out in the 'remote' realms of online activity. Even so, that romance seems to rub off on to others. Andrew Ross's essay ends by calling for fellow cultural critics to turn 'our knowledge about technoculture into something like a hacker's knowledge...capable also of generating new popular romances around the alternative uses of human ingenuity' (Ross 1991: 132): taking a cyber-subculture as inspirational for humanities intellectuals broadly speaking. McKenzie Wark's delirious homage to the hacker, *A Hacker Manifesto* (2004), begins with a dedication to the postmodern novelist 'Kathy *King of the Pirates* Acker': reproducing the romantic hacker/pirate connection, even though he seems unaware of Hakim Bey's work. Although Castells had linked them, Wark distinguishes hackers from 'entrepreneurs', sealing the former off from advanced capitalism more or less altogether. His 'manifesto' transforms the hacker into an authentically subcultural type with whom

155

(much more so than Ross) he fundamentally identifies. Andrew Ross had rightly seen the hacker as celebrating 'high productivity'. For Wark, however, hackers are one of the 'productive *classes*'; as if they have a kind of class consciousness or solidarity in which he too, as another humanities intellectual, somehow seems to participate. 'We do not own what we produce', he asserts in a section numbered 004 (there are no page numbers in his book), giving a kind of romantic neo-Marxian spin to the hacker's 'open access' libertarianism. Solidarity is stretched here to the extent that Wark imagines the hacker empathetically connected even to 'the movement of the dispossessed of the underdeveloped world, under and over every border' (088). At the same time, hackers also stand for 'abundance and liberty' (046), two of the privileges one might instead more commonly associate with First World advanced capitalism.

These sorts of investments in the image or cultural logic of the hacker work to elevate him (since the image is usually male) into a narrative of potentially epic proportions, rather as Dick Hebdige had done with punk 25 years earlier. Indeed, Wark's account of the hacker has much in common with Hebdige's account of the punk: both are distinguished from 'dominant' values and practices ('To hack is to differ'), both are cast as singularly creative, both are contrasted with mass cultural production ('The hacker interest is not in mass representation'), an attempt is nevertheless made to tie both of them to ordinary people ('everyone hacks'), and so on. Some forms of hacking, however, are much *less* able to be imagined in epic terms. The Dutch cyberactivist and media advocate Geert Lovink has written about the Syndicate Network, a small e-community of media and art culture intellectuals committed to the no doubt honourable project of developing a 'borderless' 'Deep Europe'. But the site is 'trolled' by people spreading 'disinformation' and encouraging unrest, all of which – as Lovink rather melodramatically puts it – 'accelerates the collapse of hippie dreams of the Net as a utopian, parallel world' (Lovink 2006: 291). We can wonder about how nostalgic Lovink's investment in the Syndicate Network social movement might have been; but we might also wonder about the role of *trolling* here, and how it operates. A *troll* is generally taken to be someone who plays out a disruptive role online by intervening in newsgroups, discussion lists and so on: sometimes in order to attack or 'flame', sometimes to deceive (with 'disinformation', or 'misinformation'), sometimes to parody or outrage or merely to annoy. The term *troll* is derived from fishing terminology, meaning to dangle bait, to catch the fish that *take* the bait: rather like a contemporary version of Elizabethan cony-catching (literally, to catch a rabbit), discussed at the beginning of Chapter 1. Indeed, trollers may very well be an online example of a 'canting crew', practising a roguish form of deception on unsuspecting prey – and they might also invent a set of false identities (i.e. multiple usernames) to carry this out more effectively. An online forum called Slashdot, created in 1997 and now owned by the Open Source Technology Group, hosts its own trolling activity. Here, trolls unfold according to particular protocols and logics and have evolved into what is often a sophisticated and creative form of social (or perhaps anti-social) play. There is nothing epic about this; the trolling subculture at this site can in fact seem utterly trivial, self-absorbed and inwardly turned to the point of sheer self-indulgence. Michele Tepper has looked at an earlier example of trolling on the Usenet discussion group alt.folklore.urban, which is 'dedicated to debunking misinformation', focusing in particular on the content of various 'urban legends'. This group is 'intellectually predicated on scepticism and anxious to prove [its] cultural capital' (Tepper 1997: 43). New participants or 'newbies' are put to the test with postings that are intentionally wrong or misleading. 'The hoped-for response to a troll', Tepper writes,

> is an indignant correction. It is through such a correction that the complicated play of cultural capital that constitutes trolling begins. The corrector, being outside of the community in which trolling is practised, believes that he is proving his superiority to the troller by catching the troller's error, but he is in fact providing his inferior command of the codes of the local subculture in which trolling is practiced.
>
> (41)

Here, trolling is thus 'both a game and...a method of subcultural boundary demarcation' (40), an acting-out of what Sarah Thornton had called 'subcultural capital'. But the hierarchies at work here are finely distinguished: 'The reader that the troller is fishing for shares not only his assumption of the importance of knowledge and information capital, but his cultural referents as well' (43). Usenet has been around since 1980 and is a heavily used, public system, generally easy to access. It is, as Tepper notes, 'large and heterogeneous'; but subcultures *do* form here, framing and maintaining their exclusivity in a range of different ways (most obviously, through FAQs and user guidelines). Although it is absorbed in the particularities of its difference, the subcultural activity on alt.folklore.urban is not spectacular, nor deviant, nor especially nonconformist. Primarily informational, it is really just a minor example of what Andreas Wittel – combining Castells's 'network society' with the early sociology of Georg Simmel – has called 'network *sociality*', where the social bond is ephemeral, 'project by project', and generated around 'the exchange of data' (Wittel 2001: 51). It is only trolling that holds whatever identification it has as a subculture together, with that term's trace of a connotation that links it to other kinds of subculturally understood forms of play and deception – and 'boundary demarcation' –

elsewhere. At the close of this book, we can therefore perhaps consider once again the ways in which subcultures are lent significance, the weight of the narratives they are made to carry (some trivial, some not), the investment that has been made in them, by whom, and to what end.

Bibliography

Adams, James Eli (1995) *Dandies and Desert Saints: Styles of Victorian Masculinity*, Ithaca, NY: Cornell University Press.

Adorno, Theodor W. (2001) *The Culture Industry*, intro. J.M. Bernstein, London and New York: Routledge.

Ake, David (2002) *Jazz Cultures*, Berkeley: University of California Press.

Anderson, Nels (1923) *The Hobo: The Sociology of the Homeless Man*, Chicago and London: University of Chicago Press.

Anderson, Nels (1998) *On Hobos and Homelessness*, ed. and intro. by Raffaele Rauty, Chicago and London: University of Chicago Press.

Armstrong, Jayne (2004) 'Web Grrrls, Guerrilla Tactics: Young Feminisms on the Web', in David Gauntlett and Ross Horsley (eds), *Web Studies*, Oxford: Oxford University Press.

Arnold, David O. (1970) *Subcultures*, Berkeley: The Glendessary Press.

Ashe, Geoffrey (1974) *The Hell-Fire Clubs: A History of Anti-Morality*, Phoenix Mill, UK: Sutton Publishing, 2000.

Atkinson, Michael (2003) *Tattooed: the Sociogenesis of a Body Art*, Toronto: University of Toronto Press.

Atton, Chris (2002) *Alternative Media*, London and Thousand Oaks, CA: Sage Publications.

Baker, Houston A. (1993) *Black Studies, Rap and the Academy*, Chicago: University of Chicago Press.

Baker, Paul (2002) *Polari – The Lost Language of Gay Men*, London and New York: Routledge.

Baker, Sarah Louise (2004) 'Pop in(to) the Bedroom: Popular Music in Pre-Teen Girls' Bedroom Culture', *European Journal of Cultural Studies*, 7, 1: 75–93.

Baldwin, Guy (1991) 'A Second Coming Out', in Mark Thompson (ed.), *Leatherfolk: Radical Sex, People, Politics and Practice*, Boston: Alyson Publications, Inc.

Banes, Sally (1993) *Greenwich Village 1963: Avant-Garde Performance and the Effervescent Body*, London and Durham, NC: Duke University Press.

Baudelaire, Charles (1972) *Baudelaire: Selected Writings on Art and Artists*, trans. P.E. Charvet, Harmondsworth: Penguin Books.

Bean, Joseph W. (1994) *Leathersex: A Guide for the Curious Outsider and the Serious Player*, San Francisco: Deadalus Publishing Company.

Becker, Howard S. (1963) *Outsiders: Studies in the Sociology of Deviance*, New York: The Free Press, repr. 1973.

Becker, Howard S. (ed.) (1964) *The Other Side: Perspectives on Deviance*, New York: The Free Press.

Belgrad, Daniel (1998) *The Culture of Spontaneity: Improvisation and the Arts in Postwar America*, Chicago and London: University of Chicago Press.

Bell, David (2001) *An Introduction to Cybercultures*, London and New York: Routledge.

Bennett, Andy and Kahn-Harris, Keith (2004) *After Subculture: Critical Studies in Contemporary Youth Culture*, Houndmills: Macmillan.

Bergman, David (1993) *Camp Grounds: Style and Homosexuality*, Amherst, MA: University of Massachusetts Press.

Bey, Hakim (2001) 'Temporary Autonomous Zones', in Peter Ludlow (ed.), *Crypto Anarchy, Cyberstates, and Pirate Utopias*, Cambridge, MA: MIT Press.

Bey, Hakim (2004) *T.A.Z.: The Temporary Autonomous Zone, Ontological Anarchy, Poetic Terrorism*, New York: Automedia.

Blumer, Herbert (1969) *Symbolic Interaction: Perspective and Method*, Berkeley: University of California Press.

Boyd, Nan Alamilla (2003) *Wide-Open Town: A History of Queer San Francisco to 1965*, Berkeley: University of California Press.

Bradley, James (2000) 'Body Commodification? Class and Tattoos in Victorian Britain', in Jane Caplan (ed.), *Written on the Body: The Tattoo in European and American History*, London: Reaktion Books.

Braunstein, Peter (1998) 'The Last Days of Gay Disco: The Current Disco Revival Conceals its Homo Soul', *Village Voice*, 24–30 June: http://www.villagevoice.com/news/9826,braunstein,229,1.html.

Buckland, Fiona (2002) *Impossible Dance: Club Culture and Queer World-Making*, Middletown, CT: Wesleyan University Press.

Bury, Rhiannon (2005) *Cyberspaces of Their Own: Female Fandoms Online*, Witney: Peter Lang Ltd.

Cappetti, Carla (1993) *Writing Chicago: Modernism, Ethnography, and the Novel*, New York: Columbia University Press.

Carter, Sophie (2004) 'A Harlot's Progress: Constructing and Reading a Popular Narrative of Prostitution', *Representing Prostitution in 18th Century English Popular Print Culture*, Aldershot: Ashgate.

Castells, Manuel (1996) *The Rise of the Network Society*, Cambridge, MA and Oxford: Blackwell.

Castells, Manuel (2003) *The Internet Galaxy: Reflections on the Internet, Business, and Society*, Oxford: Oxford University Press.

Castronova, Edward (2005) *Synthetic Worlds: The Business and Culture of Online Games*, Chicago and London: University of Chicago Press.

Chamberland, Line (1993) 'Remembering Lesbian Bars – Montreal, 1955–1975', *Journal of Homosexuality*, 25, 3: 231–69.

Chaney, David (1996) *Lifestyle*, London and New York: Routledge.

Chaney, David (2004) 'Fragmented Culture and Subcultures', in Andy Bennett and Keith Kahn-Harris (eds), *After Subculture: Critical Studies in Contemporary Youth Culture*, Houndmills: Macmillan.

Chauncey, George (1994) *Gay New York: Gender, Urban Culture, and the Making of the Gay Male World, 1890–1940*, New York: Basic Books.

Chisholm, Dianne (2005) *Queer Constellations: Subcultural Space in the Wake of the City*, Minneapolis and London: University of Minnesota Press.

Choquette, Leslie (2001) 'Homosexuals in the City: Representations of Lesbian and Gay Space in Nineteenth-Century Paris', *Journal of Homosexuality*, 41, 3–4: 149–67.

Clark, Peter (2002) *British Clubs and Societies 1580–1800*, Oxford: Oxford University Press.

Clarke, Gary (1981) 'Defending Ski-Jumpers: A Critique of Theories of Youth Subcultures', in Ken Gelder (ed.), *The Subcultures Reader*, Second Edition, London and New York: Routledge, 2005.

Clarke, John (1993a) 'The Skinheads & The Magical Recovery of Community', in Stuart Hall and Tony Jefferson (eds), *Resistance Through Rituals*, London: Routledge.

Clarke, John (1993b) 'Style', in Stuart Hall and Tony Jefferson (eds), *Resistance Through Rituals*, London: Routledge.

Clarke, John, Hall, Stuart, Jefferson, Tony and Roberts, Brian (1993) 'Subcultures, Cultures and Class', in Stuart Hall and Tony Jefferson (eds), *Resistance Through Rituals*, London: Routledge.

Cohen, Albert K. (1955) *Delinquent Boys: The Culture of the Gang*, New York: The Free Press.

Cohen, Phil (1972) 'Subcultural Conflict and Working Class Community', *Working Papers in Cultural Studies*, No. 2, CCCS, University of Birmingham.

Cohen, Stanley (1972) *Folk Devils and Moral Panics: The Creation of the Mods and Rockers*, London: MacGibbon and Kee Ltd.

Cohen, Stanley (1980) 'Symbols of Trouble', *Folk Devils and Moral Panics: The Creation of the Mods and Rockers*, Second Edition, Oxford: Martin Robertson.

Coleman, Julie (2004a) *A History of Cant and Slang Dictionaries, 1567–1784*, Vol. I, Oxford: Oxford University Press.

Coleman, Julie (2004b) *A History of Cant and Slang Dictionaries, 1785–1858*, Vol. II, Oxford: Oxford University Press.

Connor, Steven (1989) *Postmodernist Culture*, Oxford: Basil Blackwell.

Corrigan, Paul (1993) 'Doing Nothing', in Stuart Hall and Tony Jefferson (eds), *Resistance Through Rituals*, London: Routledge.

Cosgrove, Stuart (1984) 'The Zoot-Suit and Style Warfare', *History Workshop Journal*, 18 (Autumn): 77–91.

Cowley, Malcolm (1934) *Exile's Return: A Literary Odyssey of the 1920's*, New York: The Viking Press, 1964.

Cressey, Paul G. (1932) *The Taxi-Dance Hall: A Sociological Study in Commercialised Recreation and City Life*, Chicago: University of Chicago Press.

Cross, Robert (2004) *Steven Berkoff and the Theatre of Self-Performance*, Manchester: Manchester University Press.

D'Emilio, John (1992) *Making Trouble: Essays on Gay History, Politics, and the University*, London and New York: Routledge.

D'Eramo, Marco (2002) *The Pig and the Skyscraper: Chicago: A History of Our Future*, trans. Graeme Thomson, London and New York: Verso.

Darnton, Robert (1982) *The Literary Underground of the Old Regime*, Cambridge, MA: Harvard University Press.

Darnton, Robert (1996) *The Forbidden Best-Sellers of Pre-Revolutionary France*, New York: W.W. Norton and Company.

Davis, J.C. (2002) *Fear, Myth and History: The Ranters and the Historians*, Cambridge: Cambridge University Press.

Decker, Jeffrey Louis (1994) 'The State of Rap: Time and Place in Hip-Hop Nationalism', in Tricia Rose and Andrew Ross (eds), *Microphone Fiends: Youth Music and Youth Culture*, London and New York: Routledge.

DeMello, Margo (2000) *Bodies of Inscription: A Cultural History of the Modern Tattoo Community*, Durham, NC and London: Duke University Press.

DeVeaux, Scott (1997) *The Birth of Bebop: A Social and Musical History*, Berkeley: University of California Press.

Dinerstein, Joel (2003) *Swinging the Machine: Modernity, Technology, and African American Culture Between the World Wars*, Amherst, MA: University of Massachusetts Press.

Dionne, Craig (1997) 'Playing the "Cony": Anonymity in Underworld Literature', *Genre*, XXX (Spring/Summer): 29–49.

Dionne, Craig (2004) 'Fashioning Outlaws: The Early Modern Rogue and Urban Culture', in Craig Dionne and Steve Mentz (eds), *Rogues of Early Modern English Culture*, Ann Arbor: University of Michigan Press.

Dionne, Craig and Mentz, Steve (eds) (2004) *Rogues of Early Modern English Culture*, Ann Arbor: University of Michigan Press.

Driscoll, Catherine (2002) *Girls: Feminine Adolescence in Popular Culture and Cultural Theory*, New York: Columbia University Press.

Duberman, Martin, Vicinus, Martha and Chauncey Jr, George (eds) (1989) *Hidden from History: Reclaiming the Gay and Lesbian Past*, New York: New American Library.

Duncombe, Stephen (1997) *Notes From Underground: Zines and the Politics of Alternative Culture*, London and New York: Verso.

Durkheim, Emile (1915) *The Elementary Forms of the Religious Life*, London: George Allen & Unwin Ltd, 1976.

During, Simon (ed.) (1993) *The Cultural Studies Reader*, London and New York: Routledge.

Dyer, Richard (1990) 'In Defense of Disco', in Simon Frith and Andrew Goodwin (eds), *On Record*, London and New York: Routledge.

Ehrenreich, Barbara, Hess, Elizabeth and Jacobs, Gloria (1992) 'Beatlemania: Girls Just Want to Have Fun', in Lisa A. Lewis (ed.) *The Adoring Audience: Fan Culture and Popular Media*, London and New York: Routledge.

Elliott, Luther (2004) 'Goa Trance and the Practice of Community in the Age of the Internet', *Television & New Media*, 5, 3 (August): 272–88.

Farrell, James J. (1997) *The Spirit of the Sixties: The Making of Postwar Radicalism*, London and New York: Routledge.

Fikentsche, Kai (2000) *'You Better Work!' Underground Dance Music in New York*, Middletown, CT: Wesleyan University Press.

Fine, Gary Alan (1983) *Shared Fantasy: Role-Playing Games as Social Worlds*, Chicago: University of Chicago Press.

Fleming, Juliet (2000) 'The Renaissance Tattoo', in Caplan, Jane (ed.), *Written on the Body: The Tattoo in European and American History*, London: Reaktion Books.

Forman, Murray (2000) '"Represent": Race, Space and Place in Rap Music', *Popular Music*, 19, 1: 65–90.

Forman, Murray (2002) *The 'Hood Comes First: Race, Space, and Place in Rap and Hip-Hop*, Middletown, CT: Wesleyan University Press.

Foucault, Michel (1984) *The History of Sexuality*, vol. 1, trans. Robert Hurley, London: Penguin.

Foucault, Michel (1986) 'Of Other Spaces', *Diacritics*, 16 (Spring): 22–27.

Franklin, Rosalind and O'Neill, Cynthia (2004) *When the Nightingale Sang*, Burgess Hill, UK: Meadow Books.

Frisby, David and Featherstone, Mike (eds) (1997) *Simmel on Culture: Selected Writings*, London: Sage.

Frith, Simon (1978) 'The Punk Bohemians', *New Society*, 43: 535–36.

Frith, Simon (2004) 'Afterword', in Andy Bennett and Keith Kahn-Harris (eds), *After Subculture: Critical Studies in Contemporary Youth Culture*, Houndmills: Macmillan.

Fyvel, T.R. (1961) *The Insecure Offenders: Rebellious Youth in the Welfare State*, London: Chatto and Windus.

Garelick, Rhonda K. (1998) *Rising Star: Dandyism, Gender, and Performance in the Fin De Siecle*, Princeton, NJ: Princeton University Press.

Garton, Stephen (2004) *Histories of Sexuality: Antiquity to Sexual Revolution*, London: Equinox Publishing Ltd.

Gates, Henry Louis (1988) *The Signifying Monkey: A Theory of Afro-American Literacy Criticism*, New York: Oxford.

George, Nelson (1999) *Hip Hop America*, Harmondsworth: Penguin Books.

Gerard, Charley (1998) *Jazz in Black and White: Race, Culture, and Identity in the Jazz Community*, Westport, CT and London: Praeger.

Gertzman, Jay A. (1999) *Bookleggers and Smuthounds: The Trade in Erotica, 1920–1940*, Philadelphia: University of Pennsylvania.

Gilfoyle, Timothy J. (2004) 'Street-Rats and Gutter-Snipes: Child Pickpockets and Street Culture in New York City, 1850–1900', *Journal of Social History*, 34 (Summer): 853–82.

Gilmartin, Katie (1996) 'We Weren't Bar People: Middle-Class Lesbian Identities and Cultural Spaces', *GLQ: A Journal of Lesbian and Gay Studies*, 3, 1: 1–51.

Gilroy, Paul (1987) *There Ain't No Black in the Union Jack*, London: Unwin Hyman.

Gilroy, Paul (1994) *The Black Atlantic: Modernity and Double Conciousness*, Cambridge, MA: Harvard University Press.

Gordon, Milton M. (1947) 'The Concept of a Sub-Culture and Its Application', *Social Forces*, 26: 40–42.

Gordon, Milton M. (1964) *Assimilation in American Life: The Role of Race, Religion and National Origins*, New York: Oxford University Press.

Gray, Chris Hables (2001) *Cyborg Citizen*, London and New York: Routledge.

Greenwood, Susan (2000) *Magic, Witchcraft and the Otherworld*, Oxford and New York: Berg.

Grose, Francis (1785) *A Classical Dictionary of the Vulgar Tongue*, London: Routledge & Kegan Paul, 1963.

Gucer, Kathryn (2000) '"Not Heretofore Extant in Print": Where the Mad Ranters Are', *Journal of the History of Ideas*, 61, 1: 75–95.

Guthrie, Neil (1996) '"No Truth or Very Little in the Whole Story"? – A Reassessment of the Mohock Scare of 1712', *Eighteenth-Century Life*, 20 (May): 33–56.

Halberstam, Judith (1998) *Female Masculinity*, Durham, NC and London: Duke University Press.

Hall, Stuart and Jefferson, Tony (eds) (1975) *Resistance Through Rituals: Youth Subcultures in Post-War Britain*, London: Routledge, 1993.

Hallam, Paul (1993) *The Book of Sodom*, London and New York: Verso.

Hankin, Kelly (2002) *The Girls in the Back Room: Looking at the Lesbian Bar*, Minneapolis: University of Minnesota Press.

Harris, Anita (2003) 'gURL Scenes and Grrrl Zines: The Regulation and Resistance of Girls in Late Modernity', *Feminist Review*, 75: 38–56.

Harris, Anita (2004) 'Jamming Girl Culture: Young Women and Consumer Citizenship', in Anita Harris (ed.), *All About the Girl: Culture, Power, and Identity*, New York and London: Routledge.

Harvey, Graham (ed.) (2003) *Shamanism: A Reader*, London and New York: Routledge.

Hawes, Clement (1996) *Mania and Literary Style: The Rhetoric of Enthusiasm from the Ranters to Christopher Smart*, Cambridge: Cambridge University Press.

Hazlitt, William (1827) 'The Dandy School', *The Complete Works of William Hazlitt*, vol. 20, London: Dent, 1934.

Heaney, Peter (ed.) (1995) *An Anthology of Eighteenth-Century Satire: Grub Street*, Lewiston, NY: The Edwin Mellor Press.

Hebdige, Dick (1979) *Subculture: The Meaning of Style*, London and New York: Methuen, 1988.

Hebdige, Dick (1993a) 'The Meaning of Mod', in Stuart Hall and Tony Jefferson (eds), *Resistance Through Rituals*, London: Routledge.

Hebdige, Dick (1993b) 'Reggae, Rastas & Rudies', in Stuart Hall and Tony Jefferson (eds), *Resistance Through Rituals*, London: Routledge.

Henderson, Tony (1999) *Disorderly Women in Eighteenth-Century London: Prostitution and Control in the Metropolis, 1730–1830*, London: Longman.

Hetherington, Kevin (2000) *New Age Travellers: Vanloads of Uproarious Humanity*, London: Cassell.

Hills, Matt (2002) *Fan Cultures*, London and New York: Routledge.

History Project, The (1998) *Improper Bostonians: Lesbian and Gay History from the Puritans to Playland*, Boston: Beacon Press.

Hodkinson, Paul (2002) *Goth: Identity, Style and Subculture*, Oxford and New York: Berg.

Hoggart, Richard (1957) *The Uses of Literacy*, Harmondsworth: Penguin Books, 1990.

Howard, John Robert (1969) 'The Flowering of the Hippie Movement', *Annals of the American Academy of Political & Social Science*, 382 (March): 43–55.

Hughes, Walter (1994) 'In the Empire of the Beat: Discipline and Disco', in Andrew Ross and Tricia Rose (eds), *Microphone Fiends: Youth Music and Youth Culture*, London and New York: Routledge.

Hume, Lynne (1997) *Witchcraft and Paganism in Australia*, Melbourne: Melbourne University Press.

Huq, Rupa (2006) *Beyond Subculture: Pop, Youth and Identity in a Postcolonial World*, London and New York: Routledge.

Hutton, Ronald (1999) *The Triumph of the Moon: A History of Modern Pagan Witchcraft*, Oxford: Oxford University Press.

Ingrassia, Catherine (1998) *Authorship, Commerce, and Gender in Early Eighteenth-Century England: A Culture of Paper Credit*, Cambridge: Cambridge University Press.

Irwin, John (1977) *Scenes*, London and Beverly Hills: Sage Publications.

Jankowski, Martin Sanchez (1991) *Islands in the Street: Gangs and American Urban Society*, Berkeley: University of California Press.

Jenkins, Henry (1992) *Textual Poachers: Television Fans and Participatory Culture*, New York and London: Routledge.

Jenkins, Philip (2003) *Beyond Tolerance: Child Pornography on the Internet*, New York: New York University Press.

Jenks, Chris (2005) *Subculture: The Fragmentation of the Social*, London: Sage Publications.

Jones, LeRoi (1963) *Blues People: Negro Music in White America*, Westport, CT: Greenwood Press.

Joseph, Miranda (2002) *Against the Romance of the Community*, Minneapolis: University of Minnesota Press.

Jowett, Garth S., Jarvie, Ian C. and Fuller, Kathryn H. (1996) *Children and the Movies: Media Influence and the Payne Fund Controversy*, Cambridge: Cambridge University Press.

Judges, A.V. (ed.) (1930) *The Elizabethan Underworld*, London: Routledge & Kegan Paul Ltd, repr. 1965.

Kahn-Harris, Keith (2004) 'Unspectacular Subculture? Transgression and Mundanity in the Global Extreme Metal Scene', in Andy Bennett and Keith Kahn-Harris (eds), *After Subculture: Critical Studies in Contemporary Youth Culture*, Houndmills: Macmillan.

Kendrick, Walter (1987) *The Secret Museum: Pornography in Modern Culture*, Berkeley: University of California Press.

Kennedy, Elizabeth Lapovsky and Davis, Madeline D. (1993) *Boots of Leather, Slippers of Gold: The History of a Lesbian Community*, New York: Routledge.

Kershaw, Alister (1991) *Heydays: Memories and Glimpses of Melbourne's Bohemia 1937–47*, Sydney: Angus & Robertson.

Keyes, Cheryl L. (2002) *Rap Music and Street Consciousness*, Champaign, IL: University of Illinois Press.

King, Noel (1991) 'Mapping Hebdige', *Southern Review*, 2, 4: 80–91.

Kinsella, Sharon (2000) *Adult Manga: Culture and Power in Contemporary Japanese Society*, Honolulu: University of Hawai'i Press.

Klesse, Christian (1999) '"Modern Primitivism": Non-Mainstream Body-Modification and Racialized Representation', in Mike Featherstone (ed.), *Body Modification*, London: Sage Publications.

Koven, Seth (2004) *Slumming: Sexual and Social Politics in Victorian London*, Princeton and Oxford: Princeton University Press.

Lane, Christopher (1994) 'The Drama of the Imposter: Dandyism and Its Double', *Cultural Critique*, 28: 29–52.

Lanning, Kenneth (1992) *Child Molesters: A Behavioral Analysis*, Washington: National Center for Missing and Exploited Children.

Leonard, Marion (1998) 'Paper Planes: Travelling the New Grrrl Geographies', in Tracey Skelton and Gill Valentine (eds), *Cool Places: Geographies of Youth Cultures*, London and New York: Routledge.

Leupp, Gary P. (1999) 'The Five Men of Naniwa: Gang Violence and Popular Culture in Genroku Osaka', in James L. McClain and Osamu Wakita (eds), *Osaka: The Merchants' Capital of Early Modern Japan*, Ithaca, NY: Cornell University Press.

Lévy, Pierre (2001) *Cyberculture*, London and New York: Routledge.

Levy, Steven (1984) *Hackers: Heroes of the Computer Revolution*, Harmondsworth: Penguin Books.

Lipsitz, George (1994) *Rainbow at Midnight: Labor and Culture in the 1940s*, Champaign, IL: University of Illinois Press

Lopes, Paul (2002) *The Rise of a Jazz Art World*, Cambridge: Cambridge University Press.

Lovink, Geert (2006) 'Deep Europe: A History of the Syndicate Network', in Wendy Hui Kyong Chun and Thomas Keenan (eds), *New Media, Old Media: A History and Theory Reader*, London and New York: Routledge.

Low, Donald A. (1982) *Thieves' Kitchen: The Regency Underworld*, London: J.M. Dent & Sons Ltd.

Ludlow, Peter (ed.) (2001) *Crypto Anarchy, Cyberstates, and Pirate Utopias*, Cambridge, MA: MIT Press.

MacDonald, Nancy (2001) *The Graffiti Subculture: Youth, Masculinity and Identity in London and New York*, Houndmills: Palgrave Macmillan.

Maffesoli, Michel (1996) *The Time of the Tribes: The Decline of Individualism in Mass Society*, trans. Don Smith, London: Sage Publications.

Mailer, Norman (1959) *Advertisements for Myself*, New York: Putman's.

Mains, Geoff (2002) *Urban Aboriginals: A Celebration of Leather Sexuality*, Los Angeles: Daedalus Publishing.

Malbon, Ben (2001) *Clubbing: Dancing, Ecstasy and Vitality*, London and New York: Routledge.

Marcus, Greil (1989) *Lipstick Traces: A Secret History of the Twentieth Century*, Cambridge, MA: Harvard University Press.

Marshall, P. David (2004) 'Playing Game Cultures: Electronic Games', in *New Media Cultures*, London: Arnold.

Maurer, David W. (1981) *Language of the Underworld*, ed. Allan W. Futrell and Charles B. Wordell, Lexington: University Press of Kentucky.

Maxwell, Ian (2001) 'Hip-Hop Down Under Comin' Up', in Tony Mitchell (ed.), *Global Noise: Rap and Hip-Hop Outside the USA*, Middletown, CT: Wesleyan University Press.

Maxwell, Ian (2003) *Phat Beats, Dope Rhymes*, Middletown, CT: Wesleyan University Press.

Mayhew, Henry (1861–62) *London Labour and the London Poor: The Classical Study of the Culture of Poverty and the Criminal Classes in the 19th Century*, Vol. 1, New York: Dover Publications Inc, 1968.

Mazon, Mauricio (2002) *The Zoot-Suit Riots: The Psychology of Symbolic Annihilation*, Austin, TX: University of Texas Press.

McBee, Randy D. (2000) *Dance Hall Days: Intimacy and Leisure among Working-Class Immigrants in the United States*, New York and London: New York University Press.

McCalman, Ian (1988) *Radical Underworld: Prophets, Revolutionaries, and Pornographers in London, 1795–1840*, Oxford: Oxford University Press.

McDowell, Nicholas (2004) *The English Radical Imagination: Culture, Religion, and Revolution, 1630–1660*, Oxford: Oxford University Press.

McDowell, Paula (1998) *The Women of Grub Street: Press, Politics, and Gender in the London Literary Marketplace, 1678–1730*, Oxford: Clarendon Press.

McKay, George (1996) *Senseless Acts of Beauty: Cultures of Resistance Since the 1960s*, London: Verso.

McMullan, John L. (1984) *The Canting Crew: London's Criminal Underworld 1550–1700*, New Brunswick, NJ: Rutgers University Press.

McPherson, Tara (2000) 'I'll Take My Stand in Dixie-Net: White Guys, the South, and Cyberspace', in Beth E. Kolko, Lisa Nakamura and Gilbert B. Rodman (eds), *Race in Cyberspace*, New York and London: Routledge.

McPherson, Tara (2006) 'Reload: Liveness, Mobility, and the Web', in Wendy Hui Kyong Chun and Thomas Keenan (eds), *New Media Old Media: A History and Theory Reader*, London and New York: Routledge.

McRobbie, Angela (1989) 'Second-Hand Dresses and the Role of the Ragmarket', in Angela McRobbie (ed.), *Zoot Suits and Second-Hand Dresses: An Anthology of Fashion and Music*, Basingstoke: Macmillan.

McRobbie, Angela (1991) 'Settling Accounts with Subcultures', in *Feminism and Youth Culture: From Jackie to Just Seventeen*, Houndmills: Macmillan.

McRobbie, Angela (1994) *Postmodernism and Popular Culture*, London and New York: Routledge.

McRobbie, Angela and Garber, Jenny (1991) 'Girls and Subcultures', in Angela McRobbie, *Feminism and Youth Culture: From Jackie to Just Seventeen*, Houndmills: Macmillan.

McWilliams, Carey (2001) *Fool's Paradise: A Carey McWilliams Reader*, Santa Clara, CA: Santa Clara University Press.

Melechi, Antonio (1993) 'The Ecstasy of Disappearance', in Steve Redhead (ed.), *Rave Off: Politics and Deviance in Contemporary Youth Culture*, Aldershot: Avebury.

Mellon, John Tytell (1999) *Paradise Outlaws: Remembering the Beats*, New York: William Morrow and Company, Inc.

Merriam, Alan P. and Mack, Raymond W. (1960) 'The Jazz Community', *Social Forces*, 38: 211–22.

Merton, Robert (1938) 'Social Structure and Anomie', *American Sociological Review*, III (October): 672–82.

Miller, Timothy (1991) *The Hippies and American Values*, Knoxville: The University of Tennessee Press.

Minehan, Thomas (1934) *Boy and Girl Tramps of America*, New York: Grosset & Dunlop.

Mitchell, Tony (1995) 'Questions of Style: Notes on Italian Hip Hop', *Popular Music*, 14, 3: 333–47.

Mitchell, Tony (1999) 'Another Root: Australian Hip Hop as a "Glocal" Subculture', *UTS Review*, 5, 1: 126–41.

Mitchell, Tony (2003) 'Doin' Damage in My Native Language: The Use of "Resistance Vernaculars" in Hip Hop in France, Italy and Aotearoa/New Zealand', in Harris M. Berger and Michael Thomas Carroll (eds), *Global Pop, Local Language*, Jackson: University Press of Mississippi.

Moers, Ellen (1978) *The Dandy: Brummell to Beerbohm*, Lincoln, NB and London: University of Nebraska Press.

Mowry, Melissa M. (2004) *The Bawdy Politics in Stuart England, 1660–1714*, Aldershot: Ashgate.

Muggleton, David (2000) *Inside Subculture: The Postmodern Meaning of Style*, Oxford and New York: Berg.

Muggleton, David and Weinzierl, Rupert (eds) (2003) *The Post-subcultures Reader*, Oxford and New York: Berg.

Mumford, Kevin J. (1997) *Interzones: Black/White Sex Districts in Chicago and New York in the Early Twentieth Century*, New York: Columbia University Press.

Nakamura, Lisa (2002) *Cybertypes: Race, Ethnicity, and Identity on the Internet*, London and New York: Routledge.

Neal, Mark Anthony (1999) *What the Music Said: Black Popular Music and Black Public Culture*, New York and London: Routledge.

Nealon, Christopher (2001) *Foundlings: Lesbian and Gay Historical Emotion Before Stonewall*, Durham, NC and London: Duke University Press.

Negus, Keith (1999) 'The Business of Rap', in *Music Genres and Corporate Cultures*, London and New York: Routledge.

Newton, Esther (1972) *Mother Camp: Female Impersonators in America*, Englewood Cliffs, NJ: Prentice-Hall.

Newton, Esther (2000) *Margaret Mead Made Me Gay*, Durham, NC and London: Duke University Press.

Norman, Stuart (1991) 'I am the Leatherfairie Shaman', in Mark Thompson (ed.), *Leatherfolk: Radical Sex, People, Politics and Practice*, Boston: Alyson Publications, Inc.

Norton, Rictor (1992) *Mother Clap's Molly House: The Gay Subculture in England 1700–1830*, London: GMP Publishers, Ltd.

Ogborn, Miles (1998) 'Locating the Macaroni: Luxury, Sexuality and Vision in Vauxhall Gardens', *Textual Practice*, 11, 3: 445–62.

Pagan, Eduardo Obregon (2003) *Murder at the Sleepy Lagoon: Zoot Suits, Race, and Riot in Wartime L.A.*, Chapel Hill and London: University of North Carolina Press.

Park, Robert E. (1925) 'The City: Suggestions for the Investigation of Human Behaviour in the Urban Environment', in Robert E. Park, Ernest W. Burgess and Roderick D. McKenzie (eds), *The City*, Chicago: University of Chicago Press.

Park, Robert E. (1950) *Race and Culture*, Glencoe, IL: The Free Press.

Park, Robert E. and Miller, Herbert A. (1921) *Old World Traits Transplanted*, New York: Arno Press and The New York Times, 1969.

Parry, Albert (1933) *Tattoo: Secrets of a Strange Art*, Mineola, NY: Dover Publications, Inc, 2006.

Penley, Constance (1991) 'Brownian Motion: Women, Tactics, and Technology', in Andrew Ross and Constance Penley (eds), *Technoculture*, Minneapolis and Oxford: University of Minnesota Press.

Perera, Rushie (2006) 'Ever Winding Road', *Acclaim Magazine*, 2 (March–May): 61–63.

Peretti, Burton W. (1994) *The Creation of Jazz: Music, Race & Culture in Urban America*, Urbana, IL: University of Illinois Press.

Perkins, Roberta (1983) *The 'Drag Queen' Scene: Transsexuals in Kings Cross, Sydney*, Sydney: Allen & Unwin.

Perry, Imani (2004) *Prophets of the Hood: Politics and Poetics in Hip Hop*, Durham, NC: Duke University Press.

Polsky, Ned (1967) *Hustlers, Beats, and Others*, Harmondsworth: Penguin Books.

Polsky, Ned (1971) 'The Village Beat Scene: Summer 1960', *Hustlers, Beats and Others*, Harmondsworth: Penguin Books.

Porter, Eric (2002) *What is This Thing Called Jazz? African American Musicians as Artists, Critics, and Activists*, Berkeley: University of California Press.

Quinn, Eithne (2005) 'Gangsta Rap: Black Cultural Studies and the Politics of Representation', in *Nuthin' But a 'G' Thang: The Culture and Commerce of Gangsta Rap*, New York: Columbia University Press.

Raskin, Jonah (2005) *American Scream: Allen Ginsberg's Howl and the Making of the Beat Generation*, Berkeley: University of California Press.

Rediker, Marcus (1989) *Between the Devil and the Deep Blue Sea: Merchant Seaman, Pirates, and the Anglo-American Maritime World 1700–1750*, Cambridge: Cambridge University Press.

Reichard, William (2003) *The Evening Crowd at Kirmser's: A Gay Life in the 1940s*, Minneapolis: University of Minnesota Press.

Reynolds, Simon (1998a) *Generation Ecstasy*, New York: Routledge.

Reynolds, Simon (1998b) *Energy Flash*, London: Picador.

Rheingold, Howard (1994) *The Virtual Community: Finding Connection in a Computerized World*, London: Minerva.

Rogers, Pat (1972) *Grub Street: Studies in a Subculture*, London: Methuen.

Rose, Lionel (1988) *Rogues and Vagabonds: Vagrant Underworlds in Britain 1815–1985*, London and New York: Routledge.

Rose, Tricia (1994) 'A Style Nobody Can Deal With: Politics, Style and the Postindustrial City in Hip Hop', in Andrew Ross and Tricia Rose (eds), *Microphone Fiends: Youth Music & Youth Culture*, London and New York: Routledge.

Ross, Andrew (1991) 'Hacking Away at the Counterculture', in Andrew Ross and Constance Penley (eds), *Technoculture*, Minneapolis and Oxford: University of Minnesota Press.

Roszak, Theodore (1970) *The Making of a Counter Culture: Reflections on the Technocratic Society and Its Youthful Opposition*, London: Faber and Faber.

Rubin, Gayle (1991) 'The Catacombs: A Temple of the Butthole', in Mark Thompson (ed.), *Leatherfolk: Radical Sex, People, Politics and Practice*, Boston, MA: Alyson Publications, Inc.

Rubin, Gayle (2004) 'Samois', *Leather Times: News from the Leather Archives and Museum* (Spring): http://66.102.7.104/search?q=cache:wdwgYf_KbB8J:www.leatherarchives.org/resources/issue21.pdf+leather+resources+rubin&hl=en&gl=au&ct=clnk&cd=5.

Salgado, Gamini (1972) *Cony-Catchers and Bawdy Baskets*, Harmondsworth: Penguin Books.

Salgado, Gamini (1977) *The Elizabethan Underworld*, London: J.M. Dent & Sons Ltd.

Sanders, Clinton R. (1989) *Customizing the Body: The Art and Culture of Tattooing*, Philadelphia: Temple University Press.

Sandvoss, Cornel (2005) *Fans: The Mirror of Consumption*, Cambridge: Polity.

Schlosser, Eric (2004) *Reefer Madness: Sex, Drugs, and Cheap Labor in the American Black Market*, Boston: Houghton Mifflin.

Senelick, Laurence (2000) *The Changing Room: Sex, Drag and Theatre*, London and New York: Routledge.

Shesgreen, Sean (2002) *Images of the Outcast: The Urban Poor in the Cries of London*, Manchester: Manchester University Press.

Sibalis, Michael (2001) 'The Palais-Royal and the Homosexual Subculture of Nineteenth-Century Paris, *Journal of Homosexuality*, 41, 3–4: 117–29.

Sidran, Ben (1981) *Black Talk*, New York: DaCapo Press.

Sigel, Lisa Z. (2002) *Governing Pleasures: Pornography and Social Change in England, 1815–1914*, New Brunswick: Rutgers University Press.

Smallman, Jake and Nyman, Carl (2005) *Stencil Graffiti Capital: Melbourne*, New York: Mark Batty Publisher.

Sobchack, Vivian (1993) 'New Age Mutant Ninja Hackers: Reading *Mondo 2000*', *South Atlantic Quarterly*, 92, 4 (Fall): 569–84.

Sontag, Susan (1964) 'Notes on "Camp"', in *Against Interpretation and Other Essays*, New York: Picador.

Sparrow, Jeff and Sparrow, Jill (2004) *Radical Melbourne 2: The Enemy Within*, Melbourne: The Vulgar Press.

Spates, James L. and Levin, Jack (1972) 'Beats, Hippies, the Hip Generation, and the American Middle Class: An Analysis of Values', *International Social Science Journal*, 24, 2: 326–53.

Spears, Timothy B. (2005) *Chicago Dreaming: Midwesterners and the City, 1871–1919*, Chicago: University of Chicago Press.

Speck, Ross V. *et al.* (1974) *The New Families:Youth, Communes, and the Politics of Drugs*, London: Tavistock Publications.

Statt, Daniel (1995) 'The Case of the Mohocks: Rake Violence in Augustan London', *Social History*, 20, 2 (May): 179–99.

Strangelove, Michael (2005) *The Empire of the Mind: Digital Piracy and the Anti-Capitalist Movement*, Toronto: University of Toronto Press.

Straus, Ralph (1927) *The Unspeakable Curll*, London: Chapman and Hall.

Suttles, Gerald D. (1968) *The Social Order of the Slum: Ethnicity and Territory in the Inner City*, Chicago: University of Chicago Press.

Tepper, Michele (1997) 'Usenet Communities and the Cultural Politics of Information', in David Porter (ed.), *Internet Culture*, London and New York: Routledge.

Thomas, Douglas (2002) *Hacker Culture*, Minneapolis and London: University of Minnesota Press.

Thomas, Nicholas (2005) 'Introduction', in Nicholas Thomas, Anna Cole and Bronwen Douglas (eds), *Tattoo: Bodies, Art and Exchange in the Pacific and the West*, London: Reaktion Books.

Thompson, E.P. (1963) *The Making of the EnglishWorking Class*, Harmondsworth: Penguin Books, 1986.

Thompson, E.P. andYeo, Eileen (1971) *The Unknown Mayhew: Selections from the Morning Chronicle, 1849–1851*, NewYork: Pantheon.

Thompson, Mark (ed.) (1991) *Leatherfolk: Radical Sex, People, Politics and Practice*, Boston: Alyson Publications, Inc.

Thornton, Sarah (1995) *Club Cultures: Music, Media and Subcultural Capital*, Cambridge: Polity Press.

Thorpe, Rochella (1997) 'The Changing Face of Lesbian Bars in Detroit, 1938–1965', in Brett Beemyn (ed.), *Creating a Place for Ourselves: Lesbian, Gay, and Bisexual Community Histories*, NewYork: Routledge.

Thrasher, Frederic M. (1927) *The Gang: A Study of 1,313 Gangs in Chicago*, Chicago: University of Chicago Press.

Tobin, Joseph (1998) 'An American Otaku (or, A Boy's Virtual Life on the Net)', in Julian Sefton-Green (ed.), *Digital Diversions:Youth Culture in the Age of Multimedia*, London: UCL Press.

Tolson, Andrew (1990) 'Social Surveillance and Subjectification: The Emergence of "Subculture" in the Work of Henry Mayhew', *Cultural Studies*, 4, 2: 113–27.

Tonnies, Ferdinand (1955) *Community and Association (Gemeinschaft und Gesellschaft)*, trans. Charles P. Loomis, London: Routledge and Kegan Paul.

Troyer, Howard William (1946) *Ned Ward of Grub Street: A Study of Sub-Literary London in the Eighteenth Century*, New York: Barnes and Noble.

Trumbach, Randolph (1998) *Sex and the Gender Revolution: Heterosexuality and the Third Gender in Enlightenment London*, Chicago: University of Chicago Press.

Tucker, Robert C. (ed.) (1972) *The Marx-Engels Reader*, New York: W.W. Norton.

Turkle, Sherry (1995) *Life on the Screen: Identity in the Age of the Internet*, New York: Simon & Schuster.

Turner, Bryan S. (1999) 'The Possibility of Primitiveness: Towards a Sociology of Body Marks in Cool Societies', in Mike Featherstone (ed.), *Body Modification*, London: Sage Publications.

Turner, Mark W. (2003) *Backward Glances: Cruising the Queer Streets of New York and London*, London: Reaktion Books Ltd.

Turner, Victor (1969) *The Ritual Process: Structure and Anti-Structure*, New York: Aldine de Gruyter, 1995.

Vale, V. and Juno, Andrea (1989) *RE/Search #12: Modern Primitives*, San Francisco: Re/Search Publications.

Volcano, Del LaGrace and Halberstam, Judith 'Jack' (1999) *The Drag King Book*, London: Serpent's Tail.

Walkowitz, Judith R. (1992) *City of Dreadful Delight: Narratives of Sexual Danger in Late-Victorian London*, London: Virago.

Wallis, Robert J. (2003) *Shamans/Neo-Shamans: Ecstasy, Alternative Archaeologies and Contemporary Pagans*, London and New York: Routledge.

Wark, McKenzie (2004) *A Hacker Manifesto*, Cambridge, MA: Harvard University Press.

Watts, Jerry Gafio (2001) *Amiri Baraka: The Politics and Arts of a Black Intellectual*, New York: NYU Press.

Weber, Harold (1984) 'Rakes, Rogues, and the Empire of Misrule', *Huntington Library Review*, 47, 1 (Winter): 13–32.

Whang, Leo Sang-Min (2003) 'Online Game Dynamics in Korean Society: Experiences and Lifestyles in the Online Game World', *Korea Journal*, 43, 3 (Fall): 7–34.

White, Shane and White, Graham (1998) *Stylin': African American Expressive Culture from its Beginnings to the Zoot Suit*, Ithaca, NY and London: Cornell University Press.

Williams, Raymond (1958) *Culture and Society, 1780–1950*, Harmondsworth: Penguin Books and Chatto & Windus, 1984.

Williamson, Milly (2005) *The Lure of the Vampire: Gender, Fiction and Fandom from Bram Stoker to Buffy*, London: Wallflower Press.

Willis, Paul (1978) *Profane Culture*, London: Routledge & Kegan Paul.

Willis, Susan (1993) 'Hardcore: Subculture American Style', *Critical Inquiry*, 19 (Winter): 365–83.

Wilson, Kathleen (1995) *The Sense of the People: Politics, Culture and Imperialism in England, 1715–1785*, Cambridge: Cambridge University Press.

Wittel, Andreas (2001) 'Toward a Network Sociality', *Theory, Culture & Society*, 18, 6: 51–76.

Wulff, Helena (1988) *Twenty Girls: Growing Up, Ethnicity and Excitement in a South London Microculture*, Stockholm: Stockholm Studies in Social Anthropology.

Yablonsky, Lewis (1968) *The Hippie Trip*, New York: Pegasus.

Index

2 Live Crew 116, 117, 119

Aboriginals, Australian 121, 134
acculturation 40
Acker, Kathy 155
Adams, James Eli 124–5
Adbusters 150
Addison, Joseph 49
Adorno, Theordor 86, 97
adventure fiction 36
aesthetics 90, 93, 95, 97, 101, 112
African-Americans 28; and zoot suits
    126, 127; as hobos 34; in jazz 77–8,
    79, 81–2, 92, 107–21
Ake, David 110
alienation: bebop and 111–12, 113,
    138, 147; in the city 19, 26, 30, 39,
    44, 46: of modern society 4, 25, 26,
    147; subcultural responses to 4, 41,
    56, 62, 88, 138, 147
alt.folklore.urban 157
Althusser, Louis 89, 93
amateur media 99, 145–6
Amateur Press Association 146
Anderson, Benedict 45
Anderson, Nels 18, 33–4, 146
anomie 41, 46

anthropology: emergence of 11, 12;
    in Chicago School 27, 28, 42; in
    narratives about subcultures 26; in
    studies of tattoos 129, 130; in study
    of contemporary shamanism 137;
    of Levi-Strauss 90, 94; of Victor
    Turner 23, 24; relationship with
    sociology 18, 26, 56, 88, 121, 130,
    134, 137
anti-commercial 113–14, 120, 121,
    150
argot 14, 16, 17, 142, 154; *see also* flash,
    jargon, slang
aristocracy, the 7, 50, 72, 123, 127, 129,
    130, 153; *see also* upper class, the
Arnold, David O. 44
Ashe, Geoffrey 48–9
assimilation 40
Atkinson, Michael 129, 132
Atton, Chris 145
Austen, Jane 9
Australian hip hop 120–1
authenticity 61, 64, 121, 129–34, 147;
    and inauthenticity 58, 61, 64, 134;
    for Tonnies 25, 26; in drag 58–9
avant garde, the 93, 94, 97
Awdeley, John 5

Related titles from Routledge

BEYOND SUBCULTURE
Pop, Youth and Identity in a Postcolonial World

Rupa Huq

'An extremely accessible, comprehensive and, above all, enjoyable book. Huq's grasp of youth culture studies is impeccable as is her knowledge of the myriad of musics and styles that characterise youth culture at the beginning of the twenty-first century. A highly valuable resource for both students and experienced academic researchers.'

Andy Bennett, Professor in Communications and Popular Culture, Brock University

'This book extends the study of music subcultures into the 21st-century globalised world... ideal for students.'

Mica Nava, Professor of Cultural Studies, University of East London

'Beyond Subculture reinvigorates youth culture studies at just the right time. After the postmodern turn of the 1990s threatened to bury youth culture, and its theorists, forever, there are new, young writers shouting from the streets and the lecture theatres. Just as pop music and its culture is roaring back with a vengeance at festivals and live gigs, along comes a text for the twenty first century study of youth culture.'

Steve Redhead, Professor of Sport and Media Cultures, University of Brighton

Beyond Subculture addresses contemporary popular music cultures alongside the political possibilities of youth and youth culture and considers whether in today's diverse, globalised world it is possible to label any one type of music the 'authentic' voice of youth.

Beyond Subculture investigates a series of musically-centred global youth cultures, including:

- · hip-hop rap
- · electronic dance music grunge
- · bhangra Britpop

Drawing on first hand case studies and interviews with musicians and producers, including Talvin Singh and Noel Gallagher, Rupa Huq reexamines the link between music and subcultures. As youth culture becomes more diverse and the effects of globalisation become stronger, the late twentieth-century definition of 'Generation X' is becoming redundant.

Rupa Huq is Senior Lecturer in the School of Social Sciences at Kingston University.

ISBN13: 978-0-415-27814-0 (hbk)
ISBN13: 978-0-415-27815-7 (pbk)
ISBN13: 978-0-203-49139-3 (ebk)

Available at all good bookshops
For ordering and further information please visit:

www.routledge.com

Related titles from Routledge

THE SUBCULTURES READER, SECOND EDITION

Edited by Ken Gelder

Subcultures are groups of people which are represented – or who represent themselves – as distinct from normative social values or 'mainstream' culture through their particular interests and practices, through what they are, what they do and where they do it. They come in many different forms, from teds and skinheads to skateboarders, clubbers, New Age travellers, graffiti artists and comic book fans.

The Subcultures Reader brings together key writings on subcultures, beginning with the early work of the Chicago School on 'deviant' social groups such as gangs and taxi-dancers, and research from the Centre for Contemporary Cultural Studies at the University of Birmingham during the 1970s on working-class youth cultures and punks. In this fully revised and updated second edition, these classic texts are combined with essential contemporary writings on a variety of subcultural formations defined through their social position, their styles and language, their bodies and their sexuality, their music and their media. Subcultures can be local and face-to-face; but they can also be global, mediated and 'virtual'. This new edition gives expression to the rich diversity of subcultural locations, from underworlds, bohemias and micro-communities to scenes, 'tribes' and the 'global underground'.

The chapters in this Reader are grouped into thematic sections, each with a comprehensive introduction by Ken Gelder. There is also a new general introduction that traces the historical development and key concerns of subcultural studies.

First edition (1997) edited by Ken Gelder and Sarah Thornton

ISBN13: 978-0-415-34415-9 (hbk)
ISBN13: 978-0-415-34416-6 (pbk)

Available at all good bookshops
For ordering and further information please visit:

www.routledge.com

Related titles from Routledge

CULTURAL STUDIES: A CRITICAL INTRODUCTION

Simon During

Cultural Studies: A Critical Introduction is a wide-ranging and stimulating introduction to the history and theory of cultural studies from Leavisism, through the era of the Centre for Contemporary Cultural Studies, to the global nature of contemporary cultural studies.

Cultural Studies begins with an introduction to the field and its theoretical history and then presents a series of short essays on key areas of cultural studies, designed to provoke discussion and raise questions. Each thematic section examines and explains a key topic within cultural studies.

Sections include:

- the discipline
- time
- space
- media and the public sphere
- identity
- sexuality and gender
- value.

Cultural Studies: A Critical Introduction will be very useful in classrooms but will also appeal to anyone with an interest in keeping up or familiarising themselves with cultural studies in its contemporary forms.

ISBN13: 978-0-415-24656-9 (hbk)
ISBN13: 978-0-415-24657-6 (pbk)
ISBN13: 978-0-203-01758-6 (ebk)

Available at all good bookshops
For ordering and further information please visit:

www.routledge.com